D1131366

NEW
PIONEERS

Jeffrey Jacob

NEW PIONEERS

The Back-to-the-Land Movement and the Search for a Sustainable Future

The Pennsylvania State University Press
University Park, Pennsylvania

HT381
.J33
1997

Library of Congress Cataloging-in-Publication Data

Jacob, Jeffrey, 1942–
    New pioneers : the back-to-the-land movement and the search for a
sustainable future / Jeffrey Jacob.

        p.   cm.
    Includes bibliographical references and index.
    ISBN 0-271-01621-3 (cloth : alk. paper)
    ISBN 0-271-01622-1 (pbk. : alk. paper)
    1. Urban-rural migration—United States.   2. Country life—United
States.   I. Title.
    HT381.J33   1997
    307.2'6'0973—dc20   96-12913
                                                                              CIP

Copyright © 1997 The Pennsylvania State University
All rights reserved
Printed in the United States of America
Published by The Pennsylvania State University Press,
University Park, PA 16802-1003

It is the policy of The Pennsylvania State University Press to use acid-free
paper for the first printing of all clothbound books. Publications on un-
coated stock satisfy the minimum requirements of American National
Standard for Information Sciences—Permanence of Paper for Printed Library Materials, ANSI Z39.48–1992.

for
Florence Cordelia Johnson Jacob (1889–1966)
faithful daughter of the first pioneers

CONTENTS

PREFACE

New Pioneers had one of its beginnings in my grandmother Jacob's back-yard. A widow who survived the Great Depression on a school teacher's salary, Florence Jacob practiced pioneer frugality on a modest city lot on Salt Lake City's east bench from the 1920s through the 1960s. Self-reliance for my grandmother was more than a necessity; it was a way of life. Even in the 1950s, after she had gained a measure of affluence, she still cultivated a microfarm variety of fruit trees and berry bushes, a grape arbor, and a vegetable garden that imperialistically captured even the most marginal of her yard's empty spaces. Competing for my grand-mother's attention, I feigned interest in her horticultural preoccupations to move from the middle of a pack of nineteen grandchildren to the status of first assistant gardener. I was summarily put to work drying ripe apricots on the garage roof, and served at my grandmother's right hand in the kitchen as she made pear nectar. Growing food in the city, blocks away from a grocery store, did not always make sense to me, though I did appreciate my grandmother's attention, as well as pies made from frozen gooseberries that came out of her oven in midwinter, in part the product of our industry from the previous summer.

My next conscious encounter with the issues of self-reliance came while I was a graduate student at Syracuse University in upstate New York in the late 1960s and early 1970s. My academic interests focused on the nature of underdevelopment in the United States and the Third World, and I was putting together a research project that would allow me to see the underside of poverty by following shoeshine boys and other poor working children through the streets of Guatemala City. Though preoccupied with explanations for urban poverty in Latin America, I happened to come across the first numbers of the *Mother Earth News* and the *Whole Earth Catalogs* on the magazine racks of an off-campus bookstore I frequented. As I collected and read the first issues of these advocates of simple, back-to-the-land living, I began to entertain the idea that there could be a connection between my grandmother's pioneer spirit and the aspirations of the urban poor to live in a society that rewarded their industry and ingenuity with material security.

The primary confrontations on issues of social justice and the nature of the good society in the late 1960s and early 1970s were, and still are, between those who advocate a capitalist market, with its technological sophistication, as the solution to poverty and those who claim that the capitalist market itself is responsible for underdevelopment. In the 1960s it was still possible for capitalism's critics to maintain that the remedy for poverty was state socialism, which would appropriate capitalism's high technology for the common welfare. In reaction to the capitalist-socialist polar positions, there began to crystallize in the early 1970s a counterstream perspective that resurrected long-standing discontents with the eclipse of an agrarian way of life by a rising urban-industrial culture. This third force on issues of social equity did not ignore capitalism's responsibility in the creation and perpetuation of poverty, but it did raise serious questions whether socialism, or any social-political configuration, could transcend what it saw as the inherently alienating character of industrial technology, with the near inevitable stratification of the social order into expert planners and a relatively uninformed citizenry. Consequently, the good life was to be found in a more democratic "small-is-beautiful" society, whose everyday life would be closely connected to the sustaining power of the land. This prescription did not seem that far removed from what my grandmother had been trying to teach me during the years I spent as her reluctant apprentice, nor was it very different from what I was reading in the *Mother Earth News*.

In the decade following my bookstore encounter with back-to-the-land ideas, I was involved with research and writing projects on the relationship between culture and poverty in Latin American squatter settlements. The *Mother Earth News* still supplied much of my leisure reading material. When my Latin American research came to a natural conclusion, I decided to explore the possibility of a serious study of the back-to-the-land movement. But by the early 1980s, when I first started to track down and interview back-to-the-landers, my interests had expanded beyond social justice issues to include related questions arising out of the environmental movement. Concern over the long-term, sustainable character of industrial and postindustrial society became the focal point of my research perspective. In addition, I had become attracted to the interdisciplinary field of futures studies, whose literature contained not only predictable high-technology forecasts but also well-developed scenarios like those of Ursula LeGuin, in her novels *The Dispossessed* and *Always Coming Home,* on the possibility of future societies living simple but satisfying lives in harmony with the earth's support systems—lives that once again reflected the ideals of the back-to-the-land movement.

In translating these diverse theoretical strands into specific research problems, I decided the basic questions I wanted to ask and try to answer concerned the extent to which back-to-the-landers are actually able to break away from a mass-consumer society and find fulfillment in practicing a sustainable style of life on their smallholdings. But before going very far with my own study, I felt it was important to see just how many of my questions might already have been answered. In reviewing the literature on the back-to-the-land movement beyond the *Mother Earth News* and the *Whole Earth Catalogs,* I found, as expected, a wide-ranging and practical "how-to" collection of books and articles. There were as well a number of first-person accounts of and philosophical justifications for back-to-the-country living. There was not, however, anything resembling a systematic survey of the back-to-the-land movement in North America.

My own research odyssey in search of the practices and values of the back-to-the-landers as a group began in the fall of 1981 with a series of exploratory interviews in southeastern British Columbia. In 1983 I expanded my investigation with a mail survey of more than eight hundred back-to-the-country families in the Pacific Northwest. Employing the insights of both the interviews and questionnaire survey, I then turned to in-depth case studies to deepen my understanding of the movement, with some continuing through January 1996. In the winter and spring of 1992 I completed the questionnaire side of my study with a nationwide survey of twelve hundred U.S. back-to-the-land families. The subjects of these interviews and questionnaire surveys were almost exclusively individuals living with their families on their own small acreages, rather than commune members or large-scale farmers. While back-to-the-landers come in assorted lifestyle categories, about two in five have at least one member of their families holding down a full-time job in order to support their agriculture vocations and avocations. The rest of the latter-day homesteaders rely on a combination of part-time/seasonal work, retirement income, small-business enterprises, and subsistence and cash flow from their properties to maintain themselves back on the land.

Most of my interviews and case studies were conducted in the Pacific Northwest, in parts of the states of Washington, Idaho, and Montana and the Canadian province of British Columbia. There was as well an excursion to Falmouth, Massachusetts, on Cape Cod in the Northeast. In addition, I have freely drawn on magazine and book accounts, which, along with the surveys, take *New Pioneers* to all regions of the United States, as well as to western Canada.

I intend this study to follow the tradition of good investigative social science. The profiles of individual back-to-the-landers are here. One learns of their struggles, frustrations, defeats, and triumphs. The scope of the movement is in no way neglected. The case studies are complemented by surveys that provide insight into the character of the movement—the kinds of back-to-the-landers and their typical beliefs and experiences. But my purpose is more than a comprehensive description of an important social phenomenon. I want to ask difficult questions about the back-to-the-landers in the context of a worldwide consumer culture that is threatening the integrity of the earth's support systems.

The questions start with whether back-to-the-landers can really be considered the new pioneers they like to be called. As they enter rural communities, which often manifest the classic signs of underdevelopment associated with extraction-based economies, are they able to practice a style of life consistent with the ideals they profess? Or do they adapt, as their neighbors, to the pressures of depressed rural economies? Then, to what extent can it be said that the neohomesteaders' actual tenure on the land is a model of ecological design principles that commercial farmers and other intensive land users might emulate? And are they willing to organize for the protection of their homes and communities from a transnational economy that covets rural forests, water, and minerals? Finally, over and above questions critical to the health of rural America, there is a global one: Can the back-to-the-landers find sufficient satisfaction in simple lifestyles to suggest that a fulfilling, happy existence on this planet is possible without recourse to the high-consumption habits that jeopardize a sustainable future?

In the pages that follow, these questions are at times asked and answered directly. More often the issues and answers are found within the ongoing flow of the new pioneers' lives, played out against the backdrop of the communities they have adopted as home. Although my last chapter assesses the movement in light of the personal and social-ecological problems it seeks to resolve, my intent is that these questions remain at least implicit throughout the book. But even though this study seems incomplete to me without raising and trying to answer questions central to the nature of and the preconditions for a sustainable future, it is still the drama of the everyday life of the back-to-the-landers themselves that keeps moving back to the center of the work.

Before moving on to the world of the book's subjects, the back-to-the-landers, and the subject matter of their attempt to find satisfaction in the countryside through the practice of sustainable lifestyles, I would like to address an additional issue. On occasion I have been asked one or another version of the following question: Am I, as a chronicler of the back-to-the-country experience, aware of its dark side, the survivalist and Aryan Nation elements?

In my surveys and interviews I did not come across extremists like the survivalists or members of self-styled citizens' militias, who hoard food and weapons in anticipation of the collapse of civil society. Nor did I encounter anything resembling the claims of racial superiority associated with groups like Aryan Nation, which often try to establish rural enclaves. As I profile the back-to-the-landers in the pages that follow, I believe it will become evident that they are a generally progressive, well-educated group. Intolerance is not one of their defining characteristics. Consequently, since the survivalist and Aryan Nation movements are preoccupied with issues of conspiracy at the highest levels of government and claims of racial superiority, rather than the pleasures of a simple life in the country, they cannot justifiably be considered part of the back-to-the-land movement. They are, then, separate movements with their own distinct agendas.

ACKNOWLEDGMENTS

The University of Calgary Research Grants Committee's support of four separate studies allowed me to complete the interviews, case studies, and surveys on which *New Pioneers* is based. I express my appreciation to my colleagues who served on the Grants Committees, read my applications, and approved their funding. While the grant amounts may not have seemed large, they were, nonetheless, critical in permitting me to complete the back-to-the-land research project.

My colleagues in the Faculty of Education at the University of Calgary were supportive of and interested in my decade-and-a-half-long pursuit of North America's neohomesteaders, but their own research interests lay elsewhere. Their moral support, however, was sustaining, particularly at those times when the project was producing few appreciable results. I have been fortunate to have Merlin B. Brinkerhoff of the University of Calgary's Sociology Department as a collaborator and coauthor on the technical reports that use the surveys on the beliefs and practices of the smallholders. Merlin, who coincidentally was my first methodology instructor just over twenty-five years ago, made a number of valuable suggestions on the data-collection side of this study, suggestions that have significantly strengthened the final product.

Tracking down homesteaders at the ends of country roads has its own exhilarating moments, while stuffing questionnaires into envelopes, applying address labels, and typing multiple revisions of the same chapter are all activities with little novelty and large doses of tedium. Consequently, I am grateful to my secretary, Martha Loeman of the University of Calgary's Graduate Division of Educational Research, for cheerful perseverance in the detail work necessary to complete *New Pioneers*. I would also like to thank Joy Zimmerman, Catherine Schissel, and Sherry Kay for valuable assistance at critical stages in the research process. In addition, Thomas

Huang of the University of Calgary's Department of Sociology ably took care of my mainframe computing requirements.

When the *New Pioneers* manuscript was finally at the review stage, Peter Potter, my editor at Penn State Press, was, for me, the right person in the right place. Peter did not let my sample chapters languish in his slush pile, but called just after he received my proposal, and we went directly from his call to the review process. I thank Peter for his editorial skill, particularly his encouragement and his firm sense of editorial direction, which tamed my periodic tendency toward rhetorical excess.

The two anonymous reviewers Peter and I worked with gave us an optimum mixture of knowledge of and enthusiasm for the subject matter. Their constructive criticism played a key role in moving the manuscript I sent Penn State Press from an uneven piece of work to one worthy of publication. But since the questions the reviewers raised often stimulated revised interpretations with which they would not necessarily be comfortable, I, of course, take final responsibility for the content of *New Pioneers*.

Keith Monley, who lives close to the back-to-the-land movement in Vermont, copyedited the manuscript. I not only appreciate the work Keith did to improve the readability of *New Pioneers*, I also admire the skill and good sense he brought to the task.

The new pioneers themselves, after all the other acknowledgments, are the ones who made the book possible. Although of a generally private disposition, if not at times reclusive, they welcomed me into their homes, returned my questionnaires, and shared the depth of their feelings about their back-to-the-land experiences. I owe them a debt of gratitude that I can only hope this report of their country adventures will partially repay.

It is the rare author who works without the support of loved ones. I am no exception. Though my wife, Lynne, and my children occasionally despaired that I had been lost to an interminable research and writing project, I am grateful that we share a culture that honors both old and new pioneers.

INTRODUCTION

 The visitor who drives up the tree-lined lane that approaches Anne Schwartz's farm is assaulted by a nerve-shattering noise just before entering the homestead clearing. With the house in view the source of the noise becomes obvious. A flock of twenty-odd geese dart in and out of the shadows cast by the thirty-foot fir and spruce trees that define the boundaries of the farm's invasion of forest space. Then, as the car stops and the transient's motion becomes less threatening, the quacking, squawking chorus ebbs to occasional solos.

The geese who herald the advances on Anne's property are not of an ordinary variety. They are multipurpose animals whose contribution to homesteading only begins as gentle substitutes for the farm watchdog. These geese are Chinese weeder geese. They weed: eat the weeds in farm fields and gardens. Each morning at peak weeding times during the spring and summer Anne loads her assistants into the back of her pickup truck and heads for her five-acre organic potato patch. Upon arrival the geese scramble out of the truck, and Anne strategically places several buckets of water for the geese in the rows between the potato plants. Her charges stay close to the water as they systematically pull and eat the weeds between the rows and around the potatoes, ignoring the leaves and stems of the potato plants. As the days pass, Anne and her weeders move through the field, section by section, until the job is finished, and then come back to repeat their good work once new weeds start to compete again for the soil's nutrients.

The weedless five-acre field of mature plants in late August, with its alternating rows of bare earth and dense foliage, stands as testimony to the efficiency of Anne's scavengers. They are an effective alternative to the backbreaking and expensive farmhand labor to clear weeds from commercial acreage. It goes without saying that they carry with them none of the toxicity of herbicides. And in simply doing their job, eating weeds, they provide for themselves, saving Anne trips to the feed store.

Anne and her weeder geese preview what one part of a sustainable future might look like. But as exotic and intriguing as Anne's weeder geese are, they are not the subjects of this study. My primary interest is Anne, and the hundreds of thousands of other back-to-the-landers who over the past thirty years have left urban America in search of the sustainable life on small acreages in the countryside. Anne's use of weeder geese makes her unique among her back-to-the-country fellow travelers, though her journey in search of her mythic roots has much in common with the personal histories of the other back-the-landers I have interviewed over the past fifteen years.

Anne represents only one of a variety of ways of living back-to-the-land. Small-town residents call neohomesteaders like Anne "granolas," seemingly carefree, self-exiled urbanites who subsist from part-time and seasonal work at the margins of local economies. But the largest identifiable group that showed up on my back-to-the-land surveys was the smallholders who work full-time away from their farmsteads and spend an hour or two Monday through Friday commuting to a city job. Commuting to a full-time job may be necessary to pay the mortgage; the back-to-the-land ideal, however, is to find a way to make a living in the country, preferably on one's own property. Some of my respondents stay close to their smallholdings by setting up small businesses, like cabinetmaking shops, on their homesteads, and others are able to support themselves by full-time farming, usually the intensive cultivation of high-value fruits and vegetables. Then there are a few intrepid souls who try to provide for all of their basic needs from their farmsteads, although it does not take them long to learn that they cannot pay property taxes with blueberries. If, however, circumstances conspire against these ways of going back to the land, a prospective smallholder can always wait for retirement income to support a country-living habit, as about one in five of the survey respondents reports doing.

While these strategies for getting back on the land and staying there can be unique to each of the neohomesteaders, the majority share a common point of origin: they are returning to their metaphorical, rather than their literal, roots. Anne, like three out of four of her counterparts from my surveys, had little significant farm experience before going "back" to the country. And most of the farmsteads they end up owning are not technically working farms but smallholdings, likely on marginal land, that, according to the survey respondents, average just under twenty acres.

Anne and the other new pioneers, as they like to call themselves, are participants in a back-to-the-land movement that began as an integral, though relatively unspectacular, part of the 1960s search for counter-cultural alternatives to the corporatism of mainstream America. While it did not capture the media's attention—as did psychedelic hippies, dropping out and turning on, or the vagabonds who temporarily escaped to free-form communes—the back-to-the-land movement was, in its own quiet way, a broad-based protest against what the spirit of the sixties saw as the irrational materialism of urban life. Starting in the mid-1960s and on through the 1970s, each year thousands of urban émigrés found their way to the countryside to set up individual homesteads on a few acres of land. One student of the movement estimated that by the end of the 1970s, at the height of the urban-to-rural migration flows, there were over one million back-to-the-landers in rural North America, almost all on small acreages rather than living in communes or on large farms.[1] In the affluent 1980s interest in the movement seemed to wane, but the recessionary 1990s have revived the search for both material and psychological security in the countryside. And while it is difficult to come up with the precise number of neohomesteaders now resident in rural America, there are few small towns without smallholders shopping along Main Street on a Saturday morning.

In tracking a social movement like the back-to-the-land movement, one way to measure its scope and gauge the depth of its appeal is to examine the literature it spawns. In the case of the back-to-the-land movement a review of its books and periodicals quickly brings to light one magazine, the *Mother Earth News,* whose own history is nearly coterminous with that of the movement itself. Founded just before Earth Day in 1970 by college dropout John Shuttleworth, the *Mother Earth News* evolved from an obscure journal with a newsprint cover to a mass-circulation magazine with a glossy exterior, filled with advertisements from corporate America. By the late 1970s it counted on more than 500,000 subscribers. For over two decades it has served as a source of inspiration and information—some detractors would claim occasional misinformation—to millions of armchair homesteaders and thousands of the practicing variety, with articles like "Building with Native Stone," "Natural Flea Control," and "Build a $225 Garden Composter for $8.54."

Editor/publisher Shuttleworth is representative of both the movement itself and of the "down-home" style of the magazine. In his second issue Shuttleworth interviewed himself in "The Plowboy Interview," a feature that became popular as the *Mother Earth News* captured a wider audience. In the interview he revealed his motivation for starting the magazine, a motivation that reflects the ideological currents that run deep through the movement itself. "The magazine is dedicated to only two things," he wrote, "giving people back their lives and stopping the rape of the planet." He went on to explain what he meant by "giving people back their lives": "I want everyone to be their own man—everyone to have control and direction of their own lives . . . I want to be free, therefore I am interested in helping others be free."[2]

This preoccupation with personal freedom explains in part why Shuttleworth in the late 1950s would give up a four-year scholarship at Indiana's Ball State University after his sophomore year. As he saw it, the educational establishment does little more than provide "replacement parts for the military-industrial complex, and it turns out wonderful consumers, but doesn't teach much about living a satisfying life or developing human potential." But without some kind of credential, how does one go about finding work and making a living? Shuttleworth's *Mother Earth News* itself was his answer to the job question. "Over the years," he continued, "I've gathered whole filing cabinets of material on people who have successfully walked away from the system and started living on their own terms. I wanted to share that information."

While substantial numbers of the *Mother Earth News* readers over the past three decades have sympathized with Shuttleworth's claustrophobic reaction to urban-based bureaucracies and have tried to put space between themselves and the "system" by moving to the countryside, it is still an open question whether back-to-the-land is a legitimate social movement. To this point, I have without qualification referred to the back-to-the-country phenomenon as a social movement, but one could argue that it is more of a demographic shift or trend—primarily the movement of North Americans from urban points of origin to rural destinations.

The standard textbook definition for a social movement is large-scale collective behavior directed toward promoting or resisting social change. Unlike other forms of collective action like fads or trends, social movements possess at least a rudimentary organizational structure and well-developed ideologies, espoused by an intellectual vanguard with recognizable public identities.[3] The civil rights, environmental, feminist, and gay rights movements are examples of contemporary social movements that fit comfortably within this textbook definition.

In contrast to the well-defined organizations, groups, and coalitions that constitute the civil rights and feminist movements, for example, the back-to-the-land movement's institutions appear anemic. There are no high-profile demonstrations demanding the implementation of back-to-the-country ideals, nor are there Washington back-to-the-land organizations that retain lobbyists to petition Congress on behalf of aggrieved smallholders. While there exists no shortage of public advocates for a back-to-the-land way of life, neohomesteaders are motivated as much by defenders of ecologically sensible living like Aldo Leopold, Rachel Carson, and E. F. Schumacher as they are by those writers who focus exclusively on the importance of a simple life in the country. Given, then, the back-to-the-landers' general interest in sustainability principles, apart from their specific application on back-to-the-country homesteads, perhaps their movement might best be seen as part of the larger environmental struggle, rather than as a completely independent social movement.[4] Back-to-the-landers would likely not be uncomfortable with such a categorization, but they would just as likely claim that though their strategy and tactics differ from mainstream environmentalists, they are no less interested in seeing a fundamental change in the way Americans exercise their stewardship over their country's natural resources. While environmental organizers, and on occasion back-to-the-landers in the role of activists, agitate, litigate, and legislate for change,[5] neohomesteaders see themselves as making an equally important contribution to the overall goals of the environmental movement: actually demonstrating, or trying to demonstrate, a sustainable way of life on their smallholdings. The extent to which they are able to translate their idealism into homestead routines is, naturally, an important part of this report.

Crisis of Character I: Loss of a Rural Childhood

The 1960s was without question an exceptional decade. It is, consequently, tempting to characterize the social movements of the time, like the back-to-the-country experience, as unique historical events. While both the substantive and mythological legacy of the sixties ought not to be discounted, it is also important to recognize that the ideas that drove the decade's social movements have their own intellectual parentage. Back-to-the-land as an ideal, for example, is part of classic American agrarianism and has its philosophical roots in a rhetorical tradition that connects the thought of Thomas Jefferson to Henry David Thoreau and then to contemporary poet, novelist, and professor Wendell Berry.

Jefferson immortalized the Revolutionary War smallholder, writing that he knew of "no condition happier than that of a Virginia farmer . . . His estate supplies a good table, clothes himself and his family with ordinary apparel, furnishes a small surplus to buy salt, sugar, coffee, and a little finery for his wife and daughters, enables him to receive and visit friends, and furnishes him pleasing and healthy occupation." There was, however, a crucial precondition to this agrarian serenity. As the patrician president with common-man instincts explained: "To secure all this he [the smallholder] needs but one act of self-denial, to put off buying anything till he has the money to pay for it."[6]

The Jeffersonian vision, of course, did not prevail. Voluntary self-denial has never been a stable part of American culture. During the nineteenth century the nation chose the commercialism and large-scale industrialism of Jefferson's rival Alexander Hamilton, and the subsistence homestead became, as the century progressed, a cultural anomaly, and finally an extinct species. Thoreau's short walk, but extended spiritual journey, to Walden's Pond was a protest march against American materialism at midcentury, and an attempt to recapture Jeffersonian simplicity. "Man is rich in proportion to the number of things he can do without" were words that Thoreau genuinely seemed to live as well as to believe.[7]

More than a century after Thoreau, neo-Jeffersonian Wendell Berry continues the agrarian resistance tradition. Berry's yeoman premises collide with the logic of factory farming. Stewardship of a particular piece of earth and long-term commitment to a specific community are the themes that run through Berry's essays, poems, and novels.

Berry is an incisive critic of corporate agriculture, which he claims, in its social and environmental costs, "is a failure on its way to being a catastrophe." For Berry, the costs of fifty years of post–World War II factory farming include soil erosion and compaction, soil and water pollution, an alteration in ecological balance through the introduction of monocultures, and the destruction of farm communities. There is also the "decivilization of the cities," which results from a surplus and idle population, while "the land is suffering from the want of the care of those absent families." Since, from Berry's perspective, the damage corporate farming inflicts on the countryside is made possible by the intensive use of a finite quantity of fossil fuels, he suggests farmers return to doing their work, wherever practical, with horses. "When going back makes sense," Berry avers with practiced iconoclasm, "you are going ahead."[8]

I believe that one reason these agrarian critiques of urban society still strike a responsive chord, regardless of how impractical they may seem, is that for three out of the nearly four centuries of European settlement of this continent, the United States was an agrarian nation. This agrarian consciousness was so thoroughly rooted in American culture that when, in the early part of this century, it became clear that the country was transforming itself from a rural society to an urban one, Americans experienced something like a collective identity crisis—1920 was the first census year in which more than 50 percent of the population was living in towns and cities with more than 2,500 inhabitants.[9] A primary reason why this shift in national demographics was not accepted with anything approaching equanimity was that it carried the potential, in the popular mind, to undermine the national character. It was an article of community faith that a farm childhood was an essential component of successful character formation. The conventional wisdom held that the captains of industry and the political leaders possessing integrity were products of rural childhoods. The absence of a farm upbringing, then, for most of the country's children would mean the country's leaders and a supportive citizenry would grow up in an environment that did not require responsibility, resourcefulness, and hard work. The United States thus faced a crisis of character.[10]

Closely correlated in the public mind with the character-formation problem were the rural conditions that pushed farm families off the land. The factors promoting migration included the absence of services like medical care and schooling and of infrastructure such as all-weather roads, electricity, and telephone service. There was a generalized fear that the country-to-city exodus would take away from the farm community the most progressive of rural youth, who felt their ambitions could only be realized in the city, leaving behind the most backward elements of rural society. In response to decades of concern over the health of rural America, President Theodore Roosevelt convened a Country Life Commission to survey the status of the countryside and make policy recommendations for remedying rural underdevelopment. Composed of a high-profile group of academic and professional public figures with interest in and sympathy for farm culture, the commission crossed the country, holding hearings and distributing questionnaires. While the commission did identify the expected deficiencies in rural public services and infrastructure, it went much further by framing the overall problem in terms of the countryside's exploitation by monopolistic interests—land speculators, railroads, and grain traders whose single-minded interest in profits was seen as leading to soil erosion, excessive farm debt, artificially high land prices, and low commodity prices.[11]

The commission's report, however, had little direct policy impact. Congress was unsympathetic both to appropriating funds for rural relief and to regulating the cartels that coveted farm wealth. But even with its failure to get Congress to pass a comprehensive farm and rural improvement program, the Country Life Commission still had a significant influence in helping to define the terms of reference Americans would use for their private and public discourse on both country and city life. By using its forum to promote the virtues of farm life and implicitly, if not always explicitly, to expose the reputed deficiencies of urban life, the commission contributed to the resurrection of a national agrarian sentimentality, all while the cities' populations exploded and the rural exodus continued.

One result of this revived agrarian sentiment was a back-to-the-land movement that stretched from the first part of the century to World War II. Americans were not only talking about the virtues of life back on the farm, but were also moving back to the countryside to become either "gentlemen" farmers or commercial agriculturists. Mass-circulation magazines like *Colliers, Sunset,* and the *Atlantic Monthly* regularly featured articles on how to find one's own country property and first-person accounts of how to survive and prosper on small acreages. A 1915 article for the *Atlantic Monthly* reflects this enthusiasm for rural smallholdings. The author claims that city men are drawn to the country because "they hear the call of their elemental being, they feel the hunger of manhood for its first home—the vast open, the gleam of the untainted sky, the odor of the sod, the turmoil and conflict of the body with things, the thrilling revelations which the rough tutelage of nature forces on the expanding soul. Lacking these they are dimly conscious that the best in life is lacking."[12]

Stanford Layton, a chronicler of the early-twentieth-century back-to-the-land movement, has characterized urban Americans' infatuation with the idea of owning their own farmsteads as a "collective passion" and an "emotional contagion." The hyperbole of the back-to-the-land literature would lead one to believe, in Layton's words, that country living "makes sick people healthy, weak people strong, old people young, and young people mature. Life in the country cures tuberculosis, whooping cough, anemia, and a variety of other physical maladies. It revitalizes one's appetite, but keeps him lean."[13]

If country living can be so absolutely beneficial, then city life must somehow be profoundly deficient—and the back-to-the-land discourse was uninhibited in its denunciation of urban vices. This antipathy for city living was at times reflected in the congressional debate over rural reform measures and homestead acts. Speaking in behalf of a 1916 homestead bill, Congressman Denver Church of California declared, "I am in favor of any bill that will get people away from the cities . . . Our cities are filled with perplexities and unrest; the grind of machinery, the noise of the factory, and the shriek of the locomotive keeps the nerves of the city man strung to the key of G."[14]

While support for the back-to-the-land ideals, complimented by antipathy for city life, could be found in a variety of mass-circulation publications and became on occasion part of the politician's rhetorical arsenal, one magazine consistently and specifically promoted the cause of rural repopulation. Doubleday, Page, and Company published *Country Life in America,* a spiritual antecedent to the *Mother Earth News,* from just after the turn of the century until 1942. Coming out monthly for most of its four-decade existence, *Country Life* was a glossy eleven-by-fourteen-inch magazine that generously used high-quality photographs to promote such articles as "Could I Succeed on a Farm?" "The Philosophy of Soil," "A Five Acre Model Farm," and "Cutting Loose from the City." And *Country Life* subscribers, along with like-minded individuals and their families, were not only reading these articles but acting on them as well. According to U.S. Department of Agriculture figures, the number of people leaving cities and villages for farms in 1928 was 1.7 million, 80 percent of the figure for those who were leaving farms for cities and villages. Then, in 1932, 20 percent more migrants (1.8 million) headed back to farms than moved away from them to cities and villages (1.5 million), though the search for survival during the Great Depression, rather than the voluntary pursuit of a life on the farm, likely accounted for a significant amount of this rural-bound migration.[15]

Given the generalized enthusiasm for back-to-the-country lifestyles, one should not be surprised to learn that neo-Jeffersonian ideals influenced much of the early social policy considerations in Franklin Roosevelt's New Deal. Rex Tugwell, the Resettlement Administration's director, reported that many of the intellectuals who advised Roosevelt operated on the basis of rural nostalgia, a kind of "historic homesickness," as Tugwell described it. Roosevelt himself believed that New Deal policy should be directed toward resettling ten to fifteen million of the urban unemployed to farms and villages. These convictions were subsequently translated into actual programs, including the Civilian Conservation Corps (perhaps the most successful of the New Deal programs, with 500,000 participants in 1935), the greenbelt-cities and new-town schemes, and aspects of the Tennessee Valley Authority.[16]

The purest expression, however, of back-to-the-land sentiment in the New Deal programs was the Department of the Interior's Division of Subsistence Homesteads. Created in 1933, the Division of Subsistence Homesteads attempted to place low-income urban workers on small acreages so that they could supplement their wages with gardens and small stock animals. The administration started over a hundred of the subsistence homestead communities, but the inflexibility of centralized bureaucratic planning and low prices for farm commodities left most of the communities stillborn. By the end of World War II, the Division of Subsistence Homesteads, along with many of the other innovative New Deal rural initiatives, had disappeared.[17] Because of the war and the more than two decades of prosperity it precipitated, fascination with simple living on the land, as well as popular demands that the government keep alive the programs that supported it, appeared to fade away. But the back-to-the-land ideals stayed just below the surface of the public imagination, to resurface when the nation's commitment to materialism was called into question in the countercultural turmoil of the 1960s and early 1970s.

Crisis of Character II: Facing Up to Sustainability

From all the social movements, countercultural ideologies, and political ferment to emerge during the 1960s, perhaps the most enduring legacy of the period was the crystallization of a national ecological consciousness.

While we are still some distance from a consensus either on the gravity of the stress being placed on the planet or on how to go about remedying the problems for which urban–industrial/postindustrial societies are responsible, we do seem to have come to the point where we are beginning to recognize a collective crisis of character in regard to the environmental damage inflicted on the earth. This crisis of character parallels in part the anxiety the country experienced in the early years of the century over the prospect of losing its rural identity, engendering in the process a back-to-the-land movement.

The fear that in becoming an urban society the nation would lose its capacity for hard work and resourcefulness, of course, was not borne out by the course of twentieth-century history. More than fifty years of economic expansion and prosperity followed the early concerns over the loss of a rural identity. But progress brought with it a second crisis of national character. By the early 1970s the issue was not so much whether the country could work hard enough to produce and maintain affluence as it was whether its citizens possessed the individual and collective will to reject economic expansion as an all-encompassing solution to social problems and, as a consequence, lower overall levels of consumption to the point where the earth's support systems would have a chance to start the process of regeneration.

The last hundred years of economic development have demonstrated that a society can lose touch with the most elemental forces that sustain it, yet still become prosperous. At the same time, these last hundred years have also demonstrated that a society that loses its contact with the land places itself in danger of destroying the ultimate sources of its prosperity. Life off the land insulates a culture from the immediate repercussions of its violations of the earth's ecological integrity. Affluence, then, seduces a society into believing that there can be one-time technological solutions to problems like ozone depletion, acid rain, and overflowing municipal landfills while recessionary threats to this affluence frighten policy makers away from even modest environmental reform.

A quarter of a century after the first Earth Day in 1970 raised public consciousness on the connection between affluence and environmental degradation, the disappearance of prosperity itself has blunted the alarm over the drawdown of the planet's nonrenewable resources and the contamination of its air, water, and soil. A high-tech global economy is in the process of restructuring the world's productive capacity, and in the name of competitiveness, once comfortable workers watch their standard of liv-

ing erode and their jobs migrate or become automated.[18] Falling incomes
and shrinking tax revenues reaffirm the overwhelming impression that the
country is becoming poorer, in spite of the technological innovation that
continues to increase productive capacity. Consequently, neither governments nor their citizens believe they can afford to remedy the long-standing environmental problems created by the initial drive to prosperity and
those aggravated by the nouveau penury of the 1990s. While about one-
seventh of the population, "true-blue greens" according to Roper Organization surveys,[19] still maintains enthusiasm for a progressive environmental
agenda, affluence, once won and now jeopardized, deepens the contemporary character crisis—yielding a population lacking the discipline to
live within the earth's environmental limits.

The sustainability principles advocated by, but not peculiar to, the back-
to-the-landers hold out the promise of rehabilitating the national character. A commitment to sustainability can provide the motivation for a reassessment of cultural priorities, a reassessment conducted within the
context of the earth's carrying capacity and the ultimate sources of human well-being. "Sustainability," however, can also function as what Ger-
man linguist and medievalist Uwe Poerksen calls a "plastic" word.[20] Plastic
words are broadly connotative but lack precise denotation; in Ivan Illich's
characterization, they "make waves but they don't actually hit anything."[21]
Plastic words are able to evoke a range of powerful emotions, from frugality to fear, but they are sufficiently abstract that they require no specific
points of reference. Imported from the world of scientific discourse, experts and tyrants can use code words like "development," "debt," and
"competitiveness" to mold public consciousness without having to account
for their positions with detailed argumentation.

In the case of sustainability, there is no immediate danger that the mal-
leable nature of the concept will assist policy makers in moving the public
in directions that common sense would resist. But the abstract quality of
the word does carry the potential to render it meaningless. It has support
all along the ideological spectrum, and it is hard to imagine anyone not
in favor of a sustainable future. Since "sustainability" and its derivatives
have been and will be used frequently in these pages, I believe that the
analysis ought not to proceed without an antidote of definitional preci-
sion to diminish the fluid character of this plastic word.

The most widely accepted definition for sustainability is that of the
United Nations World Commission on Environment and Development, to
the effect that a sustainable society is one that "meets the needs of the

present without compromising the ability of future generations to meet their own needs."[22] Translating this general principle into specific terms means that contemporary economies leave future generations sufficient natural resources for them to live at a level of material comfort comparable, on an aggregate basis, to what the world now enjoys. But since urban-industrial societies are voracious consumers of nonrenewable fossil fuels (over 90 percent of energy we use comes from them),[23] it is not likely that succeeding generations will be able to replicate current energy-use habits much beyond the middle of the twenty-first century.

If world economies continue the drawdown of fossil-fuel resources at the current exponentially increasing rate over the next fifty to sixty years, the consequence will be irreparable damage to the earth's carrying capacity and, consequently, a significant drop in food supplies and population levels. In *Beyond the Limits,* the sequel to their Club of Rome report, *The Limits of Growth,* Donella Meadows and her coauthors estimate that the planet's residents will have to reduce the use of fossil fuels by 80 percent and the levels of pollution by 90 percent by the middle of the twenty-first century in order to reach a point of sustainability and avoid an ecological support-system collapse.[24]

What, however, are the alternatives to the intensive use of nonrenewable fossil fuels? The answer is a basic one: renewable sources of energy (the sun, wind, and human and animal muscle power). But one might well wonder whether a shift to renewable energy sources is practical, in the first place, and, in the second place, whether life with a restricted use of fossil fuels is bearable, even if sustainable. The lives of the back-to-the-landers, as they are played out in the pages that follow, enable us to go some distance in answering these questions. The new pioneers can help the mainstream society appreciate the difficulties in making the transition from nonrenewable to renewable sources of energy, and their experiences also permit a preview of what the quality of life might look like in a sustainable society.

The issue of overall quality of life in a sustainable society raises the critical question of what motivates an individual, a society, to practice a low-impact lifestyle. Since high consumption, driven by the need to bolster one's self-esteem and the desire to enjoy the ease of luxury, is at the root of the planet's manifold social and ecological difficulties, it follows that the essence of sustainability is the ability of an individual, and of a society, to receive fulfillment from sources that do not entail spiraling levels of consumption and the profligate use of nonrenewable sources of energy.[25] What, however, are the sources of satisfaction that might relegate consumption to an ancillary place in the hierarchy of social values?

Relationships—relationships with family, friends, and neighbors and relationships with the natural world—would seem to be good starting points as alternatives to the commercialism that permeates everyday life. Aside, then, from whatever the back-to-the-landers' technical achievements might be or whether they are able to translate very much of what they read in the *Mother Earth News* into working models on their minihomesteads, it is important to see if the satisfactions of physical labor on one's own property and the bonds of community and family life can compensate for the kinds of indiscriminate consumption that are undermining the possibility of a sustainable future.

The chapters that follow tell the story of the back-to-the-landers in a straightforward narrative contextualized within reoccurring sustainability themes. Chapter 1, "Conventional Radicals: Back-to-the-Land Profiles," is first an account of how I tracked down potential back-to-the-landers and then decided which were authentic back-to-the-country types. With the methodological issues out of the way, I outline the background characteristics of the kinds of people who take up smallholding—their age, education, marital and family status, residence patterns, property size, and farm experience. In Chapter 2, "Seven Ways of Living Back-to-the-Land: Work, Time, and Money in the Country," I develop a typology of seven different ways of living back-to-the-land, from the "weekenders" who have full-time jobs away from their smallholdings to the "purists" who attempt to support themselves completely from the resources of their homesteads. Chapter 2 includes an income profile of the neohomesteaders and introduces the time-money dilemma, with which most back-to-the-country people struggle; full-time work away from their properties leaves them insufficient time to develop sustainable homesteads, but without full-time work many smallholders would not be able to make the payments on their homestead mortgages.

This theme of the neohomesteaders' having to balance competing demands on their time and energy carries over to the subject matter of Chapter 3, "Quest for Wholeness: Back-to-the-Land Values." In Chapter 3, I explore the back-to-the-landers' encounter with two core values of the movement, self-reliance and voluntary simplicity. The description and analysis here show smallholders at some distance from becoming ideological zealots as they pragmatically juggle the often contradictory requirements of the values to which they subscribe. The chapter concludes with a discussion of the quality of country life in terms of the degree of satisfaction and happiness the smallholders feel in relation to a variety of back-to-the-land experiences. Chapter 4, "Soft Paths: Back-to-the-Land Technology," covers the practical application of smallholder values. The extent to which the neohomesteaders are able to apply ecological design principles through appropriate technologies on their farmsteads is primarily a measure of their technical success in practicing a sustainable way of life in the country. Sustainability, however, is a multidimensional concept and includes social as well as technical components. Chapter 4, consequently, looks at the farmstead division of labor, recounting how smallholders divide up the homestead chores between husbands and wives, and parents and their children.

Chapter 5, "Urban Pioneers," is a side journey into the world of the urban homesteaders, some quite content to stay city-bound, while others actively pursue strategies to make it back to the land. This city excursus permits an examination of a key variable in the sustainability equation, right livelihood. Right livelihood is a Buddhist precept that encourages one to express one's unique talents through service, regardless of how mundane, rather than in the search of wealth, power, and status. Back-to-the-land living itself could be considered an ideal-typical expression of right livelihood. But I use case studies of city residents with back-to-the-land sensibilities and plans to explore the dimensions of right livelihood.

Making a move to the countryside, setting up some semblance of a sustainable farmstead, and finding a job to pay for it all is a complicated process. There are, however, any number of additional complications that conspire to undermine the neohomestead dreams of a peaceful country existence. Chapter 6, "Organizing for Change: New Pioneers as Activists," examines what for most smallholders is an unanticipated aspect of country life. It is not an overstatement to say that much of rural America suffers from multiple crises. Rural unemployment rates are as high as those of inner cities. Farm foreclosures are common, and as the tax base erodes, rural hospitals, schools, and even entire towns are closing down. Rural wealth in the form of natural-resource extraction has been disappearing for years, and in its place are clear-cuts, polluted and silt-clogged rivers, exhausted soils, and toxic waste dumps.[26] Back-to-the-landers have the kinds of educational credentials and professional experience that could make them valuable activists working in behalf of their adopted communities. But one has to wonder, as I do periodically through the first five chapters, whether the smallholders can possibly have time or energy, much less the disposition and interest, to devote to community organizing after the last of the homestead chores are completed. On occasion, though, even the most reclusive back-to-the-landers become reluctant activists when clear-cuts arrive at their property lines or effluents from open-pit copper mines leak into once pristine rivers that flow by their farmstead properties.

By the time the narrative and analysis arrive at the last chapter, Chapter 7, "Back-to-the-Landers as New Pioneers: The Search for a Sustainable Future," it will be evident that smallholders are an ordinary group of people whose achievements fall considerably short of their dreams. The neohomesteaders' experiences, however, do demonstrate just how far highly motivated individuals can go, by themselves, in piecing together sustainable lifestyles. The distance between the back-to-the-landers' aspirations and their accomplishments raises the question of public support for those who want to align their behavior more closely with the principles of ecological responsibility. After exploring a number of policy options that would allow the mainstream society to capitalize on the neohomesteaders' idealism, I conclude the chapter, and the book, with a reconsideration of back-to-the-landers as legitimate new pioneers. By extending the definition of sustainability beyond its technical prerequisites to its more broadly based social and spiritual dimensions, the smallholders appear to be much closer to the progressive edge of a movement toward a sustainable future than their ever-incomplete farmsteads would suggest.

1

CONVENTIONAL RADICALS

Back-to-the-Land Profiles

 In 1969 Wilson Rockwell was a Colorado state senator. A Republican, he represented a district in western Colorado where his family had operated ranches from the time the area was settled. His father was once the state's lieutenant governor, as well as a four-term member of the U.S. House of Representatives. Though a rancher by profession, Wilson devoted most of his energy to writing western Colorado history and working on a variety of community-service projects, including two four-year terms in the Colorado State Senate. Wilson Rockwell was, as characterized by a *Denver Post* columnist, "Republican, rural, middle-class, middle-aged, deeply-rooted, and set-in-his-ways."[1]

Yet, in early 1970, Wilson Rockwell resigned his seat in the Colorado Senate, closed his Denver apartment, sold his ranch, and moved. The reason Wilson and his wife, Enid, moved and consequently broke with their families' financial and emotional investments in the communities of western Colorado was their opposition to the Vietnam War. Their destination was Canada: the small town of Creston, British Columbia, just across the U.S. border from the Idaho panhandle. In addition to general disenchantment with their country's foreign policy, the factor that led to the

Rockwells' abandonment of traditional moorings was the likelihood that their only child, Dan, would be drafted to serve in Vietnam. Rather than see Dan go alone to Canada to escape induction, the Rockwells decided to move as a family.

While the Rockwells cannot be considered typical back-to-the-landers, their experience does, however, share a trait with those who seek independent country living. Rather than unconsciously submit to the social forces that move most of their fellow citizens in the same direction, back-to-the-landers turn counterclockwise against the grain of prevailing fashion.

The new pioneers' independence of mind and spirit, however, is a carefully circumscribed iconoclasm. They are radical in the sense of wanting to rediscover their roots. But at the same time, as the profiles from this chapter and succeeding ones confirm, most back-to-the-landers share a number of rather conventional characteristics. Like the Rockwell family, they are superficially conservative. They possess an ingrained sentimentalism in favor of family and spiritual and pastoral values. This blend of practiced sociological independence and a traditionalist point of view finds a larger-than-life expression in the Rockwell family's behavior. Their experience, then, is worth exploring further, for its intrinsic interest as well as to illustrate an abiding commitment to the rural way of life shared by the subjects of this study.

Dan Rockwell left school at Colorado Mountain College to help his father with ranch work after a hired hand suddenly quit for a better-paying job. The family's plans were for Dan to stay out of school for a year and work on the ranch while his father finished his term in the state senate. Dan was to apply to the local draft board for an agriculture deferment to cover the year's ranch work, after which his reenrollment in school would again qualify him for an educational deferment. But as the Rockwells anticipated, the Delta County Draft Board was not sympathetic to their petition. The board turned down the agricultural deferment, and Mrs. Davidson, the board's "formidable secretary, who actually ran the show," informed the Rockwells that "according to national draft regulations, if a student quit college temporarily for any cause, no matter how necessary, he lost his college deferment."[2]

The Delta County Draft Board, a "tyrannical little bureaucracy" in the Rockwells' eyes, reclassified Dan's draft status as 1A. Although the Rockwells would have preferred to see their son avoid the draft legally, they now felt the family had no alternative but to seek sanctuary in Canada. At the end of an exploratory trip to British Columbia, they purchased a small, 240-acre ranch, only one-fifth the size of their Colorado property. They later discovered that their new property line was just two miles across the Canadian border from the United States.

Upon returning home after the acquisition of their new ranch, Wilson and Enid found Dan had just received his draft notice and orders to report for a physical examination. Since Dan missed the date for his physical examination, the Rockwells realized he was already in violation of the law. Fearing that the authorities, including the FBI, might at any time start looking for Dan, the Rockwell family immediately turned around to start the return journey to their new Canadian home. They drove twelve hundred miles night and day over snow-packed and icy roads before crossing the Idaho border into British Columbia. Reflecting on that crossing, Wilson later wrote, "We all breathed a sigh of relief when we crossed the border into our adopted country. Here Dan was safe from governmental tyranny—and for the first time since he had grown up, free to live his own life as he saw fit. There were adjustments and sacrifices to make, but Dan's freedom was worth whatever price we might have to pay."

The Rockwells' move did involve some initial sacrifice. They spent a cold first winter at their new home in a partially remodeled house without the benefit of reliable heat. It was most of a year before the electric and telephone lines reached their property. The physical conditions of their new life contrasted sharply with those of their metropolitan Denver apartment and long-domesticated western Colorado ranch house. Added to the relatively primitive beginnings at their ranch in embryo was the inevitable discomfort of leaving a secure status in one community only to have to establish it once again in a new environment. This period of transition prompted the Rockwells to reassess the direction and pace of their lives. Expressing sentiments at the heart of the back-to-the-land worldview, Wilson Rockwell later characterized his own and his family's evolving priorities in the following terms:

> I have learned that true success is based more on a day-to-day acceptance and appreciation of life than it is on achievements. That is, I have learned to accept philosophically the many things I don't have and to appreciate gratefully the few things that I do have, and in so doing to concentrate on one day at a time.
>
> I used to allow thousands of days to pass by unnoticed, believing them to be just stepping stones to the realization of great achievements and golden dreams. With my shift in priori-

ties, now no day goes by unrecognized, and I have come to value the seemingly trivial experiences of each day as important ends in themselves—like a colorful sunset, a casual visit, a good book, or a walk along the hidden trails of our mountain sanctuary.

Against the Tide: The Enduring Attraction of the Country

While the Rockwells' migration to Canada to escape the direct consequences of the Vietnam War in the United States is an experience shared by few other back-to-the-landers, their devotion to principle over comfort is a trait common to the movement. In fact, the name itself, the "back-to-the-land" movement, implies resistance to overriding social forces. One goes back—back against the tide of mainstream, urban society—to reclaim an idyllic past.

From one perspective the very growth of Western industrial society can be characterized by rural eclipse, by mass migration from the countryside to cities. In yeoman America of the eighteenth and nineteenth centuries, the farm labor of seven or eight workers was required to feed another two or three urban residents as well as the rural laborers themselves. By contrast, the contemporary farm laborer can produce sufficient food for eighty city dwellers.[3] And as the story goes, bright city lights, with assembly-line jobs behind the neon, were the magnets pulling displaced rural families into the sphere of urban domination. A revivalist back-to-the-land movement, then, when it has occurred in the industrial and postindustrial eras, can be considered a phenomenon independent of prevailing social trends—a movement against the tide.

A little more than two and a half decades ago, however, starting in the 1960s and moving through the 1970s, it appeared that the back-to-the-country movement might itself become a dominant social trend, rather than simply a counterforce to urban dominance. At a time when the *Mother Earth News* was becoming a mass-circulation magazine and the *Whole Earth Catalogs* were gaining in popularity, demographers discovered something they labeled the urban-to-rural migration turnaround. The more-than-century-long trend of relatively faster urban growth in America started to reverse itself by the late 1960s and became in the 1970s a "migration turnaround." Through the 1970s, nonmetropolitan counties, those not having a city with a population over 50,000, had population growth rates exceeding metropolitan counties. With the country growing faster than cities, the possibilities for a rural renaissance seemed genuine. Of course, only part of this migration turnaround included new pioneers, and much of it may be attributed to those for whom tracts of farm land were transformed into low-density suburbs and to upscale country residents who commuted several hours a day to city jobs. But from the late 1960s through the early 1980s, the back-to-the-landers were part of a broad population movement that reaffirmed the small-town and rural ways of life.[4]

The rural renaissance, however, never materialized. The 1980s brought a "turnaround" of the turnaround migration. The farm crisis came between many Americans and their dreams of a life in the country. Metropolitan counties grew twice as fast in the eighties as their nonmetropolitan counterparts. The ripple effect of low farm prices, debt and foreclosure, a shrinking tax base, and atrophying social services pushed migratory flows from rural America back toward cities, reaffirming the century-old trend of rural decline. Depressed prices for country property in the wake of the farm crisis might have counterbalanced rural population losses by attracting urbanites looking to escape fast-paced city lives, but these potential urban expatriates needed the jobs that disappeared along with the rural population.

But the enduring attraction of small-town America continued to pull migrants from the country's metropolitan centers through the first half of the 1990s, in spite of often depressed rural economies. After the farm crisis of the 1980s, nonmetropolitan counties are growing again, though, in contrast to the 1970s, their growth rates are now lower than the growth rates for metropolitan counties. From 1990 to 1994 nonmetro counties grew by a total of 4 percent. The same counties grew by only 2.3 percent during the entire 1980s.[5]

Rural America's revived population growth rates, however, are not the only 1990s demographic trend relevant to an understanding of the contemporary back-to-the-land movement. From the late 1980s and on through the 1990s Americans were migrating from both the nation's inner cities and its hinterland toward population bubbles that Joel Garreau has labeled edge cities—fully configured urban areas, usually at the intersections of freeways, on the metropolitan fringe. Since edge city is tailor made for the commuter, it is likely that many back-to-the-landers take advantage of the urban sprawl moving toward their country properties by driving to a city job. My nationwide survey of back-to-the-country people suggests that the metropolitan fringe plays an important role in the lives of many smallholders. Almost one-quarter (24 percent) of the respondents living on country property say they are in or close to a large or small city. Three out of five of the respondents report that they commute to work, relying almost exclusively on a car or truck (97 percent), an average of five days a week. The round-trip averages fifty miles. Paradoxically, then, the car and edge city, both dubious contributors to a sustainable society, facilitate the adventure of those who want to go against the tide of central-city dominance and take up simple living in the country.[6]

The census data that demographers use to plot population trends do not always permit precise answers to questions about what kinds of people moved to nonmetropolitan counties in the sixties and seventies and are still going back to the country in spite of the problems rural areas face. We do not know, for example, how many back-to-the-landers there are, although Terry Simmons, using detailed local surveys to interpret census data, estimates that there were in North America at the end of the 1970s more than a million back-to-the-country people practicing one brand of semisubsistence agriculture or another. But while the details in the shifting patterns of population streams over the past three decades are not altogether clear, social scientists did learn one important lesson from the migration turnarounds of the 1970s. Until the short-lived rural population growth spurt caught their attention at the end of the seventies, demographers had been working with a very basic migration equation: relatively bad economic times push people out of countryside, and economic opportunities pull them toward the city. Population flows back to rural America over the last twenty to thirty years, however, demonstrate that people move for a variety of noneconomic reasons, taking jobs and incomes that do not measure up to those they could have if they only followed their economic self-interest. Some of the noneconomic rewards of moving to the country include opportunities to be close to family and friends, to enjoy the natural beauty of the outdoors, to experience the intimacy of small-town life, and, for the back-to-the-landers of course, to try to live independently and simply on their own land.[7]

This discussion of the noneconomic motivations for moving to the country raises the issue of values—specifically the question of the extent to which there is in America support for the ideals of sustainable living, apart from their particular application by back-to-the-landers. To answer questions about general interest in what the new pioneers are trying to do, there are several surveys of public opinion conducted over the last fifteen years to which one can turn. In the early 1980s Stanford Research Institute's market surveys suggested that fifteen to twenty million Americans sympathized with a return to a simpler way of life. Consistent with these trends toward simplicity, three out of four Americans have said they would like to live in a small town. A Roper Organization survey in 1993 estimated that 14 percent of Americans can be classified as "True-Blue Greens," a group that not only supports the environmental movement but also takes action by recycling and sorting trash, refusing to buy non-biodegradable soaps, and writing politicians on environmental concerns. The Roper Organization also identified another 6 percent of consumers who support the True-Blue Greens' commitments, although they do not consistently translate their values into action. On a more impressionistic level, a 1991 *Time* magazine cover story heralded a return to simpler lifestyles as a 1990s trend. Based in part on a Time/CNN poll, the article reports that a majority of adults want to lead a more relaxed life that emphasizes time with family and friends. "After a 10-year bender of gaudy dreams and Godless consumerism, Americans are starting to trade down. They want to reduce their attachments to status symbols, fast-track careers and great expectations of Having It All. Upscale is out; downscale is in."[8]

While these surveys and the demographic trends I summarized earlier confirm that a substantial minority of Americans find back-to-the-country ideals congenial to their own values, the surveys and the census data by themselves do not bring this flow of people, ideas, and trends into sharp focus. Perhaps the best way to bring more coherence to both the hesitant and enthusiastic attempts to move toward simpler lifestyles over the past quarter century is to take a close look at a representative person whose life has been closely intertwined with the shifting fortunes of the back-to-the-land movement. A good candidate for such a case study is Jd Belanger, the editor of *Countryside,* the back-to-the-country magazine whose list of subscribers served as the source of respondents for my nationwide survey of smallholders.[9]

In the fall of 1969 Belanger placed a $25 classified ad in *Organic Gardening* announcing the publication of a $1-a-year newsletter for homesteaders. In addition to the dollar subscription price, Jd asked his readers for at least one idea, suggestion, question, or answer to someone else's question. And it was a question that prompted Jd to start the newsletter in the first place. The pigs that Jd had been raising were ready to be turned into ham and bacon, and Jd wanted to do it all himself but did not have any idea how to cure a ham. He did what farmers are supposed to do when they have questions: he called his state university extension service. The expert's answer has kept Jd Belanger in back-to-the-land journalism for more than two decades: "'*People* don't cure bacon,' [the extension agent] said incredulously, '*Oscar Meyer* cures bacon!'" Since 1969 *Countryside* has been an information exchange for the kind of practical, how-to, self-reliant lore of small-scale farming that almost disappeared with the demise of yeoman agriculture, for which extension agents, preoccupied with the promotion of large-scale family farms and agribusiness, typically have little interest or knowledge.

A journalism graduate from the University of Wisconsin at Madison, Jd's original career and life plan was to edit a weekly small-town newspaper part-time and farm full-time. Finding newspaper work was not a problem, but Jd and his wife, Diane, were penniless. They had to rent farms for several years, while Jd polished his journalism skills and tried to save money for a farm. Working two and three jobs left little time for back-to-the-land pursuits. Eventually, however, Jd and Diane saved enough money for a down payment on an abandoned two-story creamery on a one-acre lot on the outskirts of a small Wisconsin village. Jd still had to keep two jobs to help pay for the renovations and for the printing equipment he had been accumulating over the years. But the creamery finally did take the shape of a comfortable farm home, complete with a printing workshop downstairs that allowed Jd to spend more time at home to help Diane look after their four children, an assortment of livestock, a garden, and an orchard.

At a time when his one-acre homestead might have been a candidate for an article in *Organic Gardening,* Jd launched his newsletter announcement in the magazine's classified ads. Within a few months, he had several hundred subscribers. Then he came to the first of many crossroads. The *Mother Earth News* appeared in the spring of 1970. Though it was also started on a shoestring, its first numbers did have the look and feel of a magazine that would command over half of a million subscribers within a few years. Jd wondered if there was a place for his newsletter, and he thought about quitting. His subscribers, however, "truly seemed like friends." And as he recollects, "What I was learning about homesteading was both astonishing and fascinating. I couldn't quit!"

Instead of quitting, the Belangers bought a country journal, *Small Stock Magazine,* started another one, *Dairy Goat Guide,* and then in 1973 rolled the two magazines and the newsletter into the bimonthly *Countryside and Smallstock Journal, Countryside*'s full and official name. Soon there were ten thousand subscribers, and collating the magazine was much more than an evening's walk around the dining room table. Jd rented an office in town and assembled a staff that at the height of his publishing enterprise numbered twenty-five.

Complementary to putting out *Countryside* was running a small farm, one that could serve as an experimental homestead for the plans and schemes that would arrive at the *Countryside* mail box. Jd and Diane sold the converted creamery and bought a farm just down the road from their one-acre smallholding. In addition to the conventional farm chores, the Belangers tried making cheese, butter, and sausages, tanning rabbits, and spinning wool. As Jd explains, "Many of the projects were a direct result of our involvement with the magazine. During the 'sugar shortage' we planted sugar beets, made sugar, and wrote about it. We grew soybeans and made tofu; planted flax and processed it; grew comfrey and Jerusalem artichokes and amaranth, and speltz and whatever else homesteaders were talking about: we made beer, and experimented with wind electric converters and solar heat. The magazine, our homestead—and our life— became so intertwined it was difficult to say where one left off and the next started."

As the farm and magazine projects expanded, the Belangers found that smallholders were writing to ask where they could buy the kind of homestead tools they read about in *Countryside*. The Countryside General Store was just a logical extension of Jd and Diane's back-to-the-land ventures. The store became a repository for hog scrapers, kerosene lamps, cast-iron cookware, and had more than a thousand miscellaneous back-to-the-country accoutrements in its mail-order catalog. As the orders rolled into the general store and the *Countryside* subscriber numbers shot up to near forty thousand, the rented office in town was bypassed in favor of a "whole" building. Then, within a year, they acquired an even larger building, complete with a print shop that, for Jd, "would have been beyond my fondest hopes a few years before. Life couldn't have been better."

But, as Jd acknowledges philosophically, "what goes up, comes down." The Belangers' yeoman instincts told them never to touch debt. Lawyers and bankers advised the opposite: growing businesses had to have an adequate cash flow, and borrowing was the only way they could serve their exploding clientele. Debt for the Belangers, however, came at the wrong time. "Then came the 1980s," is the way Jd starts his reconstruction of the

Belangers' misfortunes; "Reagan. Yuppies. The me-first generation. The farm crisis. Interest in homesteading and small stock dropped like a bale of wet hay from the top of a 40 foot elevator." Systematic liquidation of their assets followed plunging orders and subscription renewals. By the mid-1980s all that was left was a mortgage on the farm, a substantial business debt, and a magazine headed toward oblivion. Jd thought he had no alternative but to quit. At the low point, subscriptions fell to four thousand, and the Belangers missed an issue because they did not have enough money to pay the postage.

Ironically, it was a high-tech microprocessor that saved *Countryside*, the advocate of sustainable-technology farming. Jd sold several of his Hereford steers and bought a Macintosh computer. Working with Diane, he found the Macintosh capable of doing the layout of magazine pages and producing camera-ready art and graphics. Diane could keep the subscriber list on the computer's data base, and Jd would do desktop publishing. With just the two of them and their computer, they had the potential to cut overheads radically and stay in the back-to-the-land publishing business. Though they had missed a mailing, they put together a double issue, sent out renewal notices, and advertised for subscribers. The response was heartening—subscriber numbers started to move up again. Then came the stock market crash of October 1987, which prompted many to reconsider their single-minded pursuit of wealth. Some of those turning toward basic values became *Countryside* subscribers. By the end of the eighties *Countryside* was back with pressruns of over twenty thousand. And Jd had one last worry: "Sometimes it frightens me to think that this might be the 1970s all over again, and if I'm not careful, I'll fall back into the same 'success trap' again."

With *Countryside* once again on solid ground, Jd started to reassess the family's homestead plans. Southern Wisconsin was too domesticated for Jd's adventuresome spirit. Desktop publishing freed the Belangers from dependence on print-composition shops; they could compose the magazine on their kitchen table, anywhere. A little scouting found land and a home in Wisconsin's north woods, the Chequamegon National Forest, with the nearest settlement, a small town of five hundred, fifteen miles away. In the fall of 1990 they moved, after selling just about everything except the family dog and the computer.

It might be a while before they gain their previous level of homestead self-reliance. Deer and raccoons devour the parts of their garden that survive the frost. But there are compensations. Jd describes them: "Looking over the top of my computer screen, I can see a small glacial lake about 100 yards to the west. The other day a bald eagle soared over the lake and settled in one of the tall balsam firs at the edge. Sometimes from my window I watch the otters cavorting in the water, or deer browsing in the opening between here and the lake."

Jd Belanger and all the other Americans who have gone back to small-town and rural America over the past three decades, and have tried to stay there, have not always found their moves easy. They often left careers in the city to find jobs in the country. They struggled to pay off homestead mortgages and keep their cars going for the commute to work. While agrarian sentiments in America have remained strong, back-to-the-land still means putting principle ahead of convenience; it means going back against the grain of more than a century of urban cultural and economic dominance.

But back-to-the-land is far from an idiosyncratic movement. With the urban-to-rural migration turnaround, a substantial minority of the population interested in simple living, and a generally heightened environmental consciousness, smallholders are part of a broad-based counterstream movement opposed to the unapologetic materialism of the mainstream society.

Finding Back-to-the-Landers

Individual back-to-the-landers are not hard to find. The proprietor of a small town drugstore can likely refer the curious researcher to a family or two of urban émigrés. Then these new homesteaders may know others willing to share their experiences. Further contacts follow initial ones, and soon the investigator becomes part of a network of intriguing back-to-the-country case histories.

To meet and then become involved in the personal histories of neo-homesteader families can certainly be rewarding as well as enlightening for a researcher. My feeling, however, in approaching this study of the back-to-the-land movement was that I needed to move beyond first-person accounts, as important as they have been and will be in this study, in order to give more meaning to the scope of the movement, as well as to its contours. I wanted to find something close to a representative group of new pioneers so that I could have a firm idea about the extent of the movement in America today.

My attempt to understand the back-to-the-landers both as individuals and as participants in a social movement has been a fifteen-year research investment. Early in the 1980s I began with a small number of exploratory interviews, then moved to a regional mail questionnaire in 1983, and ended the 1980s with a series of in-depth case studies. In 1992 I completed another questionnaire survey, this time nationwide rather than regional. The initial interviews were of great assistance in building the questionnaires, and the survey results in turn informed the case-study interviews.

The first problem I had to face before I could do any systematic interviewing or survey work was how I was going to define a back-to-the-lander. The initial question was just how inclusive or exclusive I wanted the definition to be. If I were too restrictive, I might well eliminate smallholders who had full-time jobs away from their farmsteads, even though they might be serious homesteaders. On the other hand, if I were too inclusive, I could end up with just about anyone living in the country who had a garden. In order to locate a manageable number of back-to-the-landers and still maintain a coherent definition of the movement, I decided to ground my definition in intent or interest. The new pioneers, then, are individuals and families who are interested in self-reliant living on their own land. More specifically, this interest in self-reliance means trying, in the best yeoman tradition, to produce on one's own property what one consumes, even if the intent falls far short of the ideal. Consequently, large-scale farmers who produce just a few specialty crops would not be considered back-to-the-landers, even though they may have just quit a city job to take up farmwork. At the same time, someone who has spent a lifetime in the country, practicing semisubsistence agriculture on a smallholding, would be for my purposes a "back-to-the-lander." Wilson Rockwell, except for living in Denver to attend to his legislative duties, is a good example of someone with a back-to-the-land perspective who, nevertheless, has spent his life in the countryside.

Being a back-to-the-lander, then, is as much a state of mind as it is a state of place. While the subjects of this study all have country property, and while almost all of them are making the move back to the country from urban America in either a symbolic or a literal sense, 7 percent of the survey respondents say they have not spent at least one year after their eighteenth birthday in an urban or suburban environment. What makes these smallholders back-to-the-landers is their philosophical point of view rather than their demographic profile. On *Countryside*'s contents page, Jd Belanger outlines what he sees as the essential elements of the back-to-the-country state of mind.

Our Philosophy

It's not a single idea, but many ideas and attitudes, including a reverence for nature and a preference for country life; a desire for maximum personal self-reliance and creative leisure; a concern for family nurture and community cohesion; a certain hostility toward luxury; a belief that the primary reward of work should be well-being rather than money; a certain nostalgia for the supposed simplicities of the past and an anxiety about the technological and bureaucratic complexities of the present and the future; and a taste for the plain and functional. COUNTRYSIDE reflects and supports the simple life, and calls its practitioners *homesteaders.*

Armed with these definitional resources, my next challenge was to find an identifiable group of back-to-the-landers. I decided that the most direct solution to my problem was to use the subscription lists to the practical, how-to magazines my prospective subjects were likely to read. Through this approach I could have missed some homesteaders too frugal to subscribe or too preoccupied to squander time and money on the obvious. But I was confident that a good many subscribers to the country how-to journals were actively practicing the applied arts of independent living, as well as keenly interested in the projects of like-minded idealists.

There are a number of back-to-the-land and alternative-technology magazines I might have chosen as the basis of my sampling lists. They range from the "down-home" approach of the large-circulation *Mother Earth News* to the relatively sophisticated *Harrowsmith,* a glossy bimonthly that tackles not only gardening issues but social-ecological ones as well. But for my first face-to-face encounter with the back-to-the-landers, I avoided the national mass-subscription magazines and approached instead a small-circulation, regional journal in the inland Pacific Northwest entitled the *Smallholder.* The *Smallholder,* based in Argenta, British Columbia, is more of an information-exchange newsletter captive to its readership than a publication controlled by its volunteer editors. It has a circulation of just over one thousand and makes a valiant, if often unsuccessful, attempt to be a monthly publication. The *Smallholder* editors allowed me to take a small sample from their subscription lists.

My first step in understanding back-to-the-landers and their movement was to find and interview the *Smallholder* sample at their homesteads. During the fall of 1981 and the spring of 1982 I pursued sixty-five *Smallholder* subscribers, the complete population of subscribers in southeastern British Columbia and western Alberta, down country back roads and along isolated lake fronts. Before actually going on the road to meet these small-holders, I wrote each one, asking permission for an interview. Many responded with invitations to visit and talk. A number of the nonrespondents did not have phones and could not be reached. A few others, in the interest of privacy, declined the interview request. In the end, my fall and spring excursions found me talking to thirty-four back-to-the-country people, as well as another eleven city dwellers with back-to-the-land dreams. The results of these semistructured interviews appear periodically throughout the rest of the book.

Once I had digested these first interviews, I felt ready to put together a mail questionnaire and seek a wider audience. The *Smallholder* interviews provided much of the specific content for the mail questionnaire, but I was now looking for a larger-circulation country magazine to provide respondents for my survey. The pages of one of the *Whole Earth Catalog*s, those compendia of tools and ideas for an alternative America, provided the source for my mail survey. Buried in the middle of a bulky, oversized catalog was the following description of *Countryside:* "The concerns and thousand odd questions of homesteaders and small livestock farmers get better regular treatment in *Countryside* than anywhere else. Separate columns for rabbits, pigs, goats, cows, woodlots, bees, feeds, marketing and more make it easy to zero in on your interests. It is also a good place to shop—there are lots of farm-related supplies advertised, many available by mail-order."[10]

I wrote Jd Belanger, *Countryside*'s editor, and told him about my back-to-the-land survey project, wondering if I might have access to *Countryside*'s subscription lists. After a couple of phone calls he agreed to send me the subscriber names and addresses for the Canadian provinces from Manitoba west to British Columbia and for the states of Washington, Idaho, Montana, and North Dakota. After I pared down the list by eliminating commercial businesses, like organic groceries and hardware stores, I had 837 potential respondents. From two separate mailings during 1983, 554 (66 percent) of the *Countryside* readers responded to a twelve-page questionnaire. Almost 90 percent of the respondents were from the Pacific Northwest, either the maritime or inland areas of the region. Washington had over half the respondents (53 percent), followed by British Columbia (14 percent), Montana (12 percent), and Idaho (11 percent).

Once the analysis of the 1983 *Countryside* questionnaires began to take shape, I came to realize that although I had the resources of my first set of personal interviews and all the detail from the questionnaire, there was still an unarticulated gap in my understanding of the back-to-the-land movement. The statistical profiles from the questionnaire were creating larger-than-life back-to-the-landers, kinds and types of individuals and families I had never met through my original interviews. I decided, then, that I really needed to go back to the field to do a number of in-depth case studies with the kind of people my questionnaire was telling me existed but whom I had yet to interview. Employing the venerable back-to-the-land technique of "networking," I met a number of individuals whose personal histories helped bring additional life to the averages and variations in the questionnaire information. I did these interviews primarily in the Pacific Northwest, with the exception of an excursion to Falmouth, Massachusetts, on Cape Cod. Most of these case studies were done in the late 1980s and early 1990s, with the last ones completed during the summer of 1995.

By the time I was finishing my last case studies, the 1983 *Countryside* survey was becoming dated. Much had happened in the eight years since I had sent the questionnaire out, including the changes in *Countryside*'s circulation from 40,000 subscribers to 4,000 and then back up past 20,000. I not only wanted to bring my understanding of the back-to-the-landers current in terms of their farming techniques and their satisfaction with latter-day homesteading, but I also was curious whether smallholders, like Jd Belanger, were taking advantage of emerging technologies like computers and modems to communicate with city offices. Prepared with the design for a revised questionnaire, I approached the Belangers once again for permission to use their subscription lists for a new survey. They agreed; but instead of replicating my previous regional study, I decided to expand the scope of the survey to a nationwide sample, representative of each of the major U.S. census divisions.

I chose six states for the 1992 survey—California (San Francisco-San Jose and north), Texas, Missouri, Minnesota, Maine, and Georgia—and then randomly selected 200 *Countryside* subscribers from each state. In the early part of 1992, I sent another twelve-page questionnaire to the 1200 potential respondents, and after a second mailing at midyear, I received 698 back, for a return rate of 58 percent, still considered to be a very good response rate for this kind of survey.[11]

In sending out the questionnaire and analyzing the returns, I was faced with the very practical problem of just how to translate my conceptual definition of a back-to-the-lander into an "operational" one, since not all respondents were likely to be practicing homesteaders. The key criterion in deciding who was a back-to-the-lander and who was not, for the purpose of the questionnaire, was a positive response to the following question: "Do you live on property that is large enough (and has no zoning restrictions if in a small town or city) to keep at least some small farm animals?" The "yes" answers to this question produced a back-to-the-country sample of 565, broken down by state into the following percentages: California, 17 percent; Texas, 15 percent; Missouri, 13 percent; Minnesota, 17 percent; Maine, 22 percent; and Georgia, 16 percent. I return to the 133 urban respondents in Chapter 5, "Urban Pioneers." But unless I note otherwise, I use the 1992 survey to describe and analyze the quantitative dimensions of the back-to-the-land movement for the rest of the book.

Beyond the technical details of the questionnaire response rates, a nettlesome question remains: Might it be possible that many of the *Countryside* questionnaire respondents are simply people who enjoy living in a country environment rather than individuals who, in addition, are dedicated to sustainability principles? While it is difficult to answer this question with absolute certainty, the survey results include, fortunately, at least one indicator of the seriousness of the *Countryside* subscribers' intent. I asked the questionnaire respondents how they would feel about spending "the rest of their lives on a labor-intensive small farm." I was apprehensive about the number of subscribers who would respond positively to this question, since I did not specify conditions, such as adequate or comfortable incomes. And also to be considered was the extent of the smallholders' attachment to the worlds of both mainstream-society convenience and back-to-the-land simplicity, which attachment would likely make them reluctant to embrace an exclusive commitment to labor-intensive farming. It was surprising, then, when 84 percent of questionnaire respondents said that they would be happy (40 percent, very happy, and 44 percent, pretty happy) to spend the rest of their lives on a back-to-the-country homestead; 11 percent would have been not too happy—and 5 percent, not at all happy—to spend the rest of their lives smallholding. The respondents' answers to this question, as well as to many other of the survey questions that attempt to measure their commitment to smallholding, demonstrate that as a group the *Countryside* survey respondents not only live in the country but also have a serious investment in the philosophy of back-to-the-country living.

The by and large fixed-choice questionnaires covered smallholder technology, number of children and how they helped on the smallholdings, satisfaction with country life, and basic values and practices in relation to a number of sustainability issues. Not quite by design the last page was left blank, and consequently I offered the following apologetic invitation: "We haven't left much room, but in the space remaining below we'd very much like to have your comments—on things we may have missed or not understood or any other aspect of country life or your feelings." The respondents took me seriously. When I transferred their comments from both the 1983 and 1992 surveys to typescript, I had over 120 pages of single-spaced text. These often insightful observations on smallholder life frequently augment the following case studies and discussions of questionnaire results.

Beyond my own firsthand research, I also draw on newspapers, magazines, and books for a rich variety of interviews with and personal accounts by smallholders. Taken together, the interviews, questionnaires, case studies, and previously published sources provide a multidimensional view of back-to-the-landers struggling to build a sustainable way of life in the country.

Origins, Transitions, and Destinations

One of the first questions I wanted answered about my back-to-the-land subjects was directed to the very words that describe the movement: Is "back-to-the-land" literal or metaphorical? More specifically, I wondered just how many of the new country people were returning to a rural way of life temporarily interrupted by city diversions, or just what part of the movement might be first-time experimenters with small-farm life. To find out how many of the back-to-the-landers have literally come *back* to the land, I asked the *Countryside* questionnaire respondents how much farm experience they and their spouses had before the age of eighteen. The four choices I allowed were: (1) a great deal, (2) some, (3) not very much, and (4) none. In Table 1, I have summarized the responses to the question on farm experience, collapsing the responses to the farm-experience question from four categories to two in order to make the differences in experience clearer and to highlight the differences between male and female back-to-the-landers. In addition, I have decided to place those respondents with a great deal of farm experience in one category, those with some, not very much, and none in the other category. Those who report a great deal of farm experience are candidates for the literal back-to-the-land designation, assuming they have spent time away from the country, an issue to which I soon turn. Table 1 shows that just 27 percent of the respondents and their spouses had extensive farm experience in their childhood and youth. Almost three-quarters (73 percent) of the *Countryside* respondents, then, have taken up a way of life with which they are not totally familiar.

Table 1.   *Countryside* respondents' childhood farm experience*

	Male (%)	Female (%)	Totals (%)
Great deal of farm experience	34	20	27
No experience, not very much, or some	66	80	73

Note: Total number of respondents = 565 (actual responses numbered 564, since not all respondents answered each question).
*Includes the respondents' reports for both themselves and their spouses. The respondents are almost equally divided between male (51%) and female (49%).

The questionnaire responses to the farm-experience question raise a number of other questions about the respondents—how long have they been living in the country? how old are they? how many years have they spent living in the city?—but before drawing on the survey to answer these questions, I want to use the experiences of three families (the Rosenthals, Strohauers, and Craigs), in a brief case-study format, to place the survey results for the back-to-the-land issue along an experiential continuum, from those returning to well-established rural roots to those trying to establish this kind of foundation for the first time.

The Rosenthals

For Anne Rosenthal moving back to the land was a simple matter of returning home—back to her childhood farm home, at which she had spent extended summer vacations as an adult.* Anne and her husband,

*Rosenthal is a pseudonym. In the early stages of the research, following the traditional ethical code of university-sponsored research, I promised my respondents anonymity in exchange for their cooperation. Consequently, in many of my interviews and case studies the names of the informants have been changed, and details have been altered, to protect their privacy. For previously published material, there is of course no attempt to hide the identity of the source. In the later stages of my research, I interviewed a number of activist smallholders who were interested in having their identities known in order to facilitate their organizing agendas. Throughout the book I clearly identify those back-to-the-landers for whom I use a pseudonym.

David, both in their early fifties, had grown restless in what they considered the confining demands of their suburban and professional way of life. When Anne's eighty-year-old father started talking about having to give up the 320-acre family farm, the Rosenthals decided they would sell their Seattle home and move across the Cascade Mountains to eastern Washington to help Anne's father keep the farm in the family.

While returning home to the land was in one sense a simple step, their motivations for doing so were somewhat involved. There was the matter of family obligation, of course—helping an ailing parent. Then there was the escape from organizational routine and the attraction of the freedom and slower pace of farm life. The primary reason for their coming back home, however, concerned their two teenage sons, Jason and Mark. The Rosenthals wanted to place their sons in situations where they would have meaningful work to do, work like farm labor, which would give them an experience of connectedness: cultivating strawberries would lead to strawberry jam on fresh whole wheat bread. And while Anne wanted to see her sons avoid the drug cultures of large suburban high schools, her first goal was to "get my boys off junk food!"

Going home required Anne and David to make a number of professional and financial adjustments. David, a geological engineer, had been employed by the federal government. Now he works part-time as a consultant, and his assignments often take him away from the family for several weeks at a time. Anne has become a substitute teacher for the local school district, an experience not altogether discontinuous with her full-time position as head of the English Department at a Seattle High School.

While the occupational adjustments mean that their income has certainly dropped, part of the trauma of moving has been cushioned by the equity from their suburban home. And their expenses have taken a sharp drop as well. They report that with a large garden, fruit trees, chickens, and a few head of beef cattle in the pasture, they are growing 75 percent of their food on their farm. They plan to become even more self-reliant with a greenhouse and fish ponds. But they have found that the 320-acre farm itself is just too large for intensive development. They keep a few horses for pleasure riding, but lease most of the farm as pasture land to neighboring dairy farmers.

The Strohauers

If the Rosenthals' move back to the country was a matter of a relatively uncomplicated transition, James Strohauer, though raised on a farm, found setting up a Maine homestead very much a novel experience. He describes his first hesitant steps in a *Mother Earth News* first-person account: "Even though I had been raised on a farm, I left it as soon as I came of age and, furthermore, had forgotten everything I ever knew about country life. What's more, my wife Claudia had always been accustomed to modern conveniences. So, it was with considerable trepidation that we set about cleaning out the old dug-out well and installing a hand pump (about which I knew nothing), rewiring the cabin (about which I knew even less), laying in firewood and making our domicile 'winter-worthy.' "[12]

Just as an adult who has learned a second language as a child finds that language returning upon taking an immersion course in the details of grammar and vocabulary, James, with Claudia as an apprentice, found his farm skills incrementally coming back as he put together a functioning farmstead, even if it deviated from ideal-typical blueprints found in the pages of the *Mother Earth News*. But like nearly all other smallholders, the Strohauers could count on their property only for part of their maintenance. Unlike the Rosenthals, with the fortunate combination of the equity from their suburban home, the inheritance of a large farm, and the possession of portable and professional occupations, James and Claudia did not have the immediate financial resources to support their back-to-the-land venture. Consequently Claudia, a registered nurse, of necessity works three nights a week at a local hospital, a schedule hardly in harmony with the country wisdom of "early to bed, early to rise," but one that does allow two to three full days a week in garden and kitchen. And James breaks away from his reacquired farm routine "to teach music as time allows and barter opportunities arise."

The Craigs

At the other end of the country experience continuum from the Rosenthals, and without a farm childhood like James Strohauer's to draw on, Rick and Joy Craig arrived five years ago at their forest-covered homestead as first-timers—back-to-the-landers in the figurative sense.* Rick was an apprentice cabinet maker who took only a passing interest in gardening until he met Joy, a social worker whose after-work time was devoted to an elaborate vegetable garden. Neither had working experience with a piece of land bigger than a large suburban lawn. Each of them, however, had

---

*Craig is a pseudonym.

been attracted to the simplicity and freedom of rural life. Together, assisted by an assortment of how-to country magazines and books, they plotted their escape from the suburbs of Spokane, Washington.

Using Joy's modest savings and a family loan, they purchased a ten-acre Rocky Mountain retreat. At the end of one school year, having made their break from the city, Rick and Joy found themselves starting from scratch on a piece of land whose scrub and older-growth pine allowed no easy choice for either a house or garden site. Though certainly neophytes, the Craigs were not without resources. Rick possessed carpentry and cabinet-making skills. Joy was an accomplished gardener. They also brought with them their small library of back-to-the-country manuals. Systematically following the blueprints and recipes from their trusted books and periodicals, they went to work to create step-by-step a self-reliant farmstead.

Joy and Rick used the first summer and early fall to clear and plant a garden and make a start on what they hoped would become a small commercial apple orchard. They also designed and built the first component of what they planned over time would turn into a spacious country home. The twelve-by-twenty-foot first-stage house was finished before winter and outfitted with a small but efficient Scandinavian wood-burning stove. During the winter Rick began to advertise a prospective cabinetmaking enterprise among his neighbors and in the several nearby small towns.

It has only taken the Craigs a few years to turn their forest-covered property into a smallholding that would fit comfortably onto the pages of the books and magazines that inspired it. As of this writing, the house is taking final form, and a root cellar holds the harvest from a large garden and an assortment of fruit trees that are just coming into production. Joy and Rick barter and sell goat's milk, eggs, and garlic, whose yearly value they estimate at between $2,000 and $3,000. Rick's cabinetmaking business, housed now in its own workshop, keeps him busier than he would like to be. He and Joy have not only coped with the demands of their expanding homestead but have the added responsibility of Kirsten, their one-year-old daughter, who has come to take precedence over the rabbits, goats, chickens, and the carefully cultivated garden and orchard.

With these case studies as reference, I want now to turn attention back to the survey results. One might naturally wonder how so many people, especially those like the Craigs and Strohauers, can make a dramatic lifestyle change without knowing very much about the kind of life to which they are committing themselves. It is quite possible, of course, that the inexperienced homesteaders did acquire some farm exposure after they turned eighteen but before they made their move to the country. Unfortunately, the questionnaire is silent on this matter. One path back to the land, however, appears to be marriage to a partner, like James Strohauer, who by virtue of previous experience can inspire sufficient confidence on the part of his or her spouse that their family can survive and prosper back on the land.

Even for those back-to-the-landers who grew up on a farm, rural experience may well have been eclipsed, as in the case of James Strohauer, by years of city-bound living. At least one more question, therefore, needs to be answered to complete an understanding of the new-pioneer separation, fictive or not, from the land. Regardless of where they grew up, we still want to know whether as adults they spent time in an urban setting. To obtain an indicator of their urban orientation, I asked the questionnaire respondents how many years they had spent in a city or suburban environment after the age of eighteen.

The answer to this question makes more sense if one first knows how old the respondents are and how long they have been living in the country. The *Countryside* respondents are well into middle age, with an average age of 47. One in twenty of the survey respondents is under 30, while just over two-thirds (68 percent) are between 30 and 60. As a group these middle-aged smallholders have accumulated a considerable amount of both country and urban experience. They have an average of 15 years of living in an urban or suburban setting and an average of 14 years in the general area where they now live, with 7 years at their principal residence.

The average age of 47 testifies to the perseverance commonly prerequisite to homestead living in the country. As I show in the next chapter, "Seven Ways of Living Back-to-the-Land: Work, Time, and Money in the Country," it takes time to accumulate the resources for a country move. The respondents on average were in their thirties before they found their way back to the land—subtracting their 14 years of residence in the general area where they now live from their average age of 47 gives them an approximate age of 33 for the start of their rural adventure. Spending a decade or more working in the city either to save for homestead dreams or temporarily to explore urban options is a common route back to the country. Coming back "home" is typically something done in one's mature years after seeing the world beyond the edge of town. Dorothy in the *Wizard of Oz* is the archetypal back-to-the-lander. After experiencing the glitter of the Emerald City, she is ready to return to the Kansas countryside, confessing, "There's no place like home." Perhaps one reason smallholders are able to tolerate the provincialism of small towns is that they have the advantage of perspective, a perspective that, after years of city living, allows them to appreciate the virtues of rural life without overreacting to its deficiencies.[13]

With the survey of the new pioneers' childhood farm experience in front of us and with an appreciation of their circuitous paths to the country, we have the resources to say what "back-to-the-land" means for modern-day homesteaders. By and large the back-to-the-landers, as they move to the country, go in search of their mythical, rather than their literal, roots (given that three-quarters of them do *not* claim intensive farm experience). Consequently, the more typical back-to-the-landers would be much like Joy and Rick Craig, relying on the pages of *Countryside* rather than reflexes conditioned by a childhood of farm chores. For most of these neohomesteaders the back-to-the-country movement is a metaphorical one, and they are reclaiming their place on the earth as descendants of ancestors who were themselves children of the land.

Educated Homesteaders

A sizable segment of the questionnaire respondents' city years after eighteen was spent going to school. The *Countryside* sample is well educated, with a substantial proportion having a college education. In Table 2, I summarize the respondents' educational achievements at the college level.

Table 2. *Countryside* respondents' college experience*

	%
Some undergraduate study	25
Undergraduate degree	15
Some graduate study	6
Graduate degree	12
Total	58**

Note: Total number of respondents = 565 (actual responses numbered 563, since not all respondents answered each question).
*Includes respondents' reports for both themselves and their spouses.
**The overall differences between males and females are minimal: 3 percent more women than men have college experience.

Almost three in five (58 percent) of the *Countryside* sample have some college-level experience, with nearly one in eight (12 percent) possessing a graduate degree, ranging from a Master of Arts in anthropology to a Doctor of Philosophy in wildlife biology. And another one in five, in addition to this academic course work, has one kind of postsecondary technical education or another, and less than one in ten (7 percent) has failed to graduate from high school. These levels of educational achievement can be further appreciated if they are compared to those of the respondents' parents. The *Countryside* respondents reported that 25 percent of their fathers and 20 percent of their mothers had college-level experience, less than half of their own 58 percent figure. In addition, just under one-third of the parents (31 percent for fathers and 32 percent for mothers) had not graduated from high school, compared to 7 percent of the respondents who did not make it through high school. These figures suggest that back-to-the-landers, to the extent that the *Countryside* survey is representative of the movement, do not come from a necessarily privileged background, at least in an educational sense, and that their moves to the country are only one manifestation of their breaking away from their family histories.

Since there are few calls for university-educated personnel in rural America beyond a dwindling number of teaching and nursing positions, and since a master's degree in English literature is not a prerequisite for rototilling a garden, one has to wonder just how the well-educated new pioneers accommodate themselves to, and are accommodated by, the demands of country life. The lives of the following back-to-the-landers show how the schooled person might adjust to a world of manual labor.

Louise Singer

Louise Singer works occasionally as a plumber's assistant in and around a small lake-front resort town in the inland Northwest.* She lives with her common-law husband and two children in a three-room cabin on one and a half forested acres two miles from town. The cabin is without electricity, and her portable radio has no batteries. Support from Ray, her partner, is unpredictable. Ray's on-again, off-again construction work is not much more reliable than Louise's casual jobs with the area's one journeyman

*Louise Singer is a pseudonym.

plumber. Louise and Ray's safety net is provided by Ray's parents, retirees who brought their young, unmarried son with them to the secluded resort community. Grandparenthood enables Ray's mother and father to maintain at least a facade of toleration for Louise's eccentricities.

Louise's divorced mother teaches business education in a suburban Philadelphia high school. Her biannual visits with Louise and her grandchildren are brief—even shorter than planned, since her repressed frustration with Louise's lack of convention takes only hours, not days, to become unrepressed.

Present peculiarities aside, Louise was conventional enough to graduate with honors from the same Philadelphia school at which her mother teaches. A year after graduation she found herself at the end of a cross-country odyssey and enrolled as a freshman at the University of Washington in Seattle. One of her English instructors was a self-styled "agrarian anarchist," and Louise was one of a small group of students captivated by this lecturer's vivid images of urban decadence in contrast to the tranquil virtues of simple living in the countryside.

The intense criticism of city life and the unqualified adulation of things rural prompted the small group of agrarian advocates to move beyond rhetoric to action. The summer after her freshman year, Louise and a small band of idealists set off on an exploratory trip to the backcountry of the inland Northwest. The reality of outdoor toilets and cold water, however, was a sobering experience for the back-to-the-land theorists. Most of Louise's companions, including her English professor, retreated to Seattle before the summer was half-finished. Louise, however, not only stayed until September, but found both friends and work enough to make her want to try to survive year-round in the imperfect utopia rejected by her academic companions.

Louise's first trial year of rural life stretched to ten. She is the first one to admit the inconsistency between the kind of life she leads and the decade-old vision that brought her to the country. More than anything, she would like to live off the land she and Ray own, rather than just live on it while they go from one low-paying job to the next. And while she still carries a wistful fondness for academic life, Louise senses that her talents are of a more applied variety. The talent or quality that lends itself to her permanence in the countryside is the ineffable one of being able to tolerate the distance, and in her case the considerable distance, between the ideal and the real.

Dan Wright

In contrast to Louise, Dan Wright had progressed much further in school before he stepped off what he considered a career merry-go-round.* Dan's master's degree in soil science from North Carolina State University brought him to the Pacific Northwest as part of a soil-survey team. He started out extracting soil samples from farmers' fields in western Washington and soon advanced to a supervisory position with the U.S. Soil Conservation Agency. But it was not long before the pedestrian aspects of government employment wore thin, and Dan began to find attractive, by contrast, the back-to-the-land lifestyle he often encountered through his work.

Dan's transformation from secure government employee to relatively precarious smallholder was more a matter of evolution than of simply dropping out. He and his wife, Heather, carefully planned their move. They concerned themselves not so much with issues like whether to exchange home equity for country property or whether to cash in a government pension but with how to maintain an independent income at the new rural home site. Their solution was to use part of their suburban house's equity to purchase a used Caterpillar tractor with a backhoe. Now, with the irregular request to dig a hole for a septic tank or to clear space for a country lane, the Caterpillar business, along with trading eggs for milk, supports Dan and Heather's relaxed and semisubsistent way of life.

The real vexation for the Wrights in their assembled paradise interestingly comes back to the credential path that Dan has left behind but that his children are just beginning. Dan and Heather's two sons attend the consolidated junior-senior high school an hour's bus ride from their front gate. The boys want to play football, and they feel conspicuous unless dressed in appropriately labeled jeans rather than a generic variety. The concession to fashion and sport are placing a considerable strain on both the Wright's modest budget and their substantial investment in country-life ideology.

In the face of the high school's assault on his values, Dan is trying to keep his perspective, a perspective that tolerates the sometimes considerable disjuncture between the real world and the one of ideals. He, along with Louise Singer, would find the academic justifications for rural life both intriguing and motivating. But he acknowledges that it takes a certain kind of educated person to survive and thrive in the country, a fact

*Dan Wright is a pseudonym.

his olfactory glands remind him each morning as he steps from the back porch, down a short lane, and into the family's outhouse.

New Pioneers: The Emerging Profile

The back-to-the-landers are well-educated city people who have made a definite break with their urban past. Typically they are middle-aged and have spent about half their adult lives in the country. Consistent with their schooling, most have elaborate justifications for their alternative way of life. But at the same time, they are far from ideological purists. Their survival in the countryside has depended on a generous pragmatism. The new pioneers' part in the movement that runs counter to urban America and its large-scale corporatism can perhaps best be seen as that of "modest revolutionaries" or "conventional radicals."

This theme of modesty and stability carries over to the last two areas of this initial profile: property size and marriage patterns. "Smallholder," for example, is an appropriate descriptor for the back-to-the-landers in the sample. The average land size for the *Countryside* respondents was 19 acres; a quarter of them have 5 acres or less, and three-quarters live on under 70 acres. While 10 percent do have 160 acres or more, Rick and Joy Craig, with their 10 acres, would be far more typical than Anne and David Rosenthal, with their 320 acres.

Although their property sizes tend toward the modest, especially in this era of the megafarm, the respondents do have a relatively secure tenure on their minihomesteads. Ninety-two percent of the sample either own the land they live on or are buying it: 42 percent are mortgage free, and 50 percent are still making payments. One in twenty respondents rents, and the other 3 percent of smallholders live with their families on communal property or are part of a room-and-board arrangement.

Regarding that family structure: a substantial majority (80 percent) of the survey respondents are married; another 4 percent report having common-law relationships; the remaining 16 percent are divorced, separated, or widowed or never married. And for the more than eight out of ten from the sample who are married or living common-law, there is an average length of relationship of fifteen years, in a group with an average age of forty-seven. Large families in the yeoman tradition, however, have not resulted from these unions. On average the respondents have two children, one of whom is still at home.

Considering this information on the new pioneers' marital status along with the other elements of this background profile, it is apparent that the back-to-the-landers are a group of people who have made substantial investments in their chosen way of life. They have committed themselves to long-term marriages; they have bought or are buying productive property; and they have invested time and energy in obtaining advanced education credentials.

The question that naturally arises is just how these considerable investments can be translated into earning a living in the country. In the next chapter I examine the ways and means these urban refugees use to maintain themselves on smallholdings that can provide only part of their material requirements. As I begin the next chapter, which addresses financial survival in the country, I want also to return to the residual questions on the role of the new pioneers in rural transformation. Given their background, what are the prospects for the back-to-the-landers working toward the rural renaissance that was anticipated after the brief wave of turnaround migration in the 1970s? Perhaps the one characteristic of the smallholders that stands out is their level of education. Combined with their considerable urban experience, one would expect them to possess the academic skills necessary to penetrate the causes and consequences of the rural maladies they share with their neighbors. But whether these "conventional radicals" will use their educational and organizational resources to work for change in their communities is very much dependent on how much time and energy they must spend in staying alive in the country, the subject of the next chapter.

2

SEVEN WAYS OF LIVING BACK-TO-THE-LAND

Work, Time, and Money in the Country

 From his "cabin in the woods" Rube Wrightsman writes a weekly column for the *Clark Fork Valley Press* (Montana) entitled "Hey, Rube." A backcountry philosopher and lay sociologist, Rube has ruminated in print on the difficulties of back-to-the-landers' finding sustaining work in his part of rural America:

> Like dark beer and square dancing, Paradise, Montana, isn't for everyone. At one time, I worried that the eastern hordes would someday discover this place and turn it into a slice of Manhattan, but that possibility doesn't bother me anymore. Every year, about a dozen people move in and about a dozen move out, often the same ones.
>
> The reason for leaving is always the same: no jobs. It's possible to make a living around Paradise, but not a good one. Most jobs are seasonal, low paying, physically wretched and still hard to find.[1]

Even while granting philosopher Wrightsman his prerogatives for classic cracker-barrel hyperbole, it takes a modest amount of demographic acumen at least to follow him to the point of noting that there is little union-scale employment and few professional opportunities beyond the town doctor and a handful of school teachers in this country's Paradise, Montana. Prospective back-to-the-landers would likely reply that they have no intention of coming to the country to work for what Rube calls "The Man." Rather, the uninitiated homesteader is in search of Wrightsman's ideal of the "elegant sense of freedom" that comes from making a living from one's own property. Though Rube Wrightsman would certainly appreciate any sentiment in favor of independent country living, he can only engage the art of the impossible when it comes to considering the feasibility of a self-sufficient smallholding. After reemphasizing that "[the dreamers] don't come here to find good jobs, because there aren't any," he turns to homesteading itself: "They don't come here to homestead, because no one is going to sodbust their way to financial independence on a 40-acre stump farm so steep and rocky that it's only fit for raising wood ticks and rattlesnakes. The reason people here endure grunt labor and low wages is as elusive and as difficult to explain as the sound of one hand clapping."

The Clark Fork columnist, of course, has an explanation for why at least some country-bound migrants stay in places like Paradise, Montana, despite the hard work and low wages. For Rube Wrightsman the holding power of Paradise, Montana, is represented in the near mystical experience of a mountainside panorama on a crisp fall day: "Suddenly, everything stops, and the world is revealed in its timeless clarity. All around, the larch are turning yellow and the mountain tops are dusted with early snow. The smell of pine rides through the air on the sound of the wind, and the afternoon sunlight filters through the dark conifers as if for the first time. Away in the distance and far below, barely visible between two steep ridges, sits the little town of Paradise beside the green ribbon of the river. Even from this far away, it looks like a very humane place to live."

As transcendent as the view is, one still has to come down from the mountain. Coming down means finding work and earning a living, so that mountain vistas, newborn lambs, freshly mown hay fields, and all the other sights, sounds, and smells of country living can be experienced many times over. And while one might allow Rube Wrightsman the characterization of back-to-the-land life as a struggle, though a qualified one, it will become evident in the course of this chapter that the *Countryside* new pioneers, as a group, are much more affluent and have much better employment than Wrightsman's "dreamers."

This issue of jobs and homesteading gets to the central dilemma of simple living in the country: time versus money. In order to develop a self-reliant farmstead, a family or couple needs time to build fences, weed the garden, milk the goats, and cut and stack wood. But at the same time, back-to-the-landers must earn some kind of income to buy, if nothing else, garden seeds, a nanny goat, or the cast-iron stove that burns the wood to keep them warm through the winter. To the extent they sell their labor in the local economies, they lose valuable time to improve their property. Working exclusively on their homestead, however, does not produce the cash to buy the durable resources like lumber, cement, and bricks that a microfarm needs to prosper. This dilemma was summarized by a forty-two-year-old smallholder from Washington: "We love our lifestyle, but it is sometimes very discouraging not to have the capital to get our place on 'its feet'; something is always needed, such as fencing, fertilizer, farm implements. We have the time, because we both work in town only part-time, but we don't have the money. If we worked full-time, we would not be living the lifestyle we want, and we would not have the time—but we would have the money. It can be very frustrating."

The same sentiments were expressed by a back-to-the-lander whose income was not so much the problem as his time. A physician, also from Washington, wrote, "My major problem is a full-time medical practice that makes it very difficult to do what I love—be a farm boy. But my friends say I'm a farmer first and practice medicine to support my habits. But the actual doing it renews my soul for my practice!"

The physician's time-money dilemma and that of the couple who worked away from their property part-time in order to live and work on their farmstead the rest of the time represent a near universal in the lives of the back-to-the-landers to whom I talked and sent questionnaires. This dilemma is so central to their lives that the ways in which they attempt to resolve it provide one with a means for moving beyond a global stereotype of the typical new pioneer to a catalog of smallholder types. The time-money dilemma also sheds additional light on the question of new pioneers and rural transformation. As the ups and downs of the smallholders' country survival adventures are plotted here against the rural landscape, it will be possible to make at least some tentative judgments regarding the extent to which the back-to-the-landers' strategies are part of the ongoing processes of rural dependence or are contributing to community and household self-reliance.

Time and Money: Ways of Living Back-to-the-Land

From the several case studies and the profiles from the *Countryside* survey in Chapter 1, it is certainly evident that the new pioneers are not all of one type. To make sense of this diversity and move toward systematic classification, while still drawing on the time-money dilemma, I want to start with the kind of work the back-to-the-country people actually have. In the *Countryside* questionnaire, I asked the respondents to tell me, both for themselves and their spouses or partners, their occupations and exactly what they did at their jobs. Most of the survey questions were of the fixed-choice variety, but for the questions on occupation I left space for the respondents to provide some detail on how they earned their living. Table 3 provides a summary of the *Countryside* subscribers' responses to the job questions broken down into seven broad categories.

Table 3.   *Countryside* respondents' job and work categories

Employment Category	Male (%)	Female (%)	Totals (%)
Farmer	7	4	6
Professional/technical	22	29	25
Self-employed	23	15	19
Skilled labor	17	5	11
Semi-/unskilled labor	13	16	15
Homemaker	0	19	9
Retired	18	12	15
Totals	100	100	100

Note: Total number of respondents = 565 (actual responses numbered 559, since not all respondents answered each question).

The information in Table 3 takes the edge off Rube Wrightsman's pessimism on the possibility of finding a good job in the country. One-quarter of the *Countryside* respondents have professional or technical employment—teachers, nurses, physicians, professors, and veterinarians. The fact that a substantial number of homesteaders do have professional work does not deny that Rube is right about the difficulty an outsider will have in parachuting into stable, well-paying work in small-town America. My case histories and the questionnaire profiles of the middle-aged back-to-the-landers who have been living, on average, in the country since their thirties show that a secure place in the country is a product of years of planning, not an impulsive trip to the hinterland. The 18 percent of the male respondents who are retired reinforce the idea that back-to-the-land is a process rather than an event and that one may have to wait for financial independence, in the absence of rural jobs, to realize homestead dreams.

If country jobs are hard to find, one can always try to start a business. This attempt to make a job where one does not exist is a survival tactic of the nearly one in five (19 percent) *Countryside* respondents who say that they are self-employed. Some of this self-employment is closely associated with portable professional skills, like those of David Rosenthal, the consulting geologist from Chapter 1. There are many other survey respondents, however, who have built community businesses—the logger, for example, who operates a small-scale shingle mill or the smallholders who turn their homes into bed-and-breakfast retreats.

Manual labor, whether on or off a small farm, is intrinsically attractive to back-to-the-landers. Just over one in ten (11 percent) has skilled work like carpentry, welding, or auto mechanics. Another 15 percent work at unskilled (or semiskilled) jobs: custodians, waitresses, postal clerks, and short-order cooks. In putting together this catalog of occupations from the *Countryside* sample, I wondered whether a good number of smallholders might have taken country work for which they would normally, because of their educations, have been considered overqualified. Doing some cross-tabulating of questionnaire responses, I found that 20 percent of the *Countryside* respondents with some college education, both graduate and undergraduate, reported that they were working at unskilled jobs. Simple necessity is the likely reason for the well-educated homesteader's taking unskilled work. For some new pioneers these jobs are the only tickets to a life back-on-the-land. At the same time, smallholders enjoy physical labor, and they are often able to see even in the most menial and low-paying of jobs elements of service that, taken collectively, carry the potential to enhance the common welfare.

Like the unskilled-labor classification, the occupational category of "homemaker" evokes a range of social judgments, from the semidivine to the uninteresting. Nearly one in five (19 percent) of the female respondents, or their spouses for them, chose homemaker or housewife as their "occupation." For many it was awkward to give a label to a role that is bound up seamlessly with the totality of their families' everyday lives. After writing "homemaker" for his spouse's occupation, a male respondent's answer to the "what does she do at her job" question was a cryptic "a lot." Female respondents who elaborated on what they do at their homemaker "jobs" would often append a list of duties that go beyond what one would ordinarily associate with homemaker: those of dairy farmer, agronomist, veterinarian, tractor driver, hay baler. A self-designated seventy-four-year-old "retired homemaker" wrote that she "took care of the kids, yard, house, chickens, barn chores, milk goats, and all the animals we ever had."

While just 19 percent of the *Countryside* females find themselves in the homemaker category, another 31 percent have occupations that put them close to home. If female farmers (4 percent), the self-employed (15 percent), and the retired (12 percent) are added to the homemakers, half (50 percent) of the women homesteaders work at or near home. Back on the male side, adding together those who are retired (18 percent), self-employed (23 percent), and farmers (7 percent), almost half (48 percent) have work that keeps them close to home.

For many smallholders, if they cannot make a living from their own property, the ideal employment would allow them to work at home and, in addition, to be well compensated. One way for back-to-the-landers to take this "second-best" option is to communicate with an office or with clients through a computer modem or fax machine, electronically sending the day's work from the homestead without ever having to leave it. I wondered, then, whether and to what extent the *Countryside* respondents had entered the information age. Thirty-eight percent of the survey respondents had certainly taken the first step into the information age by having a personal computer, compared to 15 percent who reported having one in the 1983 survey. But when the respondents were asked if they or their spouses communicated with an office or with clients by fax or modem, the percentage took a substantial drop. Just 10 percent said they or their spouses used a fax or modem.

Admittedly, one out of ten *Countryside* respondents working with a fax or modem does not, on the surface, appear significant. In defining how smallholders actually do work in the early 1990s, fax and modem telecommunication is certainly not a dominant characteristic of the sample. At the same time, these are technologies in embryo. From this perspective,

10 percent is a remarkable figure. Considering the back-to-the-landers' educational credentials and their professional and portable occupations, one can only expect that increasing numbers of new pioneers will use computer telecommunications technologies to set up homesteads at a distance from their offices or clients, all at a comfortable walk from the milking barn. But, convenience aside, there will also be homesteaders, as I show in Chapter 4, "Soft Paths: Back-to-the-Land Technology," who will dismiss the attempted synthesis of high technology and country living as hopelessly revisionist.

Reviewing briefly what Table 3 says about the smallholders' ability to find work to support their back-to-the-country habit, it is evident that they use a variety of employment strategies. Some (15 percent) have to work at unskilled jobs in order to keep their place in the country, while almost one-fourth of the male respondents (23 percent) have created their jobs by establishing small businesses. Twenty-five percent of the sample have relatively secure professional or technical positions, and nearly one in five males (18 percent) supports himself and his family from retirement income. Then regardless of their occupations, almost half of these new pioneers (retirees, the self-employed, farmers, and homemakers) have been able to arrange their work so they can be on or close to the land full-time.

Table 3 summarizes the occupational categories for those smallholders who are either employed or retired, but still leaves open the question of how many new pioneers might be unemployed, unable to find jobs in rural economies where the unemployment rate in the early 1990s fluctuated around 15 percent, or to come up with work at a manageable commute from their homesteads. The back-to-the-landers, however, fare relatively well in finding work in the countryside or nearby urban centers. Just under one in twenty (4.4 percent) of the nonretired males from the survey reported being unemployed, with nonretired females having a slightly higher unemployment rate at 6.5 percent. Rube Wrightsman aside, big-city refugees are able to find jobs to match their back-to-the-land aspirations, though not always the work they want or with sufficient remuneration to establish instantly self-reliant farmsteads.[2]

While Table 3 contains a great deal of information about how smallholders are trying to survive in the country, it lacks multidimensionality. It connects individuals to a list of occupational categories, but cannot say how the back-to-the-landers work together in family units toward self-reliance on their land. To add dimensionality to the description and anal-

ysis of how the new pioneers make a living in the country, I want to turn
back to the time-money dilemma.

In addition to finding a job in the country, a homesteader has to decide
if he or she wants, or needs, to work full-time or part-time; full-time work,
of course, severely restricts the time one can devote to farmstead improvement, while part-time work rarely generates funds for property development. Beyond full-time/part-time work considerations, the back-to-
the-lander also has to decide whether a living can be made from the
smallholding itself; if not, the only alternative may be to find outside
employment. If these time-money-location distinctions are placed against
each other in a grid, or matrix, as in Table 4, the elements of a basic
classification table emerge. For the "Primary Source of Cash Income" in
Table 4, I want to make the categories mutually exclusive, the source of
income one's own property or outside employment. The second ele-
ment of Table 4 focuses on the time side of the new pioneers' time-
money commitment: whether they work full-time or part-time for their
cash income.

Table 4.   Back-to-the-landers: a classification table

	Primary Source of Cash Income	
Time Commitment to Cash Income	Own Property	Outside Employment
Part-time	purists	country romantics
Full-time	microfarmers	weekenders

The classification in Table 4 permits the construction of four multidimensional new pioneer types: (1) the *purists,* those who devote only part
of their time to growing a cash crop on their own property for just
enough income to survive in a monetized economy but otherwise subsist
from the resources of their homesteads or through a barter relationship
with their neighbors; (2) the *microfarmers,* back-to-the-landers who devote
all their working time to the intensive cultivation of a cash crop on their
property, usually fruits or vegetables with high market value; (3) *country
romantics,* back-to-the-country people who take outside part-time or seasonal work or have a part-time business enterprise and then spend the
rest of their time at work *and* at leisure on their own property; and (4) the
weekenders, smallholders who have full-time employment away from their
farmsteads but devote most of their free time, their weekends, early mornings, and late evenings, to working on their property.

The fourfold classification in Table 4 summarizes the core survival strategies of the new pioneers. But as organizationally uncluttered as this classification scheme appears to be, there are more than a few smallholders who reside in its conceptual crevices. Two easily recognized exceptions to the initial four types are, first, smallholders who are retired and supported by pensions and, second, those whose major source of income comes from *full-time* small businesses on their property—businesses, however, that do not directly involve farming. I call these two additional back-to-the-country types the *pensioners* and the *country entrepreneurs*. And to be as inclusive as possible, there is one more category, though one very small in numbers: new pioneers who would best be labeled *apprentices*, those who are learning the back-to-the-land craft while living and working on someone else's farm. I have packaged these three additional approaches to living back-to-the-land, along with the original four, into the classification scheme summarized in Table 5. In addition to a brief outline of each type, I have included percentages for each category from the *Countryside* sample.

In order to produce a percentage for each of the smallholder types in Table 5, I had to apply a number of strict definitional rules to the *Country-*

Table 5. Back-to-the-landers: a typology

Category	Description	%
Weekenders	Have full-time employment away from their farmsteads, but spend their free time (weekends, early mornings, and evenings) working on their property.	44
Pensioners	Retired and supported by pensions (social security, investments, and retirement plans).	18
Country romantics	Take part-time or seasonal work, then spend the rest of their time at work *and* at leisure on their property.	17
Country entrepreneurs	Major source of income comes from small business on property (cabinetmaking, welding) that does not directly involve farming.	15
Purists	Invest only part of their time growing a cash crop on their property, for just enough cash income to survive in a monetized economy; otherwise subsist from the resources of their own property and barter relationships with their neighbors.	3
Microfarmers	Devote most of their working time to the intensive cultivation of cash crops on their property—usually fruits or vegetables with high market value.	2
Apprentices	Learn the back-to-the-land craft while working on someone else's farm.	1

side survey data. The purists, for example, are those homesteaders who reported "farmer" as their occupation but said they were only working part-time. In addition, the purist spouses had to be either part-time farmers or homemakers. The microfarmers, then, are the full-time farmers, who work less than 160 acres. Where both spouses' primary source of cash income comes from either part-time work off their property or a part-time self-employment enterprise, I have placed them in the country romantic category. The weekenders are those back-to-the-lander families in which at least one spouse has full-time employment away from the smallholding. The pensioners would be retired individuals or families in which the primary income earner (in most cases a male) supports himself or his family from retirement income—social security, investments, and pensions. Those family units in which at least one spouse claims full-time employment with his or her own business venture are the country entrepreneurs. The apprentices are those *Countryside* respondents who reported they received room and board as hired workers.

With these technical specifications for the new pioneer types established, it is now possible to take a case-study approach to these different ways of living back-to-the-land. In the sections that follow, I use family and personal history sketches to illustrate the essential characteristics of each of the smallholder types.

The Purists

One way for back-to-the-landers to try to solve the time-money dilemma is, on the one hand, to reduce dramatically their need for cash and, on the other, to reframe substantially their time commitment to their property. This delicate balancing act means placing priority on the process of homesteading rather than on its outcomes. Fences, buildings, and other projects become part of five-, ten-year, and even life-long plans. This long-term approach to smallholding requires only modest income, which in turn comes from the land itself. Given the difficulty of finding inexpensive land and the financial commitment required in raising a family, it is not surprising that only 3 percent of the *Countryside* sample have been able to follow the purist ideal, in spite of its low-cost appearance. The importance of the purist approach to smallholding does not, however, reside in the number of its practitioners. For back-to-the-landers it has overarching symbolic significance. It is the way of living most home-steaders have in mind when they imagine the perfect country property, and consequently, it is with the purists that I begin the detailed description of the varying ways to live back-to-the-land.

Perhaps no other modern homesteaders better exemplify the single-minded devotion to the principles of simple living in the country than Scott and Helen Nearing, who for over a half-century have practiced the arts and sciences of living on the land. In the early 1930s Scott Nearing was a fifty-year-old academic who found himself blacklisted because of his radical political and economic positions. He and his partner, Helen, twenty years his junior, turned to homesteading as both a personal solution to their employment problem and a social experiment to demonstrate an alternative to the boom-and-bust cycles of capitalism. Their next fifty years of small-scale farming in the mountains of Vermont and on the coast of Maine has been chronicled in a number of first-person accounts and in the folklore generated by the thousands of transients who have passed through their gates over the years.

The Nearings' overriding concern was "monastic simplicity." They provided for over 80 percent of their carefully sculpted personal necessities from homesteads of no more than a few acres of marginal land. A concrete example of their approach to alternative consumption was their practice of eating from their garden in harmony with its seasons. As they report, they started "early in the spring with parsnips, the first thing available in our garden [left from the fall garden]. As soon as the snow went, we dug them and had them for one meal a day for three or four weeks." This pattern continued as their garden produced asparagus, spinach, lettuce, peas, beets, squash, corn, carrots, and potatoes, with much of the harvest stored in a root cellar through the winter. "The hardiest of these vegetables would still be fresh and edible up to the time the snow melted and we were digging parsnips once again."[3]

From the beginning of their back-to-the-land experiment the Nearings resolved they would not approach the tasks of homesteading with any degree of haste; rather, they wanted to approach their work in a measured, low-key manner that blurred the distinctions between labor and leisure. Their attraction to constructing a variety of rock buildings and fences illustrates well their philosophy. "We have one strong argument in favor of building stone walls: we enjoy working with rocks." In more detail they explain their fascination with rock building: "We agreed that the project [a 420-foot fence] should be a part-time job. It could be our tennis and/or golf. Both of us preferred building with stone to playing tennis, golf or any other games. It was relaxing, in the open air, usually in sunshine. It was constructive and lasting. It was not the subject of an urgency or deadline. It would be our pleasant avocation."[4]

Just as Scott and Helen were reluctant to make hard-and-fast distinctions between work and play, they also resisted seeing work as an end in and of itself. They coveted the contemplative life. Their labor, as enjoyable as it was, was still a means to freeing themselves for other pursuits. They did not go to the country to be consumed by the full-time task of earning their living. They would work in the mornings so that the afternoons would be free to "read, write, sit in the sun, walk in the woods, play music, go to town. We earned our four hours of leisure [each day] by our four hours of labor."[5]

Part of their labor had to be devoted to the cultivation of a cash crop, since, as they conceded, they needed money, if for nothing else than to buy postage stamps. In Vermont they used the collection of maple sap and its conversion to syrup and sugar for income generation. At their Maine farm they cultivated blueberries for the same purpose.

The Nearings saw in these projects not only a way to make money but also the essence of smallholding as a way of life. Growing blueberries and tapping maple trees are livelihood activities not easily controlled and manipulated by large-scale corporate enterprise. In rural microeconomies the homesteader has the potential to control his or her own destiny. Markets are local, and earning money is not a year-round preoccupation. The back-to-the-lander need only sell in season sufficient produce to meet circumscribed cash-income requirements.

Whether from their maple trees or their roadside blueberry stand, the Nearings supported themselves on their homesteads for more than fifty years. They did not consider their lives to be self-denying or constricted. Through back-to-the-land discipline they believed they were finding liberation from the captivity of the mass-consumption marketplace. With no regrets and with a note of personal triumph, they concluded the account of their Vermont homesteading: "We dare say that during the twenty years we spent on our Vermont enterprise, we learned more things and more important things than we could have found out during twenty years in Harvard, Columbia and the University of California all rolled into one."[6]

The Nearings' total embrace of the smallholding way of life can be inspiring, as well as depressing, for nonpurist back-to-the-landers. On one level they seem to fit perfectly the sustainability criteria I outlined in the

Introduction. They receive personal fulfillment from their relationship to the land and to the ideals of smallholding, rather than as participants in the consumer culture of the larger society. They inject a self-consciously political dimension into homesteading, seeing in their routine labor a declaration of independence from corporate America. But perfection, real or imagined, can be depressing to the ordinary mortals who try to imitate it. The Nearings' strict discipline and propitious circumstances (no children or other evident entanglements) have not been easy for other homesteaders to duplicate, even by those who count themselves as disciples. Haru Kanemitsu, a member of the *Smallholder* editorial collective, explains how her circumstances led to a modification of the Nearing principles: "Although I have tried to live as they do in general, where I find I diverge from, is the keeping of animals, which I find necessary in this [Pacific Northwest] climate, in order to eat as locally as possible. Also with children, milk products seem necessary. Not having children in their homesteading lives, Scott and Helen have been able to adhere to schedules and discipline that I find virtually impossible. So as much as I admire their lives, I can only follow some of their practices."[7] And as will be seen in the accounts of the different ways of living back-to-the-land in the remainder of this chapter, most smallholders can only follow *a few* of their practices.

The Microfarmers

Even the single-minded shopper in pursuit of just one more tomato to finish off an incomplete tossed salad is likely to notice that the produce departments in Larry's Markets are not quite the carbon copies that fail to distinguish one grocery store from another. Larry's Markets are a chain of Seattle supermarkets that make a serious attempt to provide an outlet for local farm produce. Upon entering the fresh-produce section a customer may encounter a display that invites passing shoppers to compare the taste of imported California tomatoes with that of a local Yakima Valley variety. In the coolers that hold vegetables from lettuce to rutabagas, there are clearly marked signs that distinguish the locally grown products from those shipped into Seattle from outside the region. The in-store advertising for the local produce emphasizes its freshness and flavor, and competitive price.

A retailer, like Larry's Markets, that believes in the importance of fresh, local produce is an ideal complement to the back-to-the-lander, the microfarmer, who wants to farm full-time. Larry's Markets provide an easily accessible market for the microfarmers' relatively small production of fruits and vegetables. Naturally, a high-volume grocer will not be able to depend upon back-to-the-landers for an exclusive supply of produce. But since the microfarmers' harvests are integrated with agribusiness production, the inevitable fluctuation in local supply causes minimal disruption in a year-round retail operation.

While a retailer that maintains its supply connections to the megafarms can function with or without the microfarmer, the conclusion should not be drawn that these back-to-the-landers run casual operations. The individual microfarmers, committed to intensive small-scale production, often become a part of year-round, sometimes around-the-clock enterprises.

As an intensive cultivator, the microfarmer's approach to back-to-the-country living and the time-money dilemma stands in sharp contrast to the more relaxed style of Helen and Scott Nearing. As purists, the Nearings chose relative isolation and a radically simple life in pursuit of personal freedom. On the other hand, the microfarmer relinquishes family independence by entering the marketplace full-time. The microfarmer, however, would see the temporary exchange of one's immediate liberty for full-time work on the land as a more-than-equitable bargain. Making a living from work that is fulfilling for one's self and one's family is hardly drudgery or sacrifice.

While only 2 percent of the *Countryside* sample fit into the microfarmer category, their significance exceeds their numbers in terms of the struggle for a sustainable future. Corporate megafarms dominate U.S. agriculture, and medium-sized family farms are falling to a plague of foreclosures. In contrast, microfarmers can claim healthy net incomes by following a simple guideline: a farmer can make more money from an acre of strawberries than from one hundred acres of wheat. Hyperbole notwithstanding, small-scale, intensive farming with minimum capital inputs (physical labor substituted for machine energy and little or no herbicides or pesticides) can and does outperform large-scale agriculture when it comes to the bottom line on a bank statement. Consequently, microfarming deserves a careful examination for its potential to provide both fresh, quality food for American families and good jobs for those who are willing to meet its challenges. These may well be the kinds of farmers and farm families, rather than factory farmers, who are deserving candidates for major shares in the U.S. Department of Agriculture's multibillion-dollar support programs, a proposition I briefly explore in the last chapter.

Representative of this class of neoyeomen is Nevada, Iowa, microfarmer Dale Haubrick. When asked how his large-farm neighbors accepted his unconventional operation, Dale replied, "I did hear of one person who was jealous that I was making a living on four acres while he went bankrupt on 1,000, but on the whole I've had considerable local and consumer support."[8] In the late 1980s Haubrick was working fourteen acres with two partners. They grew more than one hundred tons of produce from over a hundred different varieties—from bok choy and Chinese broccoli for the international community at Iowa State University in nearby Ames to ordinary, everyday vine-ripened tomatoes, their most popular commodity. Dale Haubrick's share of this venture was more than $30,000 in net income.

While $30,000 a year on a debt-free farm in the Midwest may well be one component in a formula for comfortable rural living, Dale's way of earning his living is anything but comfortable. He supplies thirteen restaurants and five grocery stores with fresh fruit and vegetables, as well as regularly selling his produce at two farmers' markets. In order to meet his supply commitments during the peak growing seasons, he rises at 4:30 in the morning and retires at 10:30 at night. His days are full caring for a hundred thousand indoor transplants in the early spring, hundreds of hours of weeding in May and June, and picking, cleaning, sorting, and packing produce from the summer through the fall. The workload does fall off dramatically in midwinter, but Dale starts to recondition his body for the growing season by working a couple of hours a day in February, moving on to four or five hours in March, then going on to ten or twelve hours in May, before the crunch of sixteen- to eighteen-hour days hits for the rest of the summer. In reflecting on his hectic schedule, Dale says, "Oh, I get weary. I look forward sometimes to that first killing frost—no more tomatoes, peppers and cucumbers! But even then I've built up so much self-discipline, both mental and physical, that I can't stop working all at once. So, I make structures. (One October he started building an attached greenhouse by excavating over 800 wheelbarrow loads of dirt by hand.)"[9]

Though Dale Haubrick is one of just a few microfarmers in the heart of Iowa, near metropolitan areas all over America networks of the back-to-the-land microfarmers are starting to form. One such network comes under the umbrella of the Greenleaf Produce Company of San Francisco.

Greenleaf as a wholesaler has recruited one hundred Bay-area micro-farmers to grow fresh produce for one hundred restaurants. The farmers pick their vegetables or fruit one afternoon, and Greenleaf has it in a restaurant salad bar by the next afternoon, far quicker than the two or three days for the most direct of commercial channels.

Tom Phipps of Pascadero, who grows for Greenleaf, specializes in "designer" crops for San Francisco's tony restaurants. These specialty crops include zucchini blossoms, baby lettuce, thirteen kinds of string beans and five varieties of garlic. Tom says that he can make $300 to $400 a day from the zucchini blossoms alone. Less than twenty-four hours after leaving the Phipps farm, the blossoms might be stuffed with cheese, deep-fried in beer, and presented to patrons at an upscale restaurant.[10]

The Haubrick farm, Greenleaf Produce Company, and the country's other microproducers, admittedly, are at present an insignificant part of American agriculture, but Booker T. Whatley, a retired professor of horticulture at Alabama's Tuskegee Institute, is dedicated to changing the marginal position of the microfarmer and, in the process, moving the small-scale farm from an anachronism to the agricultural mainstream. Professor Whatley has systematized microfarm practice in his book *How to Make $100,000 Farming 25 Acres*,[11] though I should point out that in the title Whatley is referring to gross, not net, income. Whatley captures the secret to making money on a small farm in an analogy he is fond of using: "A good shirt has got to have two pockets and a small farm has got to have high value crops and a year-round cash flow."[12]

The "extra" pocket in the Whatley scheme is at least ten different crops. In the South they would include grapes, sweet potatoes, black-eyed peas, blueberries, strawberries, blackberries, and mustard, collared, and turnip greens. Microfarms in the Northeast would substitute brussels sprouts, cauliflower, broccoli, and sweet corn for some of the exclusively southern produce. And most farms would want to add at least sixty hives of honey bees, for both honey and crop pollination, and perhaps rabbits, quail, and pheasants.

The whole point of Professor Whatley's rescue of the small farmer is his belief that successful small farms cannot be scaled-down versions of mega-farms. Twenty-five acres of corn and soybeans simply cannot provide a living for a family, just as these crops cannot support a family on a 640-acre farm. The costs are too high, and the returns are too low. According to the Whatley scheme, the microfarms must be different. Whatley goes so far in his emphasis on difference to insist that microfarmers "can't afford to pick, grade, wash, package and haul their produce a hundred miles or more to market."[13] The alternative is to have the consumer come to the farm and pick his or her own food. Each microfarmer under the Whatley plan would form "U-Pick" clubs with membership fees, the members becoming the year-round consumers the back-to-the-landers need to survive in the country.[14]

Organizing U-Pick clubs, finding markets for zucchini blossoms, and tending sixty beehives places the microfarmer at the vortex of fast-paced market relationships and means that these smallholders need to have their marketing antennae tuned to the latest consumer trends, rather than just grow their own favorite subsistence crops. To purist back-to-the-landers, Whatley's blueprint would be unacceptably revisionist; it places the microfarmer in a dependency relationship to markets and neglects the contemplative life. In addition, the frenetic schedule all but eliminates the possibility of having time to work on rural transformation projects. But, as I mentioned earlier, as hectic as microfarm work might be, it is work back on the land, rural work that carries the possibility of a sustaining income. And microfarming has important agricultural policy implications. The purist smallholder has no intention of producing for any but neighborhood markets, but microfarmer agriculture has the theoretical possibility of becoming a major factor in a transformed rural economy, an issue to which I turn in more detail in the last chapter.[15]

Country Romantics

The country romantics are smallholders who supply a substantial part of their material requirements from their homesteads and then work away from them on a part-time or seasonal basis or at home with a part-time business for their all-important cash income. I call these back-to-the-landers romantics because they place a priority on enjoying their country property, while they take a rather casual attitude toward systematically exploiting it for a cash income—in sharp contrast to the microfarmers and even the self-disciplined purists. Second, they are less than aggressive in looking for outside work, most preferring to let serendipity lead them down the path to survival. Since their sometimes carefree attitude runs counter to the practical and even cautious approach many back-to-the-landers take toward homesteading, it is not surprising that only about one

in six (17 percent) *Countryside* survey respondents possesses the temperament to practice the country-romantic brand of smallholding.

I have already introduced a variety of these country idealists. David and
Anne Rosenthal, Dan and Heather Wright, and Louise Singer all fit more
or less comfortably into the country-romantic category. They have part-
time jobs away from their farmsteads or a part-time business, and none
raises a cash crop. But with these two points of convergence the sim-
ilarities end. The material resources they bring to their smallholding projects vary considerably. The Rosenthals are affluent professionals; Dan
Wright has traded a graduate degree for itinerant backhoe work; and
Louise Singer barely makes do from day to day, and only with reluctant
assistance from her partner's parents.

To give some additional variety to this category of mostly easygoing new
pioneers and to examine the potential transition from one smallholding
type to another, I want to sketch out a brief case study. Kevin and Cyndi
Armstrong take seasonal jobs in order to live without interruption on
their homestead the rest of the year.* The Armstrongs are tree planters.
For eight to ten weeks each year they leave their lakeside smallholding
and work in a reforesting crew. The reforesting crews are organized by a
contractor who works for both timber companies and the U.S. Forest Service. After a stretch of timber is clear-cut, the lumber companies pay to
have the stripped land replanted with evergreen seedlings. Each summer
thousands of seasonal workers, a good share of them college students, go
to the mountains to start the job of recovering the land with trees.

In the late spring, after their garden is planted, carefully mulched, and
showing signs of growth, Cyndi and Kevin trust the care of their property
to a neighbor and join the Cascade Forestry Contractors for assignment
to a tree-planting project within reasonable driving distance of their
homestead.** They have worked for the Cascade people five different summers and have always had a placement close enough to home so that they
can get back to check on their garden on their days off. They make more
than $10,000 between them in the less than two months they work at tree
planting. Given their frugal lifestyle, large garden, and ample woodlot to
keep the winter fires in their Swedish stove burning, the money stretches
to cover their basic requirements for the year. They then have the other
ten months to harvest their garden, improve their property, and spend a

---

*Kevin and Cyndi Armstrong are pseudonyms.
**Cascade Forestry Contractors is a pseudonym.

good part of the winter cross-country skiing. This ten-month tranquillity, however, comes at a price. Tree planting is hard, backbreaking work. It is also piecework: the more trees Kevin and Cyndi plant, the more money they make. The logic of tree planting, consequently, is far from the back-to-the-land ideal of the serenity of productive labor on one's own land. Then there is the problem of the toxicity of the enterprise itself. Reforesting contractors use a variety of fungicides, pesticides, and chemical fertilizers to protect and nourish the vulnerable seedlings. Many back-to-the-landers, Cyndi and Kevin included, have begun to question whether tree planting can really be consistent with the back-to-the-land quest for a healthy environment, both from an individual point of view and in terms of the long-term environmental impact of an industrial approach to the forest itself.

The Armstrongs are not likely to endure many more seasons of tree planting. They are worried about the long-term effects of the chemicals they handle as they bend to plant the seedlings and cover them with earth. Now in their early thirties, they are thinking about starting a family. The years of tree planting have allowed Kevin and Cyndi to make a number of capital improvements on their smallholding. Their major investment has been an eight-acre apple orchard that is two years away from production. With a cash crop and part-time work in and around their nearby small town, they believe they will not have to interrupt the rhythm of smallholding and family life with more tree-planting expeditions.

Not all country romantics have to leave home to find work. Many have on or near their properties part-time businesses that make enough cash to keep them going year-round. A *Countryside* respondent from Maine explained that she and her husband serve as guides and cooks for fishing expeditions that use their privately owned pond as a base camp. "The summer brings many fly fishermen and seasonal campers. The fall, winter, and spring are ours. We both tie flies for sale in the summer. Each year we get closer to self-sufficiency and less dependent on town. When the power goes out even in the winter, we are warm and have plenty to eat. It's a great life."

Although these Maine guides appear happy to play out their country-romantic roles indefinitely, country-romantic smallholding itself possess a built-in instability. For many of the case-study subjects, country romantic seems to be a back-to-the-land transition stage through which smallholders pass on their way to other kinds of back-to-the-country living. As the demands of children and the need for security press in on these smallholders, like the Armstrongs, they begin to explore the possibilities of living even more self-reliantly from their property, as purists, or looking at full-time self-employment as country entrepreneurs. At the same time, it is hard to imagine that very many of them would be attracted to the intensity of microfarming or the hectic schedules of the weekenders. And even though they are likely to avoid approaches to country living that seriously undermine their freedom, rural economies will always have a place for country romantics—part-time, casual, seasonal laborers who are somehow able to survive on the anemic and sporadic wages extraction industries pay.

The Weekenders

"Weekender" is a slightly misleading label for new pioneers who work full-time away from their homesteads.[16] They are likely to spend much more than their weekends working on their properties. Many of them devote more hours a week as back-to-the-landers than they do in their professions. Their vacations, when they come, can be stay-at-home affairs spent catching up on fence mending, orchard pruning, sheep shearing, and a thousand other farmstead chores.

For some observers the significance of the back-to-the-land movement itself could be diminished by the presence of the large number of weekenders (44 percent) in the *Countryside* sample, regardless of how diligently they pursue their homestead craft in their spare time. The ostensible purpose for going back to the country is to practice an ecologically responsible lifestyle on a few acres of land by producing much of what one consumes. The fact, however, that almost half of the *Countryside* neohomesteaders support themselves with outside full-time incomes means that a presumably defining characteristic of the smallholding movement does not apply to a substantial proportion of its membership.

There is no denying the considerable distance between the new pioneers' intentions and their accomplishments. Actually, 95 percent of the *Countryside* sample do not support themselves completely from the land itself; only the microfarmers and the purists, constituting the other 5 percent, approach technical self-sufficiency. And it is this performance shortfall that is the subject matter of much of the rest of the book. But the achievement of technical self-reliance is only one way of assessing the significance of the back-to-the-land movement. In terms of larger sustainability issues, intentions may be even more important than accomplishments. The existence of weekenders (likely hundreds of thousands across North America) in the movement demonstrates that a large number of urban residents are sufficiently devoted to sustainability principles to make the sacrifices for a country move, even though they do not have the immediate resources to support themselves from their properties. There is, then, in the movement a considerable reservoir of idealism that could, in a friendly policy environment, drive not only a revitalized back-to-the-country movement but a sustainability movement as well. From this perspective the problem is not so much the deviancy of back-to-the-land weekenders as it is the absence of public programs designed to facilitate their largely unexploited idealism.

Apart from the meaning for the movement of having weekenders as its largest identifiable group, questions still remain regarding the everyday reality of living back-to-the-land as a weekender. For the weekender, the experience of dividing a finite amount of energy between a full-time job and the full-time demands of homestead work is one of a constant collision between idealism and pragmatism, whose fallout is seemingly endless compromise. Murray Holt, a high school teacher in a small town in the inland Pacific Northwest that I shall call Pine Glen,* is a weekender who has learned to roll with the waves of necessity that reshape his dreams, transforming ideologically pure projects into tactical compromises, often leading to strategic retreats. In addition to homesteading and teaching school, Murray is an aspiring school administrator. In the middle of a master's degree in educational administration, he escapes from homestead chores one night a week for a three-hour round-trip to a college class in Spokane, Washington.

After a tour of duty in Vietnam Murray left the army to return to his hometown, Albany, New York, where he decided that he would take advantage of the GI Bill to go back to school and become a teacher. Idealism was at the core of the teaching decision. He wanted his life's work to be consequential, and teaching seemed the best way to make a difference. Going to school year-round, Murray completed his bachelor's degree with a double teaching major in English and industrial arts. The summer after he finished his courses he accepted a teaching position in one of Albany's inner-city high schools, dividing his time between classrooms and the

---

*Murray Holt and Pine Glen are pseudonyms.

woodworking shops. Characteristically, he made a major investment of energy in his students' welfare. Discipline was always a problem, but Murray tried to smooth the ragged edges of classroom order with goodwill. Nevertheless, as the months of the school year passed, he started to feel as if he were in Vietnam all over again. Drugs, dropouts, and pervasive hostility made him feel helpless. The small victories of a returned smile or a breakthrough in a grammar lesson were often erased by unexplained absences and eventually the dropout of even the most promising of his projects.

It did not take Murray long to develop a global diagnosis for his students' maladies. The world simply did not have a place for them. There were no easily recognizable good jobs or good marriages waiting for them after school. And the students more than anybody else knew it. Consequently, schoolwork, and even a dedicated teacher like Murray Holt, held little meaning for them. This reality, as well as its expression in his students' lives, was, for Murray, impenetrable.

For Murray, teaching school under these conditions slowly evolved into just another job rather than a life's work. He started to see, as a remedy for his personal problems and the public ones of his students, some kind of return to a simpler time when community welfare demanded the labor of each member of the community just to survive. Murray, a romantic turned reluctant pragmatist, realized that social transformation was not about to come to inner-city Albany and that he single-handedly could not compensate for a fragmented community. The alternative was a change of scenery. He did not want a simple escape in the sense of urban flight, but the construction somewhere of a meaningful life his students could emulate. If his idealism would not germinate in the inner city, maybe it could still grow in rural America.

Just after Murray finished his first year of teaching, he and his wife, Linda, started to discuss in earnest the possibility of moving to the countryside. The two major prerequisites for the Holts' move to the country were affordable land and a good teaching job. They spent two years looking for this fortuitous combination of factors before they found Pine Glen. First they located land through a classified advertisement in the *Mother Earth News*. Then Murray applied to the Pine Valley School District for a teaching position. It was one more year and two extended summer trips to Pine Glen before the Pine Valley School District offered Murray the job teaching tenth- and eleventh-grade English and biology (a subject for which he professed familiarity at his interview but in which he now scrambles to stay ahead of his students) at Pine Valley High.

Murray's salary in Pine Glen was one-half what he earned in Albany, and there were no immediate employment prospects for Linda. But Pine Valley had compensations. The cost of living was lower, and the equity from the Holts' Albany home made a substantial down payment on their new property. In addition, Murray and Linda felt that self-reliant home-steading with gardens and animals would more than make up for the smaller cash flows into the household economy. The translation of the theory into practice then proceeded seamlessly through their first full summer in Pine Glen. Their country garden on a strategically located plot with a southern exposure and built-up soil on their twelve acres of margi-nal Pine Valley farmland survived periodic invasions of deer, raccoons, skunks, and stray cattle to produce more than the Holts could either eat or preserve.

Hazel, however, an eight-year-old black-and-white Holstein milk cow, was Murray's first country setback. Hazel embodied all the reasons for the Holts' move to Pine Glen. Hazel made sense. Much of what Murray saw as the meaninglessness of city life was evident in the absence of a relation-ship between what one consumed and what one produced. Hazel was to take care of that unnatural division for the Holt family. Murray's children would know where milk came from because they would feed and then milk Hazel. In the early fall of the Holts' second year in Pine Glen, Hazel was purchased to provide her new owners not only milk but a sense of wholeness and connectedness.

Hazel's tenure, however, at the Holts' smallholding was short. Her less than five months with the Holts was not reflective of any inadequacy on Hazel's part. She was productive. And the Holts were certainly volume consumers of her milk and cream. Her departure was simply a matter of conflicting idealism that left Hazel low on the list of the Holts' in-practice day-to-day priorities. Murray's teaching, assistant basketball-coaching du-ties, and master's degree classes prevented him from participating in the milk-cow care and keeping, and thus those chores were transferred from the family's chief proponent of the union of production and consump-tion to the less enthusiastic hands of his wife, Linda, and Karen, thirteen, Anne, eleven, and Josh, six.

Even with the mechanical milker Hazel's schedule of two necessary and thorough milkings a day did not easily mesh with the Holts' hectic sched-ule. After several earnest family discussions on the philosophy of back-to-the-land living and two visits by the local veterinarian to treat Hazel's mas-titis, a consequence of undermilking, Murray and family decided to give

Hazel up for adoption. The owner of the dairy herd into which she was happily integrated sells the Holts a gallon of fresh milk and a pint of cream for a dollar a day as compensation for Hazel's addition. In the final analysis Murray sees the Hazel episode as a salutary experience and its final resolution only as a compromise in his idealism. Karen, Anne, and Josh do know for sure where milk comes from. While they have now reverted to simple consumers, they appreciate that their milk and cream come at an affordable price, and the intermediaries of convenience store, packaging plant, and milkman do not obscure their view of the dairy up the road.

In the ideological space Hazel left behind, Murray is working on a strawberry and raspberry enterprise he hopes will infuse his children's lives with a sense of purpose that he assumes was missing in Albany and that the misadventure with Hazel did not provide. The much less incessant demands of berry cultivation, Murray figures, will finally unite Karen, Anne, and Josh with their Mother Earth inseparably in a cycle of production and consumption. The motivation, however, for work in the berry patches is not all theoretical. Murray sees berry growing as a profitable small business that can bring the children spending money in the absence of neighborhood paper routes and part-time McDonald's or mall work.

The frustrations that subtly reshape unreconstructed idealism, as represented by the shift from milk cow to strawberries, are becoming an integral part of Murray Holt's Pine Valley life. The homestead experience is not turning out exactly as planned, and his dream of making a difference as a small-town teacher has its own frayed edges. In Pine Glen, Murray has discovered a small-town culture that tempers ambition just as much as it elevates friendliness. For the most part, his students' parents are friendly and approachable, though he characterizes as erratic their follow-through on commitments. With regard to his own ambitions, small-town cronyism is temporarily blocking his climb up the school-administration ladder. After Murray's third year at Pine Valley High he applied for the school's assistant-principal position. He believed he was the best candidate, and without question the only one that had graduate work in educational administration. But he lost the promotion to a Pine Valley native who wanted to move back home from Seattle.

The insider-outsider discrimination that stalled his administrative career would likely leave most urbanites irretrievably jaded, but Murray remains philosophical. For Murray it is this kind of particularism of personal considerations that makes Pine Valley attractive, that gives it a human face. He knows that he will have his master's degree in another year or two. He expects that with patience he will earn the administrative position he wants, and even likely serve an extended term as principal of Pine Valley High. And since Pine Glen culture does not expect the obsessive career devotion common to urban school districts, Murray expects that the days ahead will still have sufficient hours left over after teaching and administration for him to move forward with his homestead plans and schemes. He confesses, however, that the liberation of Hazel from her exile to factory-like milk production at the dairy up the road is not an item on his long list of smallholding projects.

While weekenders like Murray are chronically frustrated by the shortage of time for working as back-to-the-landers, they appreciate that they would not have the imperfect smallholdings they are trying to improve were it not for their full-time jobs. One respondent from the *Countryside* survey succinctly summed up the time-money compromise weekenders make: "While my job does not give me the satisfaction my farm gives me, it does provide the money to live this lifestyle. We are in the process of constructing what many would feel is a superior residence not commonly found on homestead property. We still want some of the advantages of modern technology: running water, electricity, gas-powered machines, etc., to help ease the tasks we must do—and enjoy doing."

The income from full-time work may be the means to buy and maintain the homestead, but the time it takes away from outdoor work is still painful. A woman respondent in her forties commented, "If I didn't have to work full-time, self-sufficiency would be a little higher. There is only so much time, and I'm spread fairly thin now. I can get the garden planted but can't keep up with the weeding and harvesting. A lot of produce goes to the chickens. At least it's not wasted. My husband travels, and so most of the work is left to me."

With time constraints closing in on them, many of the weekenders start looking toward retirement, expressing sentiments similar to the following from a female smallholder in her early sixties: "All I can say is that I don't have time—and won't have time until I retire—to do all I want to do on my acreage. However, my work as a nurse has certainly helped me care for my animals. I have big plans for when I have more time. I have a nice collection of how-to books and magazines!"

Although Murray Holt and the other weekenders chafe at the sacrifice of time their jobs demand, they would likely be even more frustrated by the absence of a reliable cash flow. One of the *Countryside* survey respondents wrote about the relief of moving from microfarmer to weekender: "After ten years of gardening, beekeeping, and all that, I decided I didn't want to work that hard. I'd rather earn money at my profession, even though I often dislike it, than be a slave for eighteen hours a day."

Perhaps one important reason that many back-to-the-landers choose the weekender style of country living is not so much to escape real or imagined penury on a subsistence homestead as to meet financial obligations they have beyond the smallholding itself. The smallholder who worried about the eighteen-hour days ended his comments by saying, "I have three kids, one in college and two about to go, and I want to be able to help them go." Consequently, Murray Holt, weekender, tries to choose the best of both worlds. A family is important. A well-equipped homestead is as well. It all takes money, and for many new pioneers a full-time job is the only means they can see leading to their goal of a fulfilling life in the country.

The Pensioners

If family and financial obligations keep one city-bound, it is always possible to put off country life until retirement. One might purchase a smallholding while still working full-time, make improvements, and then move onto the property when retirement income starts to flow. That almost one in five (18 percent) from the *Countryside* sample has taken the pensioner route to homesteading suggests that back-to-the-land is a viable alternative to Sun Belt condominiums. A farmstead stretches limited retirement income and can provide productive and meaningful work.

Though they resist easy stereotyping, pensioners come in at least two basic varieties. First are the migrants, the snow birds. They enjoy country living from the spring to the fall but start to travel once the woodstoves need all-day tending. The other kind of retired back-to-the-lander devotes all of his or her energy to building up the self-reliant homesteads whose blueprints became etched in dreams over the years. One of these full-time new pioneers in his sixties wrote the following for the *Countryside* survey: "Since retiring I have never worked harder, felt better, or enjoyed life anymore. After leaving my job five years ago, I have been developing an unimproved acreage by putting up buildings, planting trees and lawn, and adding a garden and an orchard. I updated the irrigation system and seeded pastures. Then I had to build fences, canals, and outbuildings for the livestock. I am just now ready to add sheep, a calf for meat, and poultry."

Keith and Gloria Steele were weekenders before they became pensioners.* Keith's retirement from a pulp and paper mill meant little change in work routine, though he became able to focus all his energies on the work he loved. Since retirement he has taken a number of small-holding projects off hold and brought them to completion. One of the most intriguing is a mini–hydroelectric system. Keith and Gloria rerouted one of their property's fast-moving streams through their basement. They placed a small turbine in the water's channel and harnessed the generated power through a bank of batteries. The direct-current power supplies their household electrical needs, though their vintage black-and-white television suffers from a chronic flicker.

The Steeles have an extensive raised-bed gardening system and chickens and goats, and they try to eat exclusively from their property. They do have social security and the mill pension. They see, however, real security coming from their self-reliant way of life. About fifty acres of the seventy-acre farmstead is in forest. To Keith the trees are like "money in the bank."

Walt and Maxine Gustavason can certainly appreciate the Steeles' attraction to their homestead.** But with the freedom retirement brings, they just do not see much of a reason to stay on their smallholding year-round. They spend at least six months of the year on their Pacific Northwest homestead. When the cool, rainy weather comes in November, they make plans to retreat to their winter home in a trailer community near Phoenix, Arizona.

Phoenix, however, is more a home base than a home, as they travel throughout much of the South, Southwest, and Mexico during the winter. With the return of spring they settle down to new pioneer life for six months. Self-sufficiency on their land is a self-imposed antidote to wanderlust. They plant and harvest a large garden and cook on a wood range from April through October and otherwise act out for their neighbors a good imitation of the purist version of homesteading. Perhaps if the sun

---

*Keith and Gloria Steele are pseudonyms.
**Walt and Maxine Gustavason are pseudonyms.

were to shine year-round, they would just as soon stay on their farmstead throughout the year, with an excursion or two to keep country living in perspective.

For many back-to-the-landers, however, retirement is not a simple sideways move from weekender to pensioner. Some go from a full-time city job to microfarmer or country entrepreneur. A Minnesota smallholder described the retirement of her fifty-eight-year-old husband in the following way: "My workaholic husband retired from teaching, but now he's logging full-time. He loves it. He is his own boss, plus we do all our own sawmilling and planing. And we do small wood projects for our family and friends." A mid-fifties California man explained that he and his wife made a ten-year plan in their early forties to take them from their "fast-paced, high-travel, high-tech, highly paid" urban lifestyles to a "simpler, well-balanced rural life where we could be relatively free of debt, taxes, and urban pressures." Although the couple's plan has been retirement, my respondent asks the rhetorical question, "We did?/We didn't?" His answer: "We are working harder than ever on a three-acre French intensive, complete farm. Our produce is sold at local farmers' markets, and our receipts are growing at 60 percent a year. We are going to retire, again!" The pensioner lifestyle, then, can only be equated with retirement if retirement is qualified to include moving from one kind of work to another.

The Country Entrepreneurs

Parallel to the back-to-the-land vision of self-reliance on a homestead is the dream of owning and operating a small business.[17] Small-business people, as their own bosses, appear to be in control of their destinies. If they provide good service and a quality product, they are confident they can provide a living for themselves and their families, all the while enjoying a sense of personal fulfillment. And since full-time employment in rural America is in short supply, it is only natural that a good number of independently minded new pioneers, 15 percent in the case of the *Countryside* respondents, would attempt to combine country living and a full-time small business.

Rick and Joy Craig, who, with their cabinet shop, supplied one of Chapter 1's case studies, are typical country entrepreneurs, and their experiences are representative of the range of time investments smallholders make in their microenterprises. The Craigs can see their cabinetmaking opportunities starting to undermine the quality time they want to devote to their farmstead. The problem of a business consuming all of a family's time, a problem the Craigs see themselves slowly drawn toward, is well represented by the comments of a *Countryside* survey respondent: "Our lives are presently controlled by the business we own—a ceramic-pottery shop. This is the prime source of dissatisfaction in many of our answers— lack of time to be together as a family, lack of time to work on our property and on broader aspects of life and politics. We are making progress toward business self-reliance, but we will probably always feel the constraints: too much to do in the time available. Why aren't there any questions on unfinished projects? We'd be high-end!"

While the preceding description does reflect considerable frustration, there is also evidence of hope: "*We are making progress.*" And though many of the homestead projects are still unfinished, at least they are started. More important, this family is surviving, is making a living, as are many other smallholders who have gone into business. But the chronic problem of how to fine-tune time commitments remains; one works long days to get a business started, and then, if one is successful, long hours are spent responding to customer demand.

In Paradise, Montana, the home of Rube Wrightsman, whose gloomy observations on the prospects for financial success in the country started this chapter, there are a number of surviving, and thriving, small business operations. Some are of the microfarmer variety: an acre or two of cantaloupes, sweet cherries, or grapes. One family grows four acres of baby's breath and other easily dried flowers, with delivery contracts arranged throughout California. But a more inventive project belongs to a couple who arrived in Paradise with $150 in their pockets. After supporting themselves through their first winter by cutting and selling wood, they leased land next to a local hot spring and now use the run-off steam to heat ten greenhouses. A winter lettuce crop finds its way to local stores and restaurants, and their greenhouse nursery plants can be purchased as far away as Spokane, Washington. In addition, the couple, one of whom is an acupuncturist, has established the Paradise Holistic Health Center.[18]

Small businesses, of course, have a high failure rate, and the new pioneer entrepreneurs are no less immune to the problems of unstable markets and chronic undercapitalization than are their urban counterparts. But they have their land to fall back on. If the Swedish massage studio did not work last year, then maybe an organic bakery will next year.

The Apprentices

One consistent thread running through these accounts of country living is the importance of having some kind of start-up fund. It may be a professional income, as in the case of the Holts, or a suburban home's equity, as in the case of the Rosenthals. A back-to-the-land life, however, may still be possible even in the absence of ready cash. One cashless road to smallholding is through apprenticeship—through a government grant or program that teaches farming skills or by working for room and board on someone else's smallholding. Only a handful (less than 1 percent) of the *Countryside* respondents are taking the apprentice path to homesteading, though apprenticeship is certainly a viable back-to-the-land strategy, even if its compensation leaves little room for a *Countryside* subscription.

Don and Karen Jensen work as hired hands on a medium-sized cattle ranch.* Part of Don's salary comes from a government subsidy program that encourages young rural families without land to learn farming skills. Although they are apprenticing on a commercial enterprise, they use their small home and allotted acreage in typical smallholder fashion. There is of course the large garden. With the garden and access to meat from the ranch, they produce 50 percent of their own food, and they buy most of the rest through a consumers' cooperative.

Over the few years they have been working on the apprenticeship program, they have been able to purchase a small cattle herd. They plan to raise the animals on their own miniranch if and when they can persuade the rancher for whom they work to finance the sale of a small part of his property. Toward the goal of ownership, Karen works part-time as a ski instructor during the winter months, though their first child is only a year old.

Ways of Living Back-to-the-Land:
A Concluding Note

I have taken the *Countryside* respondents and placed them into seven categories, from purist to weekender. The classification scheme presents a clear-cut image of the way back-to-the-landers try to operationalize their

*Don and Karen Jensen are pseudonyms.

country dreams. One has to recognize, however, that the categories are still frames of a group in motion. Smallholders often move from one category to another and may at times find themselves acting out the roles of more than one kind of back-to-the-land adventure. In concluding this review of the different ways smallholders support themselves, I would like to do one more case history, this time a "hybrid" new pioneer type, in order to counterbalance the necessarily static quality of the typology with the everyday flux of back-to-the-land life.

An interview with David and Cathy Williams that appeared in the *Smallholder* is a good source of insight into the daily life of a couple who are trying to juggle both the country-romantic and microfarmer approaches to country living, all the while coveting a more focused, purist lifestyle. The Williamses live on a fifty-two-acre farm on Salt Spring Island, one of the Gulf Islands off the coast of Vancouver, British Columbia. Thirty sheep provide the main farm income, but there are also 250 free-range chickens and a market garden that provides carrots for the local health-food store. In addition, the family makes a small amount of money from a sawmill operation. "Sometimes I sell poles," David reported. "I have a saw-mill and I cut a little bit for people but not very much. We do a lot of trading too, trading with our neighbors."[19]

In the year of the interview the Williamses had a net return of about $1,800 from their homestead. During the same year David earned another $2,500 working off of his property. "I do butchering for people. I butcher lambs, do fencing, work a little bit at the feed store. I do carpentry. I do just about anything."

With a low cash income the Williamses use their property to supply most of their food. In addition to lamb, they graze a steer for meat, and each fall David usually shoots a deer for venison. Their garden gives them fresh vegetables for six months of the year. And they hope eventually to be able to shift all their cash generation—as they have shifted most of their subsistence needs—to their smallholding. They would, for instance, like to integrate their sheep farming vertically. Rather than double or triple their flock, they plan on keeping the thirty sheep, while growing all the grain for them, shearing them for wool, butchering some of them to sell as meat, and then tanning and selling the hides. The smaller flock is, in addition, much more suited to the carrying capacity of their land.

In talking about their plans for an independent farmstead, David reflects on their progress and their dreams: "We always say to ourselves,

'Well, we're building our farm now.' And we said, five years ago, 'In five
years it will be built.' Now we say in another five years it will be built. By
'built,' I mean to the point where we've reached a plateau where we can
make a living from it and not have to go off the farm to work and maybe
not work the long hours we work now."

The Williamses case study, though it combines several smallholder
types, shares with the other back-to-the-country lifestyles the time-money
dilemma and the ever-unfinished nature of so many of the smallholding
projects. But as careful and comprehensive as I have tried to be with my
back-to-the-land classifications, I would not want to pretend, even with the
David and Cathy Williams case history, that I have exhaustively covered all
the different ways smallholders survive and prosper in rural America.
They are, after all, an inventive collection of individuals. The ambitious,
though destitute, will always find some way to make it back to the country.
One often, for example, runs across smallholders looking for help or
working partners in the classified sections of back-to-the-land magazines.
One intriguing invitation is the following from the *Smallholder:*

> HELLO, THOUGHT OF SHARING LAND? Five acres of prepared
> land on east shore of lake, suitable organic stone fruit orchard,
> nuts, berries, grapes, vegetables. Unpolluted air, gravity water.
> Roads in, water and electricity; surrounded by convivial neigh-
> bors. Prefer vegetarian couple, non-smokers, non-drinkers with
> small regular income. Now US, less easily described in a few
> words: we follow a spiritual path, but will not invade the psy-
> chic space of others; interested in ecological agriculture and
> Conserver Society lifestyle; cooperation not competition; aim-
> ing for a high degree of self-sufficiency, but recognize benefits
> (including monetary), as well as necessity, of working off the
> land part-time; developing mind as well as bodies. If still inter-
> ested WRITE TO US! and introduce yourselves.[20]

The classified ad concluded with a name and address for interested
correspondents. I have no information on the volume of response to the
invitation or whether there occurred a happy convergence of interests
and temperaments. In the absence of any hard data, I assume that this
kind of country matchmaking likely has about the same success rate as
any first-time marriage.

Money and the Good Life

Smallholders come back to the country to find the good life. The good life, as practiced by Helen and Scott Nearing and exemplified by the purist ideal, means tranquillity—a measured approach to small-farm living in contrast to the frantic pace of city life. From the purist perspective, it is the earth itself that sustains its stewards. Urban families, on the other hand, must somehow connect themselves to an abstraction called the economy, to find jobs and earn money, in the pursuit of both survival and affluence. The stress points of a life off the land center to a large extent on the elusive quest for "enough" money, rather than on the physical encounter with the natural environment of farmsteads. With few exceptions, however, back-to-the-landers also find themselves preoccupied with money, and as a consequence their relationship to tranquillity becomes a precarious one. Whether as weekenders, microfarmers, or country entrepreneurs, more than half of them believe they need full-time employment. Admittedly, this rural pursuit of income can have compensations unmatched by urban occupations. Work and money translate into an investment in country property calculated to allow the smallholder to retire on a modest pension or move from full- to part-time work. Then the latter-day homestead provides its families not only with the pleasure of working the land but also the food and fiber that permit the back-to-the-lander the luxury of having to earn less from outside sources.

This discussion of money and the homesteader leads to one obvious question: How much money do back-to-the-country people actually make? In the *Countryside* survey I asked the respondents to tell me their yearly incomes, gross from all sources, and those of their spouses or partners. I used this information to calculate their family incomes, which I believe is the best indicator of their financial status. I have summarized the *Countryside* respondents' family income levels in Table 6.

The new pioneer incomes are modest. Not quite one in four (24 percent) has a family income over $50,000, and 43 percent live in families that make less than $30,000. Table 6 incomes are certainly not reflective of country gentry. And while the *Countryside* respondents' earnings do confirm Rube Wrightsman's pessimism on the possibility of getting rich in rural America, Table 6 also shows that 46 percent of the questionnaire respondents have family incomes between $30,000 and $70,000 a year.

Table 6. *Countryside* respondents' family income levels

Yearly Income	%
Under $9,999	7
$10,000 to $19,999	15
$20,000 to $29,999	21
$30,000 to $49,999	33
$50,000 to $69,999	13
$70,000 to $99,999	7
Over $100,000	4
Total	100

Note: Total number of respondents = 565 (actual responses numbered 533, since not all respondents answered each question).

These incomes are consistent with the respondents' educational credentials and often qualify as affluent in the depressed rural economies.

Productive property, of course, can compensate for modest incomes. Consequently, I asked the *Countryside* respondents, "What percentage of the food your family eats is produced on your property?" They reported that on average they raise just over a third (36 percent) of their families' food from their smallholdings, with 25 percent of them eating half or more of their food from their own land and 10 percent able to grow 80 percent or more of their families' food. This food, of course, is in no way "free." It comes from an investment not only of time but of money as well, money in farm implements, outbuildings, and feed. Still, a one-third reduction in the cost of food, an increase in wealth that is not taxable, is certainly a significant contribution to a family's financial well-being, and the pleasure intrinsic to producing what one consumes is certainly a significant contribution to a family's temperamental well-being.

A homestead is not only a subsistence venture, but in addition can be a commercial enterprise. Wondering whether the smallholders might be able to earn substantial portions of their incomes directly from their property, I asked the *Countryside* respondents to tell me the gross farm income they had received from their properties over the past year. The average income from property was only $300, confirming that the study's subjects are country residents whose property can best be characterized as semi-subsistent. This characterization should not obscure the fact that some smallholders, like the microfarmers, do make a living from their property. Ten percent of the respondents, for example, had a gross income from their property of $14,700 or more.

To understand the relationship between money and the good life for the back-to-the-landers, it is necessary, in addition to pulling together their sources of support, to turn as well to their own assessment of their financial situations. From an outsider's perspective it is not difficult to summarize what the income figures seem to mean: smallholders have modest incomes supplemented by gardens and livestock, very little earnings from their properties, and some bartering and trade activity. This summary leads one to wonder whether the neohomesteaders feel constrained by their modest resources. Is there evidence of frustration from trying to build self-reliant homesteads on a shoestring? To answer this question, I asked the *Countryside* respondents, "How satisfied are you with your current financial situation?" I allowed them one of four answers: (1) not at all satisfied, (2) fairly unsatisfied, (3) fairly satisfied, and (4) very satisfied. In the overall response to this question, 79 percent of the *Countryside* smallholders said they were either very (26 percent) or fairly satisfied (53 percent) with their current financial situation, while the remaining 21 percent were either fairly unsatisfied (13 percent) or not at all satisfied (8 percent). Naturally, how much a family was making did influence the degree of positive response to the question, but even those reporting family incomes under $20,000 a year still expressed clear satisfaction with their finances—66 percent answering that they were very or fairly satisfied with their current financial situation.

The *Countryside* respondents' answers to the financial-satisfaction question does not demonstrate a preoccupation with money or chronic frustration at its absence. This sanguine attitude, however, should not conceal the homesteaders' residual anxieties over financial matters. In the open-ended-response section of the questionnaire many of the respondents wrote to express their general dissatisfaction with government tax and support policies for small and part-time farmers. Though they were satisfied with their immediate finances, they were nevertheless uneasy over the long-term prospects of maintaining their farmsteads. Specifically, one concern surfaced more than any other—health-care insurance. A thirty-two-year-old homesteader from Texas summarized the problem: "Concerns over access to health care are keeping many people from abandoning jobs with health-care benefits and pursuing a better life in the country." Rube Wrightsman's minimum-wage jobs, of course, rarely carry health-care benefits.

Absence of accessible health-care insurance evidently keeps potential back-to-the-landers, who are otherwise financially prepared for country life, in the city. As one urban survey respondent explained, "We hope to move to the country in the next five years. Our concern is health care in the future, so we are tied to a job until we can qualify for a health plan." And those who have made it to the country often stay, for the sake of health-care benefits, at jobs they would like to leave. "If this slowpoke country ever manages a decent health-care system, I'll ditch the town job in a blink—I could do much better managing if I could be on my land more" was the way a single mother from Maine put the problem. A California smallholder, living in an economically depressed logging community with little work for men, makes essentially the same point: "In order to have health insurance it was necessary for me to go to work for the local elementary school four hours a day, five days a week, ten months a year. They pay part, and I pay part [for the health-insurance premiums]. I had not worked for twenty-seven years, but there is no work here for men. I find at fifty-six, after working all day, that I don't have the energy I need to really enjoy our little farm."

Even if one has health insurance, medical care is not always nearby. A Minnesota smallholder framed the accessibility issue in the following way: "Health care is a very important issue to us because our youngest son was injured at birth due to the negligence of the doctor at the local hospital. This is the only disadvantage that I see to living in the country. Right now we have to travel seventy miles round-trip to take him to a doctor, and even farther to take him to the specialists that he needs."

But even with anxieties over health insurance, one can still find in rural America vestiges of yeoman self-reliance applied to medical care. While the following comments from a forty-one-year-old smallholder from Maine are not representative of the *Countryside* questionnaire's open-ended response section, they do illustrate homesteading carried to its logical conclusion: "I am losing my teeth because no money can be spared to repair them. Last year I removed infected bone fragments from my jaw myself with a scalpel and forceps purchased from an animal supply house. My anesthetic was homemade beer."

In reporting this somewhat bizarre example I do not mean to diminish the health-insurance crisis. But at the same time, the respondent's home-based dental care exemplifies back-to-the-land independence. This independence is not restricted to the material self-reliance of gardens and milking barns; it is a spiritual autonomy that has an ambivalent relationship to the American mainstream. A good example of this shift toward nonmaterial values is the absence of a correlation between the *Countryside* respondents' incomes and their assessments of their own personal happiness. I asked the questionnaire respondents, "Taking all things together, how happy would you say you are now?" and allowed them one of four fixed choices: (1) very happy, (2) pretty happy, (3) not too happy, and (4) not at all happy. More than nine out of ten (94 percent) said they were either very or pretty happy. As remarkable as this high level of expressed happiness is, the fact that family income has little to do with personal happiness is even more significant. *Countryside* respondents with modest incomes were just as happy as, and in some cases happier than, affluent respondents. Ninety-one percent of the respondents with family incomes under $20,000 and 86 percent of those with family incomes over $100,000 said they were either very or pretty happy.[21]

The lack of a defined correlation between income and happiness leads one to wonder whether money has no more than an incidental connection to the back-to-the-land good life. Given their devotion to building self-reliant homesteads and the importance of both time and money to this endeavor, I am at least a little surprised that more evidence of frustration did not surface in their responses to the financial-satisfaction and general-happiness questions. This apparent equanimity does not mean that the time-money dilemma with which I started this chapter is not a chronic concern; rather, the back-to-the-landers are not willing to allow this dilemma to erode the pleasures of country living.

It is obvious that something other than money motivates the smallholders. And the most obvious candidate for this motivation is back-to-the-land values. The narrative and analytical accounts of the movement, through the end of this chapter, have presented, in context, the ideals that shape the new pioneers' perspectives on their lives in the country, but these ideals have yet to receive a systematic examination. This is the task to which I turn next, in Chapter 3. In dissecting smallholder values, one naturally comes back to the central criterion of sustainability: the ability to derive personal satisfaction primarily outside of the consumer culture. The absence of a relationship between personal happiness and family income among the back-to-the-landers is one piece of evidence in favor of the argument that smallholders can be emotionally independent of the mainstream society. But of course the sustainability issue is a multifaceted one. New pioneers are in reality caught between two worlds. How they balance the demands of these two worlds, using the resources of back-to-the-land values, influences both the quality of their back-to-the-country experience and their progress toward their sustainability goals.

3

QUEST FOR WHOLENESS
Back-to-the-Land Values

 "The beauty of watching a foal being born or other things like that" was the way a *Countryside* respondent from Idaho summarized the smallholding experience on the back of his questionnaire. Another, from Maine, wrote, "There is so much to enjoy. All of nature—a fox bark at night, the hoot of an owl, the call of a loon, lilacs and apple blossoms in spring, the scent of new mown hay. I could go on and on, but I think you know what I'm saying."

These expressions of reverence for the everyday encounters with the small wonders of the universe appeared frequently in my interviews and in the open-ended sections of the questionnaires. The smallholders' reports of their apprehension of the natural world often carry a transcendent quality. At the same time, for the neohomesteaders, these experiences possess an easily appropriated concrete reality. In the country, the ethereal seems to evaporate; the concrete has the potential to endure. A woman in her early thirties from Washington State captured this subjective dimension of country living as follows:

> Morning chores at seven,
> Wind blows to beat the band.

Comfort is two new laid eggs,
One to warm each hand.

As this homey verse intimates, it is not only the closeness to nature that
captivates back-to-the-landers; there is in addition the satisfaction of seeing the results of one's own husbandry in action. One respondent in her
late twenties from Idaho wrote, "There is so much more to say, and all I
can start with is—this is a most beautiful way to live. We feel joy in just
watching a gate we built open and close."

Standing for minutes watching a gate open and close might strike the
time-conscious urbanite as a form of mind*less*ness—simple indolence. But
for the back-to-the-country people, the awe they experience in their encounters with the ordinary and the taken-for-granted is better represented
as a kind of mind*ful*ness. Psychologists studying the mindfulness phenomenon have identified it as a calm, yet focused, engagement with the present, not unlike a meditative experience, but usually shorter and less intense. At the moment of a foal's birth or the opening and closing of a
newly built gate, time, for the smallholders, seems to stand still. The anxieties of the future have space to recede to the background, and the past's
residual fears can be replaced by peace of mind. The world for one moment appears whole, and the mind moves toward a stillness. For those
reporting mindfulness experiences, there is little place for the scores of
thoughts, ideas, and concerns that typically race across the mind. One's
being, then, is not seen as separate, apart from a world outside of consciousness; rather, one, if only for an instant, appears to be drawn into the
ongoing stream of a perceived universal reality, with the potential for finding tranquillity, union, and wholeness.[1]

Invigorated by the occasional excursion into mindfulness, the new pioneers come back to collect the rest of the morning's eggs or to complete
a day of fence building. But even outside the moments of transcendence,
the ordinary can still bring sustained pleasure. A woman in her early sixties from Montana confirms, "We keep goats because they are our therapy.
They get us out in the mornings when otherwise we'd have no occasion to
go out. Early morning is the most beautiful time of the day. And one of
my little goats turned out to be a six-quart milker, a little love! 'For it is in
the dew of little things the heart finds its morning and is refreshed.'"

On reviewing these anecdotal accounts of the smallholders' experiences with mindfulness, I wondered if it might be possible to probe systematically the homesteaders' everyday feelings of peace and wholeness,

to find out how common they are. In the *Countryside* survey I included questions on seven dimensions of mindfulness and asked the respondents how often they occurred, with five choices from never to very often. The seven aspects of mindfulness were: (1) a sense of wonder, (2) a feeling of union with nature, (3) a sense of peace of mind, (4) a feeling of wholeness, (5) a feeling of joy, (6) a feeling of living in the present moment, and (7) a sense of being accepted within the universe. In Table 7, I report the percentage of respondents who said they experienced each of these aspects of mindfulness either often or very often.

Table 7. *Countryside* respondents' reports of their mindfulness experiences

Experience	% Reporting Often or Very Often
A sense of peace of mind	81
A feeling of union with nature	75
A feeling of joy	74
A feeling of living in the present moment	65
A sense of wonder	64
A feeling of wholeness	61
A sense of being accepted in the universe	51

Note: Total number of respondents = 565 (actual responses numbered from 535 to 557, since not all respondents answered each question).

Although I was confident that the mindfulness questions reflected an important dimension of back-to-the-country living for some smallholders, I thought that many respondents might find them foreign to their experience—perhaps even consider them peculiar. Consequently, I did not expect the string of high percentages in Table 7. While feelings of wholeness, peace, and wonder may not be universally experienced by the *Countryside* respondents on a frequent basis, they are nevertheless common, with a range from 51 percent feeling "accepted within the universe" to 81 percent who experience "peace of mind" either often or very often.

Table 7 supports my impressions, from interviews with smallholders and their families, that significant numbers of the back-to-the-landers have made personal happiness a primary objective in their lives. Of course, happiness, regardless of its source, can be elusive. When dependent on material possessions and the perishable goodwill of peers, it is not only elusive but fragile. But when defined in terms of a relationship to the natural world, the experience of happiness is not contingent on marketplace fluctuations. In contrast, the immediate pleasures of rural life are theoretically available to any who single-mindedly pursue them. As a sixty-four-year-old male homesteader affirms, "We have five acres, raise 90 percent of all our food, and supply all our heat with wood. We raise llamas for both hobby and profit and have fourteen of them. Our house is four hundred square feet, but the barn is five thousand square feet! Seven dogs and all kinds of birds live at our place. We give llama rides to children. We enjoy life!" Whether back-to-the-landers can unproblematically pull back from their often hectic schedules and so easily lose themselves in the flow of homestead life is a question I want to keep in view as I continue to examine the values that motivate smallholders.[2]

The wholeness the new pioneers covet, however, is rarely pursued directly. It is more a by-product that comes from a commitment to values central to the back-to-the-land movement itself. In the next two sections I probe the meaning of two ideals at the core of the back-to-the-country vision, self-reliance and voluntary simplicity. As I examine these values, along with their translation to action, I want to be sensitive to the possibility that their obsessive application might well complicate smallholder life to the point where mindfulness itself becomes elusive.

The Self-Reliant Homesteader

"Self-reliance," "autonomy," "freedom," "independence," and "responsibility"—these words, their meanings, connotations, and applications, are the beginning of the back-to-the-land journey toward a sustainable future. The self-reliant smallholding is a microcosm of sustainable living. The mainstream economy shifts waste to landfills, the sea, and air and temporarily postpones the confrontation with pollution. Both producer and consumer, as a consequence, do not immediately confront the consequences of their actions. The direct encounter with the debris of human activity, however, cannot be deferred on the self-reliant homestead. The self-sufficient smallholding constitutes a closed loop; disagreeable waste has to be retained and reused on site rather than become part of a refuse stream that pollutes neighbors' properties.

Smallholders themselves, however, do not always see self-reliance in terms of its generalized social value, but often define it in more immediate, personal terms. Self-sufficiency can be satisfying as an end in and of itself, rather than as a means to the end of planetary sustainability. As one of the back-to-landers has already put it, "We feel joy in just watching a gate we built open and close." And beyond the gratification that comes from the process of smallholding itself, self-reliance can bring to its adherents an intoxicating sense of personal freedom. On an individual level, self-sufficiency is an escape from all the organizational entanglements that are packaged with the urban way of life. While it is true that urban life does come with convenience and organization can empower the individual, the prospective back-to-the-lander typically feels caught in a web of relationships that profoundly frustrates the need for a feeling of independence and personal impact. For those weary of the push and pull of hierarchies and seemingly interminable negotiations with peers, smallholding can be an attractive alternative to the constraints of organizational life. A retired back-to-the-lander in his mid-sixties summed up this escape ethic in the following way: "I have been retired for nine years. I always said that when I retired I would get a small place and run it as I damned well pleased! I would do it not to make money, but to produce food—and not have anyone tell me how to do it!"

Might it be possible, nonetheless, that one value or set of values, like self-reliance and autonomy, however laudable in and of itself, if single-mindedly adhered to, could in practice become distorted? While self-reliance is central to the back-to-the-country good life, there are other ideals it needs to be balanced against. The conviviality of relaxed community life and a sense of wonder for the natural world, for example, could well have a difficult time surviving in an environment where self-reliance were elevated to a position of prime importance. Investing all one's energy in the solitary pursuit of self-reliance might leave one more isolated and exhausted than trying to scramble up the corporate hierarchy.

Self-reliance extracts a price from those who embrace its demands for exclusiveness. A case in point comes from an article written for *Countryside* magazine by a disillusioned reader who became caught in the trap of pursuing self-sufficiency to the exclusion of other back-to-the-land values.[3] The *Countryside* correspondent and her husband had studied and reread copies of the *Mother Earth News* and *Organic Gardening* for a number of years before venturing in their mid-thirties from the comfort of New York City to a nine-acre farmstead in small-town Tennessee. The books and magazines the couple read "made everything sound so wonderful and grand—so easy and so rewarding," and all the smallholders "sounded so happy."

The *Countryside* correspondent was soon to discover, as she phrased it, "the other side of the coin." She and her husband planted a garden and purchased goats and chickens. Self-sufficiency, the couple's preoccupation, proved elusive. They immediately became dependent on the feed store for both the goats and the chickens, and they then found out it cost them more to produce their milk than to buy it at the grocery store. In addition, she reported that her husband had to "work in the city to afford this place, with its unending bills." In my terminology he became a "weekender," literally as well figuratively, since "he [hadn't] much time or energy to do a lot in the evenings, so everything heavy [had to] wait until the weekends."

It was the garden, however, that really discouraged the *Countryside* correspondent. Northwestern Tennessee was much hotter *and* dryer than she imagined possible. Despite considerable quantities of green manure, the clay soil remained rock hard. Then the organic material attracted thousands of pill bugs, which ate the newly planted seeds. In addition, watering the garden became a major problem. The couple had to buy city water for their plants because the well water was alkaline. At the same time, not only was watering the garden with city water expensive, but this only viable source of water contained lead and cadmium, as well as insecticide residues. In addition, the inevitable weeding of the garden turned from an enjoyable interlude to an unbearable task. As she admitted, the garden, "instead of being a pleasure," became "a time-consuming chore."

Rather than enjoy the freedom of rural life, the novice homesteader found herself trapped by the attempt to be self-reliant. She goes on to explain her predicament in more detail:

> We haven't had a vacation in five years. No one can be found to take over for us for even an overnight stay . . . So, for 365 days a year, we're tied here. This helps kill the fun, pleasure or joy in doing night or morning chores, since there is no relief, no change, no break in the daily routine.
>
> Yes there are rewards, but the price is very high. The endless chores, the endless bills, the lack of free time, the constant drain on our resources—both financial and physical—are quite a price to pay for some country fresh eggs, cow milk and veggies . . . wood heat that costs hours and hours of labor when so many other chores sit begging . . .
>
> Is this what country life is all about?

I am pleased to report this story does have a happy ending. In an exchange of letters printed in *Countryside*, editor Jd Belanger acted as country therapist, and his client experienced a remarkable recovery. Jd confessed that he also had been "overloaded and despondent, lots of times." "It usually doesn't last long," he added, "and as long as the good times outnumber and outweigh the bad, wouldn't you say that is a fairly normal life?" In terms of practical advice, Belanger went on to suggest that his correspondent not try to do nearly so much, not try to be technically self-reliant. He mentioned that he had given up raising rabbits and that he had stopped "weeding most of the garden several weeks ago. But we're still getting an awful lot of produce out of it, even if it doesn't look pretty." He then summarized his own approach to country living and self-reliance by writing, "In other words, we've cut back on a lot of things, neglect some others, and manage to lead a fairly pleasant life."[4]

In closing his reply to the discouraged homesteader, editor Belanger asked her to think "as hard as she could" and send him the "three happiest moments" she had experienced on her homestead. In time Belanger received his answer, but with five, not just three, "happiest moments"—from a farm birth to playing Monopoly by candlelight with her family after an electrical power outage. His correspondent started by saying she had cut back on her goal of technical self-sufficiency by selling a number of her goats and chickens and then just letting the drought kill off some of her garden. She started to take regular minibreaks by visiting friends in the afternoon or even going shopping in one of the local malls, knowing the place would still be here when she got back, "and who really cares just when the barn gets painted or that decrepit gate fixed." In conclusion she wrote therapist Belanger, "I do believe I've let the chore list get to me—I've been putting too much pressure on myself to get all these things done as soon as possible. I had to stop and ask myself, 'Who really cares?' The answer is no one. I want you to know that I do enjoy woodcutting, animal care and things most of us find rewarding. Each of these things by itself is fine—it's just when you combine them all together that they become overwhelming."[5]

Seasoned smallholders, in contrast to Jd's correspondent, typically see back-to-the-land living as more a marathon race than a sprint. They have learned to pace themselves. With years of country living behind them, the survey respondents are likely to be back-to-the-country survivors, and surviving is an art a smallholder refines over time. One of my correspondents, a woman in her thirties from Washington, explains this evolutionary process of learning to balance self-reliance against serenity: "When we first came out here, we did have self-sufficiency in mind. So we grew a lot of things (animal and vegetable), and we've butchered and put away a lot of chickens, and I've seen a goat butchered (through tears!), and a pig, but real self-sufficiency is a twenty-four-hour-a-day job. And I like to read a lot, have a part-time job, and I want to spend my evenings with our kids. So I'd like to think I know enough to do it if we had to, and having the animals has been a real love affair. We love our lifestyle even if it is not self-reliant."

While many smallholders have backed off from the obsessive pursuit of self-reliance in favor of a more measured style of life, the ideals surrounding self-reliance, even if not actually put into practice, are still very important to them. A number of the survey respondents wrote to say that they could become self-reliant "if the need arose"—"if things ever get to the point where we have to, we and our neighbors could get along without much outside aid." And as the Washington correspondent above concluded, "So I'd like to think I know enough to do it if we had to . . . We love our lifestyle even if it is not self-reliant."

Self-reliance as a distant goal, rather than a hard-won accomplishment, allows the smallholders to appropriate the sense of freedom that comes from potential, if not actual, independence. Refusing to chase the phantom of self-reliance, they move with, rather than against, the flow of their lives.

A preoccupation with self-reliance, however, is not the only vexation that can come packaged with a commitment to independent country living. Even if one takes a relaxed approach to smallholding, the homestead is still there: the goats have to be milked, and the woodstove must be fed a supply of fuel that has been collected, cut, and stored for winter burning.

Given the necessary constraints of homestead life, I wondered if there might not be a feeling among some of the back-to-the-landers of being locked in or tied down to their country properties. Even though they originally came back to the country to escape all the urban and organizational compromises of their freedom, perhaps the new pioneers were now finding the obligations of smallholding to be just as confining as the city life they left behind. A comment from a respondent to the 1983 survey confirmed my suspicions that at least some homesteaders could be victims of country burnout. He wrote, "I really love every aspect of homesteading except for one. The lack of freedom to be able to come and go as you please can really get you down sometimes. Animals are an everyday, 365–

days-a-year, responsibility, and it's not easy to go off and leave them in someone else's care."

To come to an understanding of how the back-to-the-landers react to having to surrender their independence to the demands of a homestead, I asked the *Countryside* questionnaire respondents the extent to which they felt tied down to their property (unable to leave easily), allowing them one of four answers from very tied down to not at all tied down. Interestingly, almost half (48 percent) of the *Countryside* respondents considered themselves to be either very or fairly tied down (16 percent and 32 percent respectively). And just 13 percent said they were not at all tied down.

On a superficial level the high number of new pioneers who feel tied down raises questions about the possibility of "getting away from it all" in the country. In trying to answer these questions, however, one has to start by appreciating that being "tied down" does not necessarily carry a negative connotation for all smallholders. In fact, the "tied down" question prompted a number of spirited reactions from the *Countryside* respondents in defense of the voluntary commitment to a smallholding way of life. Typical of these reactions to my question was the following from a forty-five-year-old homesteader: "We beg to differ with the implication that 'tied down' is a negative thing. We choose to be 'tied down' if this means a regular farm schedule. True it means more arranging to get away for vacations, etc., but when you enjoy your farm and animals, you don't need to get away so often. We do not feel lacking in 'freedom.'"

These comments highlight an inevitable paradox of back-to-the-land life: one often comes back to the country seeking an independent way of life, but homesteading is a package that entails a cluster of obligations that limit one's freedom. For those who accept the limitations with grace, self-reliance can be a very satisfying, even exhilarating, experience, while the new pioneers who pursue it single-mindedly often find themselves exhausted, plodding after an elusive, constantly receding goal.

Most of the *Countryside* respondents appear, however, to have learned to approach self-sufficiency from a perspective of moderation; for them self-reliance is partial and a matter of potential rather than an immediate objective. Nevertheless, balancing self-reliance against other homesteading goals is a far from easy task. As one smallholder observed, "Working nine-hour days and many nights and weekends here in central Minnesota we have found the road to self-sufficiency slow and winding. Many lessons learned, many to come." In learning and applying the lessons of homesteading, a natural corrective to the excesses of self-reliance is another prominent back-to-the-land value: simple living. And it is to the simple life that I now turn, aware that it is likely not without its own brand of inherent contradictions.

Living the Simple Life

"We could produce much more net income from the land if we wanted to, but by living more simply, we have more time to do as we wish." This straightforward statement from one of the *Countryside* survey respondents succinctly captures a central back-to-the-land survival strategy: when self-reliance, or any other part of country living, starts to become too complex, too frustrating, then life just has to become simpler.

Simple living, then, as actualized in the back-to-the-landers' lives, has the potential to fulfill two important needs in the smallholders' hierarchy of values. First, it can bring peace of mind by helping to uncomplicate a life that becomes preoccupied with external goals, even goals as worthy as self-reliance. Second, simple living is part of the path, both directly and indirectly, to a sustainable society. Simple living in the sense of making modest demands on the biosphere is certainly synonymous with sustainability. The simple life, then, the life that is uncluttered, can bring to homesteaders an enabling power that allows them, at least in theory, to move incrementally, if not dramatically, closer to their goals of sustainable living.

What constitutes the "simple life," however, is far from simple. It often means no more than uncomplicating life by cutting back on one's obligations—selling the family cow or quitting a part-time job—but "simple living" is a much more involved process than merely streamlining commitments. It is not only something one does or does not do; it is a way of life. And like self-reliance, with which it has a dynamic, if often uncomfortable, relationship, simple living represents a belief system that carries an admission price for its adherents, as well as offering the possibility of considerable rewards.

The rewards and the price of simple living have been described in detail by Duane Elgin in his book-length treatment *Voluntary Simplicity: Toward a Way of Life That Is Outwardly Simple, Inwardly Rich.*[6] Elgin makes a distinction between "voluntary simplicity" and "involuntary simplicity."

Voluntary simplicity is consciously chosen and means "to live more deliberately, intentionally, purposely."[7] Involuntary simplicity, on the other
hand, is unadorned poverty; one has no choice but to live a materially
simple life. Poverty, then, is limiting, confining, and ultimately oppressive,
while freely chosen simplicity can be liberating. But even in choosing the
voluntary brand of simplicity, there is no requirement that life be either
rudimentary or primitive. Rather, a kind of "esthetic simplicity" is the
ideal.

The attractions to the simple life come from seemingly polar extremes:
the desire for inner peace and the desire for world peace. Small acts of
voluntary simplicity, if magnified and multiplied in the lives of millions of
practitioners, can naturally have an impact on worldwide problems as diverse as pollution, inflation, and war. The simple life is cooperative and
gentle, rather than competitive and aggressive. Its path to peace is a "soft"
one[8] and follows Gandhi's dictum: "We must live simply in order that
others may simply live."[9]

Admittedly, simple living by back-to-the-country people constitutes just
one small variable in the world-peace equation. Inner peace through voluntary simplicity, while elusive in its own right, is naturally much more
accessible than its global counterpart. And for the back-to-the-landers
tranquillity is found, in part, by rejecting the "goods life" in favor of the
"good life."[10] But the good life is more than technique; it possesses a spiritual dimension. Beyond any recipe stage, simple living is an attitude, an
attitude that includes a reverence for the earth and its inhabitants. Still,
this reverential attitude and the other ideals of the simple life need to be
translated into concrete action. The direct application these feelings of
reverence can extend as far as foraging for foods like wild berries, mush-
rooms, and herbs or, for nonvegetarians, hunting game birds, deer, elk,
and moose. This approach to alternative consumption is part of the practical art of "making do, making over, and doing without." Haru Kanemitsu, a former member of the *Smallholder* editorial collective, explains
her practice of simple living in terms of the gentle science of frugality:

> I am a frugal person—I wince when a beautiful clean (advertis-
> ing on one side) piece of paper is thrown away, or when un-
> eaten soup is not put back into the soup pot to be boiled
> again. These little picky annoyances make me keep food scraps
> separate for goats and chickens; dig in rummages for wool
> cloth for snow pants or braided rugs; use handkerchiefs, cloth

napkins and hand towels instead of paper ones; use diapers for sanitary napkins; use sourdough instead of yeast for bread; use old envelopes and address them on the other side; scrounge to find canning jars that use rubber rings rather than buy new lids every year; keep string from packages and wrapping paper; pick up paper clips, nuts and bolts, buttons, washers, and pins whenever I see one unclaimed.[11]

The kind of frugality practiced by Haru can dramatically lower one's expenses. One *Smallholder* correspondent, for example, who used water and "elbow grease" for tooth paste, baking soda for deodorant, bar soap for shampoo, and stopped shaving her legs, in addition to generally following Haru's style of personal conservation, found that she averaged just $576 a year in cash expenses during a period from the late 1970s through the early 1980s.[12] This kind of savings is certainly attractive, but it does come at the price of time and energy. One of Elgin's correspondents summarized the time and energy dilemma of simple living when she reported, "It's sometimes the harder way to do something . . . I can't rely on fast food, fast service, fast buying. Everything takes longer—cooking, buying, and fixing. But it's worth it—most times."[13] But since nearly half the back-to-the-landers from the *Countryside* survey have full-time jobs, they likely have neither the time nor the necessity for a fully conscious effort at conservation in the interest of radically reducing cash expenditure.

With this sketch of voluntary simplicity as background, the next, and natural, question is how smallholders go about reconciling their frugal ideals with the sometimes hectic pace of full-time jobs and full-time homestead responsibilities. A number of the comments from the *Countryside* survey suggest ways and means back-to-the-landers use to balance convenience and creature comforts against self-reliance and material simplicity. These responses show that the smallholders, much as they do in their commitment to self-reliance, pull back from a rigid application of voluntary simplicity to practice a more modest version. I am tempted to say at this point that the back-to-the-landers seem to be working out a dynamic balance between simplicity and convenience, but perhaps it is more accurate to conclude that they selectively employ those aspects of voluntary simplicity considered compatible with whatever stage of homestead life they find themselves passing through. This kind of mix, as much as balance, is captured in the declaration of a *Countryside* respondent: "Yes, I want running water and electricity when I want it! We have a dishwasher, stereo, TV, etc., but we also have a wood cook stove, generator when electricity fails, and heat totally with wood during the winter (hot-water heat, fired by a homemade boiler), and we cut the wood off our own place. We desire not to be dependent on the outside world, but very dependent on friends."

Convenience, of course, is relative. What one homesteader takes for granted another will struggle with, either somehow to acquire or to find a way to live without. The observations of a Montana survey respondent illustrate well the relative nature of simple living: "We really do love our lifestyle, and as the girls mature, they'll assume more of the mundane household chores. That'll create more time for the camping and hiking and other outdoor activities that we enjoy but [that] are shelved for the time being. Our leisure activities now include enjoying our farmstead. We do have material things—convenience appliances. But we feel they free us to enjoy our lifestyle. We have bought no milk, eggs, very little meat, and no veggies for seven years. We would, however, like a new passive solar, insulated home—with closets!"

A house with closets can certainly uncomplicate life, though perhaps only those who live without them ever come to appreciate their utility. But in addition to highlighting the unusual in the ordinary, the comments of the Montana homesteader point to a common experience for smallholders in their encounters with voluntary simplicity. Just as the survey correspondent hopes to move on to a house with closets, back-to-the-landers typically start out with a very idealistic version of the simple-living homestead and then, as time passes and children come, move to a more moderate interpretation of their original dream. "We've gone from no running water and no electricity back to the conveniences. Wonder if lots of others have gone to similar extremes only to return to modern conveniences?" This reported experience and question from the *Countryside* survey reflect and are sensitive to a not uncommon back-to-the-land experience. A couple, may, for example start out with a very rustic farmstead: a small cabin with wood heat and without the symbolism of electric power lines, virtually independent from the world outside its boundaries. A small concession may be a battery-powered radio to hear an occasional news broadcast. But the hard physical labor does take its toll, especially with the arrival of children. As a California respondent explained:

> We live in a nice big house which we built ourselves. But before
> that we lived for seven years in a two-room cabin with an out-

house, outside bathtub, outside wringer washer, clothesline, outside frig. So now, for the first time in my life, I have a washer-dryer, and—yeah—it's important to me. I feel guilty, but washing used to take a whole day once a week. We used to try to do everything ourselves, but now do only what we enjoy. We could do a lot more if we had to. Between the two of us, there's very little we couldn't figure out. With my doctor husband, we cover a lot of bases. It takes a lot of flexibility, hard work, awareness, discipline, and humor to live in the country and love it the way we do (and a good pickup truck!).

The simple life, then, comes back to selection. Conveniences like electricity, running water, telephones, and washers and dryers make life a little less complicated and free the homesteader for more time in the garden or at the goat barn and to care for the children, as well as work at full- and part-time jobs. There is no simple recipe for living out the good part of the simple life. It is a matter of experiment, contingent on a family's resources and requirements. But perhaps more than anything else it is the art and science of keeping self-reliance within manageable bounds.

To this point, however, I have treated the juggling of the demands of simple living and self-reliance essentially as an individual or a family project. Little has been seen of the new pioneers' communal spirit as they pursue their separate visions of the good life. In the next section, however, I describe tribal rituals known as barter fairs and earth song festivals. They are the back-to-the-country equivalents of garage sales. On a borrowed farm field, usually in the fall, hundreds of back-to-the-landers congregate over a weekend to trade the fruits of harvest and a miscellany of household and farm artifacts. The fairs and festivals are community expressions of the individually held values of simplicity and self-reliance.

"No Drunk Dogs with Guns": Barter and the Simple Life

About one-half mile from the entrance to the Columbia River Barter Fair and Earth Song Festival,[14] a sign attached to a tree along the road announces, "NO DRUNK DOGS WITH GUNS." At the entrance to the barter fair, there is an easy explanation to the mysterious sign. The organizers ask registrants to take no alcoholic beverages into the fairgrounds, to leave their dogs at home, and to keep any and all guns sheathed and out of sight. The festival is a community celebration where children and their parents and grandparents need to be able to wander and browse, negotiate and trade, without incident.

The Columbia River Barter Fair and Earth Song Festival is held each October on a forty-acre pasture that overlooks the Columbia River in northeastern Washington. It is one of many barter fairs and festivals held throughout the Pacific Northwest and the rest of the country. Back-to-the-landers and their neighbors follow a circuit from one fair to another from April through November, much as the indigenous people of highland Latin America ritually pass from one village fiesta to another.

More than two thousand people attend the Columbia River Barter Fair and Earth Song Festival. Many of them buy a $10 camping pass for the weekend, and the rest purchase a $5 day pass. By the start of the fair the pasture is nearly covered with cars, tents, teepees, recreational vehicles, and school buses converted to family traveling machines, a favorite new pioneer mode of transportation. More than a few curiosity seekers come just to watch, to enjoy the evening camp fires and listen to the music, or to join in the freewheeling volleyball games that dominate the center of the campsite.

In the late afternoon attention shifts to the earth song festival. Festival organizers have erected a performing stage on the edge of the campground. A succession of bands with names like Tribal Therapy and Zumak, the Wild Bioregional Band, take turns at center stage. The electric guitars and keyboards are amplified by a bank of photovoltaic cells and storage batteries. Performers in bear robes imitating spawning salmon gyrate to the rhythm of classic rock refrains—"and the salmon circle from sea to sea, up the rivers of life endlessly."[15] When the bands' energy subsides, the Colombia River Dance Collective pulls both willing and reluctant participants into the large field in front of the stage, where they arrange their recruits in a circle, holding hands, a circle that moves in time to the hypnotic beat of African drumming. Eventually the circle breaks apart, and the dancers sway alone or in small groups, as they celebrate their gifts from Mother Earth.

Most barter fair participants are amused though respectful observers of their neighbors' ecstasy. They are at the fair to display their wares for trade, from surplus harvest to long unused paraphernalia from the goat shed that someone, they hope, will take home as a special treasure. Both the ordinary and the exotic are up for trade. Two boys sit by a cage of rabbits, waiting for an offer, while a long-haired new pioneer with a llama walks through the grounds looking for takers. Bathtubs, lavatories, tables, chairs, and rusted plowing implements are strategically placed throughout the grounds. Trade, however, is not limited to produce, livestock, and durable goods. Impromptu restaurants from Mexican to Thai move in and out of operation, a function of their proprietors' supplies. Here cash, rather than carrots or squash, is the usual payment for a burrito or a spring roll. Then, after food for the body, there is sustenance for the soul. Rustic signs in front of both tents and trailers offer services in rebirthing, breath release, polarity, modulation therapy, reflexology, and spiritual yoga.

Naturally, the barter fairs are much more than a convenient place to trade goods and services. They are archetypal gatherings of the primal clan. But after the communion and the celebration, the smallholder goes home. Trade and barter, however, remain as institutions important to the quality of the new pioneer way of life. These venerable yeoman institutions allow one to improve one's standard of living without working away from home or selling farmstead produce. A dozen eggs for a pint of straw-berries mimics the specialization of the formal economy without its imper-sonal quality.

Bartering is an everyday activity for a good number of smallholders. Sixty-five percent of the *Countryside* respondents say they have barter and trade relationships with neighbors, with 29 percent saying that these rela-tionships are either very or somewhat important to them. Bartering is a reflection of not only individual self-reliance but also community self-reliance. One survey respondent wrote, "My main hassle is laundry which I do at a friend's in exchange for milk." Another commented on a more extensive trading network: "Our garden is smaller than we'd like because we live on a steep hillside. Our neighbor, a master gardener, gives us 'tons' of produce, both out of friendliness and out of appreciation for our keeping her supplied with eggs all year. Another neighbor lets us cut fire-wood on his property—and we care for his animals during his frequent trips."

These reports evoke a sentimentality of relaxed neighborliness, but bar-tering can easily strain a relationship. "I think that trading, rather than using money, places a lot of stress on friendships" was the way one *Country-side* subscriber put it, and then went on to explain, "It mixes up having a personal relationship with having a business relationship. I'm tired of being friends with people so that we can trade!" For at least this smallholder, and likely many others, the impersonal nature of the monetized economy has definite advantages.

While this negative reaction to barter relationships was not a common theme in my interviews or the survey responses, it does reflect the anxiety that surrounds the trading networks. I was sensitive to the reluctance of back-to-the-landers to talk in detail about the extent of their bartering activities. There is among many smallholders a fear of the "Bigholder." In this case Bigholder is government incarnated as Internal Revenue Service agents. The informal economy's bartering and trade transactions are technically subject to taxation, just as the formalized ones are in the monetized economy. In the rural resistance tradition new pioneers want to avoid the Bigholder intrusion into the self-reliant world they have created for themselves, particularly if they are trying to minimize their dependency on a cash income in the first place.

Bartering, integral to both self-reliance and the simple life, is much like these two ideals, as well as being a part of them. It is an activity seen to be of worth but whose affirmation is a matter of struggle, particularly for those smallholders who covet the uncomplicated privacy of homestead life. From escaping the oversight of Bigholder to establishing community trading relationships of trust and conviviality, barter is a new pioneer ideal that requires a conscious involvement, in contrast to the depersonalized transactions that routinely take place in the formal economy. As with self-reliance and simple living, it has rewards along with inconvenience, and this inconvenience comprises the trade-offs and compromises that define the new pioneer way of life.

The Quality of Country Life

To this point in the study of the back-to-the-landers and their values, I have included frequent smallholder testimonials to the effect that country life is very satisfying. At the same time, threads of discontent have shown through the fabric of overall new pioneer satisfaction. The weekender families who have full-time employment away from their property are chronically frustrated by time constraints. Finding enough money to equip their farmsteads is another obstacle almost all smallholders face. But there are also any number of other aggravations that go beyond the time-money dilemma. An Idaho homesteader, for example, wrote, "My satisfaction with the way we live has been greatly hampered by a very short supply of water." She went on to say that she had not been able to have a garden or a green lawn for the past six years, and then added, "If this would turn around so we could again be more self-reliant instead of having to purchase all of our livestock feed and vegetables, it would make this type of living much more pleasant." But even if the elements cooperate, there are always the neighbors. A Maine smallholder recounts her predicament: "Some of your questions hit a nerve. My lifestyle can be described by the old adage 'Use up, wear out, make do or do without.' Most of what I own is secondhand, much of it needs repair, and a lot of it is old enough to vote. I AM TIRED OF DOING WITHOUT. I am surrounded by YUPPIE, NIMBY [not in my backyard] people from out of state who do not understand the difference between a hamster and a Hampshire."

Given the kinds of frustrations that the new pioneers face in their pursuit of self-reliance and voluntary simplicity, I wondered, on balance, what the quality of country life might be as seen through the eyes of the smallholders. In particular I was curious to see if the back-to-the-landers as a group would express dissatisfaction with specific parts of their lives, even though, as I reported earlier, 94 percent of the *Countryside* respondents consider themselves to be either very happy or pretty happy. To measure the potential dissatisfaction, I used a series of statements and phrases representing specific aspects of the *Countryside* respondents' lives, and then asked them to give their reaction to each of them on a four-point scale from not at all satisfied to very satisfied. In Table 8, I have summarized the responses to seven different aspects of the *Countryside* respondents' experience.

Table 8. *Countryside* respondents' satisfaction with selected aspects of their lives

Aspects of Respondents' Lives	% Very or Fairly Satisfied
Family life	96
Area where they live	93
Current housing	91
Relationship with neighbors	91
Current employment	82
Current financial situation	78
Progress toward self-reliance	75

Note: Total number of respondents = 565 (actual responses numbered from 430 to 554, since not all respondents answered each question; some questions were not applicable to all respondents).

Although in my interviews and in the questionnaire comments the back-to-the-landers were rarely shy in expressing their unhappiness over the obstacles in their way to the good life, Table 8 shows them reluctant to translate their grievances into a declared dissatisfaction with specific areas of their lives. On four of the items in Table 8 (family life, area where they live, housing, and neighbors) more than 90 percent of the respondents say they are either very or fairly satisfied. The satisfaction level does erode marginally on the issue of employment, with those either fairly or very satisfied declining to 82 percent. This drop in satisfaction is understandable when one reflects back on the struggle homesteaders go through to find a job to support their smallholding habit, but it is remarkable that less than one out of five respondents (18 percent) takes the opportunity to express frustration by choosing the "not at all satisfied" or "fairly unsatisfied" categories. Further, with the perennial problem of personal finances, still over three-quarters (78 percent) of the respondents express satisfaction with this contentious part of their lives.

The last item in Table 8, progress toward self-reliance, continues the trend of high satisfaction levels, with an even 75 percent of the respondents feeling either very or fairly satisfied with this elusive aspect of their lives. The high satisfaction with a decidedly problematic part of homesteading likely reflects as much the compromises the survey respondents have made with the goals of self-sufficiency as any technical proficiency they may have in the area of self-reliance.

The consistently high percentages of satisfaction in Table 8 raise questions about the source of the back-to-the-landers' equanimity. They have set for themselves the challenging goals of self-reliance and simple living, while constrained by work commitments and chronic underfunding. Yet, as a group, they are able to find extraordinary levels of satisfaction in their admittedly imperfect lives. In searching for the roots of this contentment, one is naturally led to consider the religious sources of smallholder tranquillity. Are the back-to-the-landers able to transcend the imperfections in their day-to-day lives by reliance on a religious tradition? If the question is framed in terms of formal, organized religion, the answer is a qualified no. Forty-two percent of the respondents say they are not part of any religious group. Just 14 percent belong to conservative or evangelical Christian churches, while 11 percent are Roman Catholic, 1 percent Jewish, and 25 percent identify with either mainline Protestantism or nondenominational and community churches. One percent claim an Eastern or New Age religion, and the remaining 6 percent are divided among Seventh Day Adventists, Quakers, Latter-day Saints, Christian Scientists, and Jehovah's Witnesses.

Perhaps more telling than church affiliation is the question of church attendance. Forty-one percent of the *Countryside* respondents report they never attend church, and another 17 percent attend less than once a month. On the other hand, 20 percent of the survey respondents do go to church at least once a week. For this minority of the *Countryside* subscribers, organized religion may well provide the resources for tranquillity, but it does not appear to be a powerful force in the lives of most of the new pioneers.[16]

Intriguingly, these same, mostly unchurched respondents admit to possessing spiritual dispositions. Only 13 percent saw themselves as less than average in terms of being spiritually minded, when being spiritually minded was qualified as not necessarily being related to formal religion. The back-to-the-landers, then, consider themselves to be spiritually sensitive but decline to express their spirituality exclusively in terms of organized religion.

This emerging characterization of the back-to-the-landers as nonconforming, spiritually minded people leads one back to the question of the smallholders' apparent serenity in spite of their sometimes hectic lives. And this brings the discussion back as well to the phenomenon of mindfulness, with which the chapter began. From my interviews and the comments on the questionnaires, I have concluded that it is the process of living in the country itself, often expressed through mindfulness experiences, that accounts for the high satisfaction levels seen in Table 8, even though homesteading entails a multitude of complications. While the values of self-reliance and voluntary simplicity are central to their view of the world, smallholders subordinate them to the priority of simply enjoying the tranquillity of rural life, of living close to nature. Whether they express this sentiment through a system of formal belief or through an ineffable communion with the natural order of things, it is this spiritual-mindedness that seems to be the best candidate for the empowering force that allows them to hold on tenaciously to country life.[17]

Many of my correspondents, as has been evident, were not hesitant to complain of the vicissitudes they face, but they quickly qualified their discontent by adding that they could never leave their homesteads. One Maine respondent whose family had to give up its health insurance said, "I would rather worry about bills than change my way of life." Another smallholder elaborated on this theme: "All improvements and projects take FOREVER. Almost nothing has gone as we thought. But we hated city life and had to get away. We love this wild place, and neither of us would move back! But it is extremely difficult too. I'm *not* complaining, please understand. Just the FACTS you asked for." And then a California respondent, after reporting that her husband had just been hired full-time with medical and dental benefits, summarized as well as anyone the smallholder attachment to the land when she explained, "It was a lot harder for us to survive here than we ever thought it would be. We feel we are over the hump now. We would never go back to the city, even if my husband did not get this job. We would have just gone on doing without and enjoying country living."

Country Values: Finding Balance

"Are we self-sufficient? No. Are we aware? Yes." In this question-and-answer sequence a *Countryside* survey respondent succinctly captures much of the back-to-the-land experience with sustainable living. Smallholders come back to the country to fashion self-reliant lifestyles through simple living and homestead technology. But while their intentions may be "sustainably correct," compromise is the near inevitable product of the back-to-the-landers' encounter with the real world of small-town and rural America. Most have to work full-time to support themselves and their homesteads. The paraphernalia of small-farm technology can be expensive, and the homemade versions exchange precious time for cash and credit. And the pressures of moving back and forth between farmstead and job make the allure of convenience all the more seductive, undermining a strict application of voluntary simplicity.

Rather than magnify the technical deficiencies in the back-to-the-landers' attempt to practice the values of self-reliance and simple living, one could perhaps more effectively appreciate the prerequisites of the overall sustainability project by focusing on the smallholders' ability to balance the demands of homestead efficiency against the pleasures of living in the country. In a world where worthy projects fall victim to the single-minded obsession with principle, a single-mindedness that can undermine the quality of life, the new pioneers' pragmatism is perhaps more a virtue than a weakness. In a commencement address at Brandeis University, novelist E. L. Doctorow recognized the efficacy of balance. Drawing on Sherwood Anderson's "theory of grotesques," developed by Anderson in the introduction to his *Winesburg, Ohio,* collection of short stories, Doc-

torow explains how admirable principle can distort a truth when it is elevated to an exclusive status: "All about us in the world are many truths to
live by, and they are all beautiful—the truth of passion and love, the truth
of candor and of thrift, the truth of patriotism, the truth of self-reliance,
and so on. But as people come along and try to make something of themselves, they snatch up a truth and make it their own predominating truth
to the exclusion of all others. And what happens, says Anderson, is that
the moment a person does this—clutches one truth too tightly—the truth
so embraced becomes a lie and the person turns into a grotesque."[18]

By balancing mindfulness against the ideals of simple living, back-to-
the-landers avoid turning self-reliance into a grotesque.[19] They transform
self-reliance from a rigid to a relative principle and appear not to allow
frugality to overwhelm convenience. Many of them are able to let the
sights, sounds, and smells of farm life compensate for both the contingent
and existential aggravations with which they cope. Nevertheless, voluntary
simplicity, self-reliance, and mindfulness do not constitute the complete
constellation of back-to-the-country values. There are also the principles
of neighborliness, cooperation, and community activism. Might it be possible, however, that in emphasizing the *private* pleasures of country living,
the back-to-the-landers carry the potential for turning mindfulness itself
into a grotesque? Is the smallholding phenomenon primarily one where
solitary individuals on scattered homesteads experience moments of
transcendence while rural America's community and natural resources
slip away?

These considerations raise once again the nagging question whether
the new pioneers can be an organized force for positive change in a dete-
riorating countryside. While I am still two chapters away from tackling the
activism question directly, to this point it appears that the smallholders'
contribution to rural renewal is one of individual example more than of
collective action. Change may never come to rural America without community activism; still, taken together, the new pioneers' individual experiences with voluntary simplicity and self-reliance constitute guidelines for
the society-wide search for a sustainable future. As a group the smallholders do seek their primary sources of satisfaction outside of consumer
relationships.

In many ways the back-to-the-country experiences reflect the struggle
that lies ahead for the larger society in its journey toward sustainability.
There will be false starts, compromises, defeats, as well as small, and even
significant, victories along the way. As country survivors, the back-to-the-

landers have been through it all before. But how have they survived? It is in the answer to this question that perhaps the value of the smallholding experience most clearly reveals itself. The back-to-the-landers' perspective on the potential of simple living in the country may be much more important than their technical achievements, though these are not inconsiderable. They have learned to tolerate a seemingly endemic disjuncture between their aspirations and their performance. Though not without discouragement, they have persisted in inching toward their goals. Their appreciation of the ordinary and their ability to live in the present appear to renew their ability to endure and to persevere. The road to a sustainable future will be a difficult one. If one can enjoy the journey, it will likely make the difficulties all the more bearable, and the chances of arriving at one's destination will be all the more probable.

4

SOFT PATHS
Back-to-the-Land Technology

 Anne Schwartz and her weeder geese, who introduced this report on the back-to-the-land movement, possess many of the attributes of an ideal, sustainable, back-to-the-land technology. Having geese eat weeds in a potato patch rather than rely on backbreaking physical labor or the application of herbicides is a kind of "convivial" technology—one that is agreeable and friendly.[1] The Chinese weeder geese exemplify convivial technology not only because they eliminate the toxic by-products of herbicide spraying but also because they make a number of other contributions to the sustainable farmstead. The birds' primary fringe benefit is the manure they leave behind as they go about their work, a not inconsiderable contribution to fertilizing a crop. And they do not compact the soil as they move in and out of the crop rows, as a tractor pulling a chemical sprayer would. Of course, the tractor is also a fossil-fuel user; the geese are less intensive users—if they cannot walk from field to field, they can be chauffeured in a pickup truck. Their value, however, is not exclusively related to their field work. They also provide goose down, as well as eggs. When age catches up with them and they become too old to work, they still have one more contribution to make. They take their turn as part of the smallholder's stew pot. All this from animals who pay for their own upkeep by the very work they do: eating weeds that are of no value to anyone else.

At this point I should stop to say that the Chinese weeder geese are far from an essential homestead technology for most smallholders—only 14 percent of the *Countryside* survey respondents reported using them. But apart from how many people actually employ these multipurpose animals or how practical they may be, the fundamental logic behind their use can provide additional insight into the kind of technology that has the potential to make a major contribution to the building of a sustainable world.

In addition to "convivial," alternative (or appropriate) technology has also been labeled "soft" technology, in contrast to the conventional "hard" variety. Just below I have listed six contrasting characteristics of hard and soft technology, and I shall briefly discuss them in relationship to the weeder geese.[2] My purpose here is to place into relief the design principles that underlie the specific applications of the soft technological path.

Hard and Soft Technologies: A Comparison

Hard	*Soft*
Ecologically unsound	Ecologically sound
Intensive use of nonrenewable energy	Reliance on renewable energy
High pollution	Low or no pollution
High specialization	Low specialization
Complex—difficult to understand	Easily understood
Capital intensive	Labor intensive

In describing the work of the weeder geese, I have already outlined the first three characteristics: pollution free, nonrenewable-energy-conserving weeder geese are an ecologically sound technology, one example of a soft-path approach to sustainable living. The next two parallel characteristics, items four and five from my list, lead to the larger issues of access and control, issues that center on the degree to which ordinary people can understand both the technical details and the policy ramifications of a technology like the chemical control of weeds, or, conversely, the degree to which these matters, because of their complexity, have to be entrusted to experts.

Herbicide use is a typical hard technology because its continued application depends on a hierarchy of specialists and high-technology research-and-development organizations impenetrable to the nonexpert. It is, of course, easy enough for a farmer to hook up a sprayer to a tractor and apply herbicides across a field of crops. But at the same time, the farmer depends on the assurances of experts that the chemicals used are safe and necessary. These assurances come by way of a research establishment whose pronouncements are clouded by the mysteries of the scientist's laboratory.

On the other hand, Chinese weeder geese are a human-scale technology. It is by nature democratic, and access can be universal. The techniques and the policy issues are relatively transparent. There are of course critical prerequisites to its successful use. These prerequisites, however, are personal; conversance with the technology does not require an extended initiation into a priesthood based on esoteric knowledge. The personal attributes that lend themselves to the care of a flock of weeder geese are patience, a love of animals, and an affinity for physical labor. Given Anne Schwartz's attraction to her animal assistants, it is difficult to separate her interests in the geese as a naturalist from her need for their work as weeders.[3]

The close relationship between physical labor and soft technology is most apparent in the final distinction on my list: hard technology is capital intensive while soft technology is labor intensive. In many ways it is the labor-intensive nature of soft technology that defines its overall character. After all, it is the smallholder's hands-on encounter with the geese that makes them effective. Physical labor is a substitute for the high energy input of hard technology. The energy for hard technology comes primarily by the way of nonrenewable fossil fuels. The muscle, solar, and wind power of soft technology not only allows future generations to inherit their share of what will be left of the earth's finite supplies of fossil fuels, but soft technology also permits significant reductions in the pollution trail from the combustion of fossil fuels.

This case study of weeder geese, however, demonstrates that soft technology is more than just a physical encounter with the natural world. There are of course the very real physical pleasures of farmwork. But it is the design of the work plan itself, as much as the sweat from its implementation, that can give the smallholder a sense of accomplishment. For smallholders soft technology is more than the primitive expression of muscle power. While depending on intensive physical labor, it is also designed to save labor—in this case backbreaking weed pulling. Soft technology, at its core, is a plan for working in harmony with nature rather than against it. Consequently, the advocates of soft technology can claim that it represents one, though not necessarily the exclusive, path to a sustainable future and that hard-technology competitors need to be judged in terms of soft technology's sustainable precedents.

My purpose in describing the work of the weeder geese is not so much prescriptive as it is illustrative. Acknowledging that the relationship between Anne and her geese is not an easy one to duplicate, even among dedicated smallholders, I want to make the point that the weeder geese possess a value that is more symbolic than practical. Turning for the most part from the esoteric to the prosaic, the review of back-to-the-land technology in the rest of the chapter reinforces the notion that the value of the weeder geese is not so much that they offer a pollution-free solution to weeds in a potato patch as that they illustrate the distinctions between sustainable and unsustainable technologies. In the final analysis, the distinctions between hard and soft technology are meant only to sensitize one to the possibility of a range of alternatives, not to force a choice between Anne's geese and toxic herbicides. Using a green or plastic mulch to cover the ground and suffocate the weeds in a potato patch or periodically tilling between rows to uproot the weeds are two sustainable alternatives to herbicides, as is just letting the weeds grow, once the potato plants are strong enough to compete with them, as Jd Belanger advised his overcommitted Tennessee correspondent in the last chapter. This kind of divergent and creative thinking, rather than dogmatic solutions, will likely be soft technology's lasting contribution to a sustainable future.

Since the human factor in the form of physical labor is critical to the soft paths of homestead technology, it is only natural that in order to understand both its potential and its shortcomings, one would want to know more about the personal histories of the people who use it everyday. This brings us back to Anne Schwartz and a basic question: How did a young woman from New Jersey end up tending Chinese weeder geese on the western slopes of the Cascade mountains?

Growing up in suburban New Jersey, Anne became, as she puts it, "horse crazy." Her father paid for riding lessons, and she spent much of her teenage years working at local stables. Her affection for horses in particular and animals in general led her to Rutgers University's School of Agriculture, with the goal of becoming a veterinarian.

In college Anne's interests broadened from a love of animals to environmental activism. After two years mixing college classes and student politics, she dropped out of school in 1976 to find her place in small-town America. She headed west, alone, driving a red 1972 Toyota. Three thousand miles later, on her way to California, Anne met up with college friends in Washington State's Skagit River Valley, a hundred miles northeast of Seattle. The friendliness of the local people and the natural beauty of the mountain valleys captivated her, and Anne has been a back-to-the-lander a continent away from home for the last twenty years.

Although Anne's dream of becoming a veterinarian never did materialize, animals have been, and still are, a very important part of her life. In addition to the weeder geese, the Schwartz family consists of a shifting assortment of dogs and three riding horses, the animals who initiated Anne's back-to-the-land odyssey, and Mike Brondi. Anne first met Mike while they were both at Rutgers. Mike finished his degree in forestry and took a job with the U.S. Forest Service in the Skagit River Valley, while Anne stayed in New Jersey. Shortly after their Pacific Northwest reunion Mike and Anne pooled their resources and started living together—the valley's first Jewish-Catholic union. When their wedding came ten years later, it was a major social event in the local community.

After a decade and a half in the country Anne and Mike move to the rhythms of rural life, while still maintaining the spontaneity of the nomadic instincts that brought them to the Skagit River Valley. In addition to helping Anne with her incorporated Blue Heron Farm, Mike is an apprentice carpenter. He also experiments with growing bamboo, hoping eventually to supply commercial quantities to Seattle's large Southeast Asian population, who now import bamboo from Thailand and the Philippines. Both Mike and Anne belong to the local volunteer fire department and serve as emergency paramedics in the community. And though so much of her life and work are centered in the mountain valley she has adopted as home, Anne still nurtures the 1960s kind of activism that was part of her college experience. She keeps in touch with a network of correspondents throughout the country, sharing her own experiences and offering support for an assortment of back-to-the-land projects.

With this profile of Anne Schwartz and the underlying soft-technology logic abstracted from the case study of the weeder geese as background, it is time now to ask to what degree the back-to-the-landers actually employ soft technologies. In the following sections of the chapter, I summarize the *Countryside* survey, looking at the kinds of technologies smallholders use and their reported effectiveness, from gardens to draft horses. I also describe the family division of labor on farmsteads, focusing on the varying contributions of men and women and children. As has been my approach to this point, I ground the discussion within the everyday reality of

the new pioneers, who find themselves caught in the time-money dilemma while trying to build self-reliant microfarms. But before examining
the variations in the smallholders' use of soft technology, I want to highlight selected aspects of the homestead of their dreams, in order to understand the demands, and the rewards, of one approach to a sustainable
lifestyle.

Homestead Dreams

Anne Schwartz's Chinese weeder geese are a small-scale expression of the
design principles of self-reliant, soft technology. The homestead dream,
however, does not comprise only a technology or two like the weeder
geese. Rather, the ideal smallholding, as transferred from the pages of
Countryside to the subconscious of even the most dissolute of back-to-the-
landers, is a series of soft technologies knit together through automatically reinforcing feedback loops, in much the same way the weeder geese
constitute an integrated technology, with their digestive systems turning
potato-choking weeds into manure that enriches the soil. This approach
to farmstead technology mimics the way the elements of an ecosystem
interact to regenerate life continually. The sustainable homestead of back-
to-the-land dreams would, for example, reflect the design characteristics
of a small pond, where algae exposed to sunlight give off oxygen necessary for the survival of the animal life forms, which in turn generate the
carbon dioxide required by the pond's algae and other plants.[4] In the
same way, the ideal back-to-the-land microfarm enhances, rather than de-
grades, the piece of earth on which its human operators hold a stewardship.

   In the paragraphs that follow, I present a series of snapshots of the
sustainable farmstead designed on the basis of biological principles. Few
of these integrated homesteads exist outside of the pages of back-to-the-
land magazines and books and the imaginations of new pioneers. Their
occasional incarnations come primarily in the form of demonstration
farms. The partial blueprint that follows, however, stands as a point of
reference for judging the back-to-the-landers' progress toward the kind of
technical self-reliance that is one of the prerequisites for a sustainable
future. While neither my surveys nor interviews led me to much more than
an approximation of the homestead of back-to-the-land dreams, I found

few smallholders who did not entertain the possibility that good fortune, hard work, and propitious circumstances could conspire to turn their farmsteads into exemplary homesteads.

Trees and gardens are basic components of the self-reliant homestead. Deciduous poplar and maple trees, for example, shade the farmstead home in summer, and in winter their bare branches let sunlight flow through to the solar greenhouse, which traps and radiates the sun's heat to the rest of the building. On the north side of the farmstead, there might be a bank of coniferous fir and spruce trees to break the sting of cold fronts moving south toward the homestead residence. An orchard occupying perhaps an acre of space on one side of the smallholding would be desirable, with apple and apricot trees strategically and decoratively positioned over much of the homestead grounds. There is as well the possibility of a woodlot, whose deadfall would provide fuel for the woodstove that heats the farmstead house on those winter days when the solar gain through the greenhouse cannot do the job. The trees, with their shading, wind-breaking, and fuel- and food-producing properties, not to mention the contribution their leaves make to the compost piles, are prototypical examples of both the ecological integration and multifunctionality of a soft technology structured around the principles of biological design.

But as important as trees are, most homestead plans start with an ordinary vegetable garden. While the traditional farm garden occupies a large rectangular plot of ground, with long straight rows of peas, corn, carrots, and beets that can displace up to an acre of land, most neohomesteaders, working marginal land, usually favor a more compact design. Seeking maximum production from limited space, new pioneers feel little inhibition in covering their raised garden beds with polyethylene sheeting supported by a skeleton of PVC (polyvinyl chloride) pipe, turning the beds into miniature green houses—even though the generous use of plastic constitutes a break with conventional gardening. Of course, the smallholders are also attracted to the time-tested, natural methods of integrated pest management, whereby companion planting, natural insect predators, frogs, toads, and song birds control garden pests.[5]

Moving from the plant side of the homestead blueprint to the animal side, one must first ask whether the ideal integrated smallholding will accommodate animal husbandry. Few back-to-the-landers, as it turns out, are vegetarians, and most have no problem with the prospect of eating animals they raise. They see animals not only as part of the life cycle that sustains the human component but also as part of the chain of life that supports an entire ecosystem. Consequently, raising animals to eat, in moderation, is usually considered as being in harmony with ecological design principles rather than in conflict with them. But at the same time, the crowded factory-like conditions of commercial feedlot methods of turning animals into meat are foreign to smallholder sensibilities. Most back-to-the-landers believe that the animals who are eventually to nourish them are due the dignity of an uncrowded existence, with sunshine and fresh air. And apart from when or how they might end up on a family's dining table, farmstead animals are companions—companions who allow children to learn responsibility as the children take over their care.

But aside from ethical considerations concerning their use, animals make a considerable contribution to a family's self-reliance project. With a garden, orchard, and berry patch, a family might be able to produce in the neighborhood of 25 percent of its own food. The addition of animals (eggs, milk, and meat), could push that up toward 75 percent, a signifi-cant advance in family self-sufficiency.

This rise in productivity is an irresistible argument in favor of animals. The question for most back-to-the-landers is, then, how many animals and what kinds—more specifically, cows or goats, or both—as the farmstead's primary milk-producing animals? Cows have a productivity edge over goats, but they also eat considerably more—and leave as a consequence more manure. Goats, however, have a size advantage. They can be easily loaded into the back of a small pickup truck, or even a station wagon. And their diminutive stature makes them attractive family pets, as well as much less intimidating when milking time arrives.

Chickens present the homesteader with little of the strategic planning decisions connected to the cow-goat dilemma. Chickens are multipurpose creatures, providing eggs and meat as well as taking care of their share of barnyard insects. Satisfaction in raising them comes not only from their utility but from allowing them the freedom to peck their way around the farmstead yard in the sunshine and fresh air. Airy, well-ventilated chicken coops with doors open to the outside world are light years from the con-centration-camp-like existence of their commercial cousins—crammed to-gether in banks of cages, beaks blunted, and fed hormones and anti-biotics during their short and confined lives.[6] Free-range chickens, of course, do constitute a homestead nuisance factor, though salmonella-tainted eggs and meat are not one of them. Ideally the homestead chickens are trained to lay their eggs in their coop, though the search for the eggs of free-range chickens carries elements of a low-grade adventure and the source of some diversion, for children, if not adults.

Aside from all their remunerative benefits perhaps the compelling reason for keeping chickens or goats or any other homestead animal is an intangible one. "We keep chickens in large part because they make good friends and neighbors" is the way the *Mother Earth News* contributor John Vivian calculates the cost-benefit equation for having chickens. In classic *Mother Earth News* folksiness, Vivian goes on to make his pitch for chickens:

> Give [them] a try, if you have or can wangle the space. You may have to scrape droppings off your shoes now and again, but that never hurt anyone. In compensation, you'll have your eggs and fried chicken fresh, wholesome, and on the cheap. That's worth a little cash money. And then, spared an existence cooped up in a pen, your birds will live out as close to a natural chicken-life as their breeding permits. Maybe freeing them up will free something in you. It works that way with me, or I like to think it does. Looking to live and let live in the natural condition is as near a state of grace as I'll ever approach in this life. Can't put a dollar value on that.[7]

Taken together, all the nonhuman elements of these homestead dreams work together for a renewable, sustainable approach to living on the earth. But what happens when human activity is entered into the sustainability equation? Answering this question brings one directly to the door of the farmstead residence, the habitat of the smallholders who occupy the property, and suggests another question: Is it possible to entertain any reasonable hope that the homestead residents can enjoy an approximation of urban amenities while giving as much or more back to the earth as they take from it? This question leads from the front door of the farmstead house to the bathroom and a direct confrontation with the toilet.

Toilets consume 40 percent of household water supplies, and at five gallons a flush they discharge potentially valuable nutrients into public water ways, where they pollute rather than enrich the medium that carries them. A family of four uses forty thousand gallons of fresh drinking water a year to move just six hundred pounds of fecal matter, which, if it were composted, would only fill two gallon cans.[8]

With a flush toilet thousands of gallons of polluted water are added to the community's waste stream. For rural people, an option to moving family wastes into a community sewer system is an on-property septic tank. While the septic tank does to a point keep waste water within the confines of the homestead, in terms of sustainability, it is not much of an improvement over the sewer system. The tank has to be pumped out periodically; part of the waste, then, still ends up in someone else's backyard. And since the typical septic tank holds only a thousand gallons, there is a constant flow of effluent into a leach field, which raises concerns about both groundwater pollution and the extravagance of dedicating a large field on a small property to waste-water seepage.

There is, of course, the classic latrine, and a three-foot-by-four-foot, four-foot-deep pit can accommodate a family of four for several years. But, though the traditional privy does not involve any direct water pollution, the comfort factor is clearly absent. The odor is noxious; frosty mornings do not encourage a reflective constitutional. In addition, the excretion deposited, if it does not seep into the groundwater, will take a generation and more to become part of healthy soil.

To combine comfort with the satisfaction of transforming a once disagreeable waste into useful product, while avoiding the contamination of either the homestead property or the community beyond it, the smallholder can install an in-house composting toilet in the farmstead residence. A composting toilet goes right in the bathroom just like its water-flush predecessor. Under the seat is a chute that allows the fecal matter to fall into a bin, located in the basement, where over time it goes through a composting process.

The composting of human excreta in the composting toilet takes from two to three years. The farmstead residents can add through another chute in the kitchen food and greenhouse wastes in order to prevent compaction of the fecal material and to maintain optimal aerobic conditions. The point of the careful composting of the human waste is to kill the parasites and polygenic organisms that transmit disease. And if the compost pile can be maintained at the proper temperature and moisture levels, there should be, at least in theory, little more odor from the composting toilet than from the conventional flush variety, since they are both vented in the same way, though the composting toilet does not have a water trap that seals off the transfer of gases.

The basement bin is an inclined one, and during the composting process the fecal matter moves down through a series of baffles until it finally comes to rest as a finished product next to the bin's bottom doors. What one finds upon opening the doors is a substance much like peat moss— with one person's waste in a year composting down to somewhere between one to two cubic feet of the stuff.

Once a cubic foot or two of human compost accumulates, the question becomes what to do with it. Since there still remains the possibility that the composting has not taken care of all the pathogens and since the quantity of compost is small, smallholders will likely want to use it on their inedible landscape—flowers, shrubs, and trees.

Even though prospective country residents, accustomed to the immediate convenience of a water-flush toilet, might be reluctant to embrace the reality of composting toilets in their bathrooms, they would have little difficulty in understanding their technical feasibility. Composting toilets, along with passive solar space and water heating, and gray-water recycling, possess a straightforward logic, even if they demand a change in attitude and habit from their users. In contrast, it is far from evident how a sustainable homestead goes about detaching itself from the electrical grid and starts producing its own power. Generating electricity on a farmstead is admittedly a complicated and relatively expensive undertaking, but there are, nevertheless, three viable options for renewable power production on a smallholding. The first is a mini–hydroelectric system whose small turbine takes advantage of the current of a fast-moving stream or small river. In addition, windmill technology that pumped water on American farms before rural electrification has been refined over the past several decades for use on small, self-sufficient properties. And the third alternative to hooking onto a distant energy source through a utility's electrical grid is photovoltaic cells, which transform sunlight into electrical current. Each of these three power sources has unique advantages, though the first two are limited to locations with either quickly moving water or dependable winds. Regardless of which source a smallholding draws on, however, the process of getting the current to power a toaster or a compact disc player is roughly equivalent. The electricity generated is first captured by a bank of storage batteries as direct current and then run through a converter to transform it into alternating current before it passes into the farmstead residence or its outbuildings.[9]

Although the alternative power generators perform well, the smallholder still has to monitor the parts of the system carefully in order to ensure a reliable source of power. When the power goes off, the public utility is not going to send a lineman out to get the lights back on. Faced with a tangle of wires connecting batteries to windmills and converters, while imagining the inevitable power outages that could require long nights of troubleshooting, even the most conscientious of back-to-the-landers may well wonder if independence from public utility is worth the kind of involvement that alternative energy demands. It is, however, just this kind of intense involvement that characterizes both the separate elements and the totality of the back-to-the-land homestead dreams. Working with soft technology, rather than the conventional hard variety, has been compared to driving a car rather than riding as an unconcerned passenger.[10] But the integrated, ecologically grounded farmstead design I have just described, from chickens to composting toilets, takes the analogy at least one or two steps further: placing the smallholder behind the wheel of a sensitive touring car over a switchback route perilously skirting oceanside drop-offs.

For some, the journey over a difficult road in a demanding sports car is both an inconvenience and a nuisance. For many others, however, such a trip is an exhilarating experience. The difference in sentiments is largely a matter of how one defines the situation. In the case of soft technology, from sprinkling urine mixed with gray water on a vegetable garden to wearing a sweater inside on a sunless winter day, one can define the conscious encounter with material survival in diametrically opposite ways. On the one hand, physical labor is seen as demeaning, a subordination of intellect to muscle power. On the other hand, it is possible to define the application of soft technology as both an intellectual and spiritual enterprise. There is an aesthetic dimension, a thoroughgoing elegance, to the design of integrated convivial technology that functions on the basis of biological principles. Composting toilets, for example, may provide their owner-operators with only modest amounts of compost, but they allow them the satisfaction of working with nature by stopping pollution at its source and, as a consequence, becoming participants in the cycles that regenerate life. The process, as the authors of *The Integral Urban House* have observed, brings one to "a dramatic view of one's fecal matter at close range. Although there is no odor, the sight may be disquieting to some. To others, of course, it is a challenge to overcome taboos and a pleasure to know they are turning a problem into an asset."[11]

But apart from its aesthetic or nuisance character, it is likely that one version or another of soft technology will have to be adopted by the human beings on this planet in order for the earth's support systems to maintain a growing population through the midpoint of the next century.[12] Over the past two centuries, however, the hard technological path has prevented any significant gravitation toward soft-path options. Although it has not been without selective success, the soft technological path as a package still carries the stigma of antimodern primitivism and has generally been ignored by sponsored, wide-scale research and development. But if policy makers, with popular support, come to the point where they are ready to pursue a soft technological path before irreversible damage is done to the earth's ecological integrity, the back-to-the-landers' reservoir of experience can be a valuable resource in understanding the human-scale difficulties of switching from unsustainable to sustainable technologies. Consequently, in the next section of this chapter I want to review the smallholders' attempts to realize their homestead dreams, with the inevitable dilemmas, contradictions, and qualified accomplishments that come when idealism collides with reality.

Soft Technology: Homestead Realities

"We're doing things, but it's not all fancy. One example would be a gray-water-recycling system. In our case all our drains lead to a ditch that ambles across the yard. The ducks and chickens work it for snacks, and the liquid fertilizes the grass, which the goats then graze on. So, the kernel of the idea is there, but we don't have the specialized equipment you read about in a lot of back-to-the-land magazines."

With this brief description of her homestead's rudimentary approach to gray-water recycling, a smallholder from an island off the coast of British Columbia summarizes much of the back-to-the-land experience with soft technology. For most smallholders soft technology's homestead dreams, in terms of an overall integrated design, remain pretty much just that— dreams waiting generous amounts of time and money magically to appear and transform them into reality. While they have plans and schemes to move parts of the soft-technology dream from the pages of the *Mother Earth News* to their own smallholdings, most back-to-the-landers remain relatively content with a considerable gap between intent and achievement. The new pioneers tend to settle for the simple pleasures of a mindful apprehension of the natural world around them rather than to labor single-mindedly on building a farmstead that works in harmony with it.

It would be misleading, however, to suggest that soft-technology proj-

ects are unimportant to the back-to-the-landers or that alternative-technology dreams are not a powerful force in shaping the back-to-the-country
experience. The contingencies of country survival simply get in the way of
full-scale implementation. But to move this discussion of smallholder
technology beyond an impressionistic stage, I want to draw on the *Countryside* survey in order to report the actual levels of soft-technology adoption
for a representative group of back-to-the-landers. In the survey I presented the respondents with a list of homestead technologies, from the
prosaic (gardens and goats) to the relatively complex (mini–hydroelectric
and photovoltaic power systems). In addition, I asked the respondents to
indicate—on a four-point rating scale from not at all effective to very
effective—how effective each of the technologies was in "providing their
families with independence or self-reliance." In Table 9 I have listed the
most common homestead technologies, based on the percentage of smallholders who say they have the particular item, and then I have included
the effectiveness score for each technology.

Table 9. Homestead technology: the common elements

Item	%	Effectiveness Score (1–4)
Garden	95	3.1
Fruit trees	78	2.6
Woodstove heat	73	3.6
Woodlot	63	3.2
Chickens	60	3.3

Note: Total number of respondents = 565 (actual responses numbered from 561 to 564,
since not all respondents answered each question).

Though the data in Table 9 are straightforward, they do come with
interpretive complications. On the one hand, Table 9 shows that more
than half of the *Countryside* respondents do employ the basic elements of
homestead technology, from chickens (60 percent) to gardens (95 percent). Though basic, these elementary technologies appear to be productive, at least in a subsistence sense; only fruit trees, at 2.6, have effectiveness scores below 3.0. The uncomplicated conclusion here is that most
smallholders effectively use the fundamental elements of a soft technological approach to sustainable living. And as a result of these prosaic technologies, the *Countryside* subscribers report that on average they produce

36 percent of the food their families eat. But at the same time, it is surprising that these simple technologies have less than a universal application among the *Countryside* sample. Only gardens, at 95 percent, approach universal implementation, and then there is a sharp drop-off to fruit trees (78 percent) and woodstove heat (73 percent). After chickens (60 percent in Table 9) there is an even sharper decline to goats (28 percent in Table 10). One would think that a group of people, like the *Countryside* respondents, who go to all the trouble to make it back to the country and by the fact of subscribing to a back-to-the-land magazine demonstrate their interest in self-reliant, sustainable technologies might be sufficiently motivated to have up and running most, if not all, of the ordinary and inexpensive soft technologies. Such a supposition, however, does not fully appreciate all the energy expended on a move to the country in the first place or the sometimes paralyzing effect the time-money dilemma can have on the country survivors.

The absence of motivation, however, is a poor candidate as a primary factor for explaining the smallholders' modest use of farmstead technologies. The soft-technology checklist itself provides evidence on the seriousness of the neohomesteaders' intent. While it was innocuous enough, the questionnaire checklist nevertheless distressed a number of the survey respondents. This straightforward list seemed to touch a nerve deep within the back-to-the-land psyche. One respondent complained that I should have had a category for work in progress or planned. A number of respondents wrote of their specific plans, including intended dates for completion of fish ponds and chicken coops. In many of the comments there was clear discomfort at not being able to report more progress toward self-reliance through alternative technology. But at the same time, many of the comments reflected a certain equanimity in the face of the technology deficits. "We built a house, shop, two barns (peeled hundreds of poles) with only family labor and from paycheck to paycheck. Greenhouse and root cellar are coming—each takes a turn," reported a male *Countryside* respondent in his late thirties from Washington State by way of explaining his family's measured approach to homestead technology.

"Each takes a turn." This kind of persevering attitude helps one understand why three-quarters of the *Countryside* respondents report they are satisfied (either fairly or very) with their progress toward self-reliance, as I reported in Chapter 3, in spite of modest technological accomplishments. Their plans, schemes, and dreams seem to energize more than overwhelm them. This appears to hold true even when they move from one homestead to another and have to start all over again. On the back of her questionnaire a woman in her mid-thirties from British Columbia shared her perspective on second-time-around smallholding:

> We have recently moved to an island, where we hope to do some subsistence farming. We bought raw land and are in the process of building up our homestead. We brought our mobile home with us, but as yet we have no power or water. We have been part-time homesteaders for twelve years, and during that time we have raised all sorts of animals for food, had gardens, orchards, greenhouses, and cold frames. We plan to take all the information we have learned over the years and apply it to our lifestyle here on Cortez Island. Because we are just starting, we had to check "no" for many of the items on your technology list. We haven't gotten around to them yet, but we will have them—or we have had them.

While appreciating that smallholding is more process than product, I still wanted to know the extent to which the *Countryside* respondents had moved the rest of homestead dreams from magazine pages through their front gates. In Tables 10 and 11, I have summarized the *Countryside* respondents' reports on their possession of another fourteen elements of soft technology. The first set, in Table 10, contains for the most part rather ordinary but, for the smallholders, less common technologies (goats, greenhouses), while Table 11 includes the relatively exotic (workhorses and photovoltaics).

Table 10.   Homestead technology: the less common elements

Item	%	Effectiveness Score (1–4)
Goats	28	2.9
Root cellar	22	3.0
Greenhouse	22	2.8
Fish pond	22	2.1
Bees	15	2.7
Weeder geese	14	2.3
Milk cow	11	3.3

Note: Total number of respondents = 565 (actual responses numbered from 561 to 563, since not all respondents answered each question).

As is obvious from Table 10, there is a considerable difference between tending a garden (Table 9) and keeping animals. While goats and small-holding are often seen as synonymous, the reality is that just over a quarter of the back-to-the-landers feel that they can dedicate the time and energy to these sometimes captivating animals; "goats are like potato chips, it's hard to stop at one" is a sentiment that is part of smallholder folk wisdom. But the twice-daily milkings make them a luxury that most smallholders forgo. The milk cow is even a rarer fixture on the back-to-the-land homesteads. Just 11 percent of the *Countryside* respondents have one, perhaps an understandable figure when one considers that a cow is a very large animal whose sheer bulk inspires trepidation in dairy-barn novices. Cows, after all, do not fit into the backs of station wagons, as goats do. Still, for those homesteaders who can see their way clear to make a commitment to a milk cow, the payoff is a large volume of milk and cream, as the relatively high effectiveness score of 3.3 for these animals testifies.

One can certainly appreciate busy and often peripatetic smallholders feeling reluctant to take on the responsibilities of animal care, even for bees and fish, who take care of themselves most of the year round. But in Table 10's list there are two inanimate homestead technologies, greenhouses and root cellars, which share a relatively low possession rate of 22 percent. Perhaps more than anything else these low percentages, for what one would normally consider standard equipment for the homestead dream, demonstrate what a substantial undertaking it is just to move to the country. There are all the financial sacrifices associated with changing jobs and buying property and then likely either building or renovating a home. While a garden may seem like a low-commitment endeavor, a productive one requires considerable amounts of energy for soil revitalization, weeding, pruning, thinning, and irrigating. Consequently, even what one might think of as common homestead technologies, such as greenhouses and root cellars, still reside a considerable distance down on the typical back-to-the-lander's list of priorities—"Each takes a turn," as the Washington smallholder explains.

Before leaving Table 10 and moving on to Table 11, I should take at least brief notice of weeder geese, whose contribution to sustainable, soft technology I used to open this chapter, as well as the Introduction. While they are far from ubiquitous on back-to-the-land farmsteads, they are still present on one out of seven (14 percent) of the *Countryside* subscribers' homesteads. The respondents, however, do not report high utility scores for the geese; their effectiveness rating of 2.3 is close to only a "somewhat effective" characterization. The weeder geese possess a great deal of theoretical potential, but in order to be effective they require the kind of concentrated attention an Anne Schwartz is willing to give them. The geese are not automatic weed-removal devices. With few of the neo-homesteaders having the time or dedication to exploit their unique talents, on most back-to-the-land smallholdings the weeder geese are not promoted beyond the status of farmyard pets.

If the effectiveness scores of the technologies in Table 10 are compared with those of Table 9, it becomes evident, as in the case of the weeder geese, that there is a tendency for the effectiveness ratings to be lower with the less common technologies; only fruit trees in Table 9, at 2.6, are below 3.0, while only milk cows (3.3) and root cellars (3.0) in Table 10 are at 3.0 or above. This trend toward lower effectiveness scores continues with technologies reported in Table 11, the relatively sophisticated, and often expensive, homestead technologies.

Table 11.   Homestead technology: the uncommon elements

Item	%	Effectiveness Score (1–4)
Composting toilets	15	2.9
Gray-water recycling	14	2.7
Workhorses	7	2.6
Solar water heater	5	2.8
Wind power	3	2.4
Photovoltaics	3	2.6
Mini-hydroelectric system	1	1.9

Note: Total number of respondents = 565 (actual responses numbered from 430 to 554, since not all respondents answered each question; some questions were not applicable to all respondents).

The soft technologies of Table 11 carry a high profile in the back-to-the-country homestead dreams, and collectively they take up considerable space in back-to-the-land magazines. They attract attention for very good reasons. As important as gardens, chickens, and greenhouses are, it is the alternative-energy and waste-disposal systems of Table 11 that have the potential to establish renewable energy sources and recycling as viable options to the hard technologies that are exponentially consuming the planet's nonrenewable resources and saturating its adaptive capacity with toxic wastes. But regardless of their theoretical attractiveness, technologies like photovoltaic power cells and windmills find themselves on few back-to-the-land farmsteads.

Even with their "each takes a turn" approach to soft technology, it is an open question whether another survey of these same *Countryside* respondents ten or twenty years into the future would discover more than a significant minority of the smallholders with the kinds of alternative technology listed in Table 11. While only the workhorses require constant attention, the other technologies, like composting toilets and photovoltaic cells, still demand continual monitoring. They are not technologies one can walk away and forget. In addition, they are expensive, requiring from several hundred to several thousand dollars of start-up funds. Given, then, the expense of these alternative technologies, in addition to their time-consuming character, one has to wonder whether it is reasonable to expect, in the absence of public policies that encourage their adoption, anyone other than the fanatical, and the wealthy, to possess and use the sustainable soft technologies.

It would be a mistake, however, to end the discussion of alternative technology on back-to-the-land farmsteads with the information from Tables 9 to 11.[13] In addition to the specific technologies these tables report, there are the supporting tools smallholders choose to do the work of homesteading itself. The choice of tools has the same sustainability implications as the choice of technologies. A garden, for example, can be worked exclusively with hand tools or with the assistance of a garden tiller or tractor. Muscle power, of course, is renewable. While tractor and motorized-tiller power in aid of vegetable self-sufficiency is hardly a back-to-the-land vice, it nevertheless takes the smallholder across a technical line to nonrenewable energy use.

To understand where the *Countryside* respondents stand in respect to the issues surrounding the kinds of tools they actually use and would be inclined to use, I first presented them with a list of ordinary household and small farm appliances or tools and asked them whether they had the particular item in question. The results were predictable. The respondents reported the following levels of possession: chain saw (86 percent), truck (85 percent), freezer (84 percent), clothes dryer (83 percent), garden tiller (69 percent), and tractor (58 percent). These possession figures, while unexceptional in themselves, do identify the *Countryside* respondents as steady customers of nonrenewable energy sources: gasoline for the tractors and tillers, and electricity for the freezers and probably most of the clothes dryers. However self-reliant back-to-the-landers might be in other areas of their lives, their generally uncritical use of nonrenewable energy, as unavoidable as it might often be, does not constitute a clean break with hard technology.

Given this contradiction in smallholders' pursuit of a sustainable future, I wondered to what extent the *Countryside* respondents might feel uneasy about the way they use energy, perhaps feeling trapped by the time constraints of their often hectic lifestyles. Then by extension I wanted to know if the respondents at least theoretically favored muscle power over nonrenewable petro-chemical or electrical energy. In the list of survey statements that I used to measure how the smallholders feel about a cross section of sustainability issues, several items were either closely connected to or had implications for energy use. In Table 12, I have summarized the *Countryside* respondents' reactions (on a four-point scale from not at all important to very important) to six of these statements.

Table 12.   *Countryside* respondents' reactions to energy-use issues

Statement	% Considering Important*
Using human or animal, rather than electrical or petro-chemical, power	43
Walking or riding a bike rather than riding in a car or truck	38
Working with hand tools rather than power tools	37
Having a microwave oven	29
Having a clothes dryer	52
Having an indoor toilet or bathroom	82

Note: Total number of respondents = 565 (actual responses numbered from 544 to 557, since not all respondents answered each question).
*Either important or very important.

Table 12 shows the back-to-the-landers, as a group, not to be overly concerned with substituting muscle for nonrenewable power or with radically reducing their energy consumption. Less than half of them believe it is important to replace petro-chemical or electrical power with muscle power or to use hand tools rather than power tools (43 percent and 37 percent respectively). And it is only to be expected that a group in which 60 percent of the members commute fifty miles on average for five days a week would have a minority (38 percent) who felt it was important to walk or ride a bike rather than travel by car or truck. But when it comes to assigning importance to having two ordinary but convenient appliances, the survey respondents demonstrated some restraint, with only 29 percent considering a microwave oven important and 52 percent feeling the same way about a clothes dryer.

There are, however, very few mixed feelings among the back-to-the-landers about indoor toilets or bathrooms—82 percent considering them to be important. Such feelings, of course, do not rule out the use of an indoor composting toilet. But overall it would appear that smallholders are not prepared to embrace the entire soft-technology package. The ease and comfort hard technology brings to them, even with its unsustainable character, is not something they seem prepared or able to give up, at least in the near future. Still, a significant minority hold reservations about the exclusive reliance on power tools over hand tools or nonrenewable power over muscle power—and even about driving over walking or riding a bike.

This division over the importance of a soft technological preference was reflected by the survey respondents' comments on the last page of the questionnaire, where many of them wrestled with the contradictions of trying to work toward sustainability while still taking advantage of the convenience of hard technology. The responses in favor of an exclusively soft technological approach to homesteading were both mild and ambivalent. One respondent summarized her approach in the following way: "I'm just trying to tread a little lighter on this earth. I'm trying to practice a lifestyle that mirrors all the things people talk about—use fewer resources, recycle, precycle. I only drive when I need to haul tools or pick up something I can't carry on my bike." A Texas smallholder explained his mixed feelings about the use of power tools: "I'll use power tools because it is easier and faster with all I have to do. But I don't like it and use hand saws where I can."

There are, however, smallholders who take a less compromising position on the importance of always taking the soft path. In defense of manual smallholding, a Washington State correspondent wrote the following response to a *Countryside* "question of the month" ("Tools that homesteaders wouldn't want to be without"):

> For myself, the only concession I make to the internal combustion engine is a pickup truck to carry payloads since I do not choose to submit a horse and wagon to the perils of a modern highway. When possible I use foot power or the appropriate technology of my bicycle. I have no problem choosing crosscut

and bow saws over chain saws. I opt for shovel and hoe rather than a rototiller, a rake rather than a leafblower and a hand powered reel mower rather than a gas model. My choices are motivated by esthetics and health as well as environmental concerns. I want to hear birdsong when I cut wood rather than have my hearing impaired by engine noise. I want to enjoy fresh air . . . not exhaust fumes. These are major reasons we moved to a rural area. Moreover, using my own energy saves the time and money I would need for a health club membership to exercise engine pampered muscles.[14]

A Maine reader, in response to the same question, wrote to say that he gave up his chain saw one spring when it would not start and a neighbor with a two-man crosscut saw offered to help him cut his wood if he would return the favor. "I agreed and it was great! We worked, talked while we worked, listened to the warbles sing . . . and never had a breakdown." After this positive experience the *Countryside* correspondent and his friend formed a sawing club that had, as of his report, five members. He subsequently sold his chain saw and learned how to sharpen his hand saws. The reader went on to say, "The more I avoid electric and gas powered tools the more serene I stay . . . techno-tools and machinery give me only an illusion of power, while in reality they sap my strength and self-confidence. How helpless I initially feel when they break down! Techno-tools steal from me the skill and artifice I learn every time I use a hand tool. They isolate me from other animals and inhibit my contact from the world I live in. I don't feel like much of a man when using techno-tools—more like an emasculated technician—whereas using simple, people-powered tools always heightens my self-esteem."[15]

This kind of anti-hard-technology sentiment, which could have been read into my survey questions on the possible desirability of hand tools over power tools, provoked a vigorous response from a number of the *Countryside* survey respondents. They wanted to make clear that back-to-the-land does not have to be equated with primitivism. "If by a small, labor-intensive farm you mean a meager primitive existence of drudgery day in and day out like a Third World peasant for the rest of my life—no way!" was how a California respondent summed up his feelings. More specifically, a Texas smallholder added, on behalf of himself and his wife, "Just a note for those who voted for no indoor plumbing and no electricity—both of us grew up under those conditions and we sure don't want to revisit those times, especially on a cold winter night."

But in addition to discomfort, soft technology can entail a great deal of hard work. Another Texas respondent made this clear in her comments on using a chain saw: "Personally we would not want to have to cut firewood or maintain our wooded area with an ax alone. Work is hard enough with a chain saw (clearing, stocking, and hauling). Same thing with mowing and planting our pasture. We have a tractor—*not* a new, airconditioned one. Chain saws and flatbed trailers are a necessity for us."

Many of the *Countryside* respondents' objections to the exclusive reliance on muscle power were dictated not so much by considerations of comfort as by logistics and practicality. "You can't ride a bike with five kids twenty miles to shop" was the unequivocal declaration of a Maine respondent in her late thirties. She went on to write, "Also, clothes won't dry here for three or more days if left outside, or inside—depending on the wind. We live on an island off the coast, so it's quite damp here. A clothes dryer is pretty much of a necessity if you want to blend in (at least sometimes) with the rest of humanity." Then, in addition to all the practical considerations, there are matters of personal priorities. Another smallholder with a clothes-drying dilemma, this time from the Pacific Northwest, made the decision to give in to electric clothes-drying convenience in order to have more time with her children: "I enjoy more conveniences than I might otherwise like to, so that I can do things I prefer—local outings with the children as opposed to hanging up diapers in the living room (our rainy climate makes outdoor drying unbelievably difficult, and a dryer really simplifies things)."

With the demands of sustainability at times threatening their efforts to piece together their own private versions of serene country living, back-to-the-landers are forced to make technological choices that are not always in harmony with either the particulars or the overall design of soft technology's homestead dreams. But even when smallholders make taking the soft technological path a matter of first priority, dilemmas and contradictions seem to increase rather than diminish. A classic statement on technological choice, which illuminates the intractable struggle with and for sustainability, is Wendell Berry's essay "Why I Am Not Going to Buy a Computer."[16] Berry's essay is not so much about computers as it is a conditional declaration of independence from centralized hard technology. "As a farmer," he writes, "I do almost all my work with horses. As a writer I work with a pencil or a pen and a piece of paper." His wife, serving as typist, copy editor, and critic, transfers Berry's handwritten work to typescript. He characterizes their work together as "a literary cottage industry that works well and pleasantly. I do not see anything wrong with it."[17]

Berry feels that his working arrangements are both sufficient and satisfying, and believes that using a computer would not only fail to improve the quality of his writing but also compromise his moral integrity. Since electricity in his native Kentucky comes by way of strip-mined coal, he wants to do everything he can to be independent of the grid, and a computer plugged into a public utility shortens the distance he is trying to put between himself and corporate energy interests. "The history of the exploitation of Appalachia is long, and it is available to readers," he writes, and then adds, "I do not see how anyone can read it and plug in any appliance with a clear conscience."[18]

There are, however, aesthetic as well as political reasons for Berry's technological noncompliance. He enjoys the tactile pleasures of pen on paper, shaping, molding syntax and meaning, and being able to trace the progression of his work from handwritten sheets through the typed page. Berry's literary endeavors, then, parallel his small-farm labors. In his novel *The Memory of Old Jack,* Berry has his protagonist, Jack Beechum, plowing in the 1930s behind his team of mules, as he has done for most of his seventy-five years: "The sun gleamed on the young grass. He was plowing an old bluegrass sod, and it broke well, the furrow crumbling as it turned, dark to light. With deep pleasure, with his familiar sense of blessedness of that old return, he watched the earth roll dark off the mouldboard and settle and lie still again in the long straight furrow." But Jack Beechum cannot accept tractors any more than Wendell Berry can tolerate computers. "Old Jack hates tractors. They seem to him suddenly to be everywhere, roaring and stinking. With a sort of fierce grace, he has kept his hatred to himself, not wanting to interfere with a world that he is so nearly out of. But he hates their heaviness, their hulking and graceless weight. They remind him of groundhogs. They have the look about them of being just ready to burrow into the ground."[19]

In drawing on Berry's work, I may be leaving the impression that he is an ideological purist and the practitioner of exclusively neolithic technologies. If true, his thought and its application would possess little more than curiosity value for the generally pragmatic back-to-the-landers. But though his prose is clear and his logic consistent, Berry confesses bewil-

derment. While his values are sharply defined, Berry has no master plan
to implement his vision of a simpler, more agrarian society. He is particularly baffled on how to go about reducing the profligate levels of commuting forced on country people. To the readers of his essay who see
hypocrisy in his giving permission to have it reprinted in a magazine,
Harper's, that accepts advertisements for the National Rural Electric Cooperative Association, Marlboro, Phillips Petroleum, and McDonnell Doug-
las, Berry confesses that he "is a person of this century and implicated in
many practices that [he] fully regret[s]." And although he is certain he
will not be persuaded anytime soon to purchase a computer, and though
he does most of his work with horses, Berry does concede that the exigen-
cies of his day-to-day life have forced him to use a chain saw. He does not,
however, like having to use one, and writes of a neighbor who did not
abandon his handsaws: "He was a healthier and saner man than I am. I
shall let his memory trouble my thoughts."[20]

Wendell Berry may agonize over his inability to break his dependence
on machinery he does not like, but at the same time, he refuses to be
overwhelmed by technological innovation. In what for him is a strategic
battle, a person who is committed to the ideals of sustainability has to take
a stand, to draw a line that he or she is determined not to cross. For Berry
and most back-to-the-landers this line cannot be dogmatically defined. It
is more situational. A computer may be the appropriate tool for the back-
to-the-land activist publishing a newsletter, who may well use handsaws
rather than a chain saw. Nevertheless, the short-term sacrifice of sustainability by smallholders is a near constant; using tractors or milking machines, they want to get the homestead chores over with in order to move
on to other priorities like their families, thinking and reading, and sleep-
ing after all day at a town job and all afternoon and evening with farmstead work. Compromise, then, is inevitable, as is struggle. Berry himself
exemplifies the tension between pragmatism and idealism when he writes,
"I'm afraid I won't live long enough to escape my bondage to the machines. Nevertheless, on every day left to me, I will search my mind and
circumstances for the means of escape."[21]

Wendell Berry's anguish over the distance between conviction and performance underlines just how difficult it is to practice sustainable living in
a consumer society. Given their circumstances and conflicting loyalties, it
is admirable, even remarkable, that the back-to-the-landers have achieved
at least economy-model versions of homestead dreams, with gardens, or-

chards, woodstoves, and chickens. But I am reluctant at this point simply to acknowledge the smallholders' survival instincts and move on to the next topic. The need to reduce substantially the pressure on the earth's support systems through soft technology is sufficiently compelling that I cannot allow the back-to-the-landers' motives to escape a more penetrating examination. Could it be that, for many back-to-the-country people, living in the country is one variation on a consumer-culture theme? One buys a country place with the primary objective of living in the country: one "consumes" the country-living experience. And are soft technologies seen as ends in and of themselves, an experience, a recreation, rather than as a means to a sustainable future?

Living in the country for the sake of living in the country is certainly central to the back-to-the-land experience. But the back-to-the-landers' motives are also complex. My own analysis leads me to believe most smallholders are serious about self-reliance, voluntary simplicity, and soft technology and consciously weigh their behavior in terms of its contribution to a sustainable future. Consequently, I believe that the smallholders' modest levels of soft technology should not be attributed as much to personal inadequacies on their part as to the nature of incentives and rewards in the larger society. Although back-to-the-landers as new pioneers are making valuable contributions to the understanding of soft technology in practice and its relation to the overall sustainability project, they receive little recognition for their efforts. Government and business neither acknowledge nor support their experiments. Back-to-the-landers not only pursue their soft technological dreams in the absence of institutional encouragement, but the time-money conflicts conspire to undermine their experiments.

This line of argument, coupled with the review of the smallholders' adventures with soft technology, brings me to the conclusion that designing and building sustainable homes, farms, and communities is much too difficult for individuals and families to accomplish alone. Such a conclusion does not necessarily open the door to a government bureaucracy taking over the sustainability project, but it does mean that government needs to take an active role in structuring a series of incentives that reward and smooth the way for those who want to align their behavior with sustainability principles. The kinds of policies that can encourage the back-to-the-landers' best instincts are a topic I turn to in more detail in the last chapter.

Soft Technology: Dividing Up the Work

To those confronting the ideals of soft technology for the first time, its prominent characteristic is likely its labor intensity. Making soft technology work in an overall design requires smallholders and their animal assistants to supply muscle power in place of commercial power—milking goats a short walk from the kitchen door rather than having milk delivered to one's front step from a distant dairy, for example. But once the goats are in the barn, the question becomes, Who is going to make the trip to the barn, on icy winter mornings when one is late for work, as well as on leisurely summer evenings? Since it is unlikely that all members of a smallholding family will be equally enthusiastic about doing the chores that sustainable homesteading requires, getting the work done will have to be a matter of negotiation and compromise. Just as the back-to-the-land farmsteads deviate significantly from the ideal blueprints for homestead dreams, the actual division of labor on smallholdings rarely matches their proprietors' intentions.

Drawing first on the written comments from the *Countryside* surveys, I want to outline the range of ways back-to-the-landers divide up smallholding work, moving back and forth along a continuum from conflict to compromise to relatively harmonious cooperation. Once the outline of the back-to-the-country division of labor is in place, I turn to the questionnaire's structured responses for a more precise description of how the homestead work gets done.

"Please send an additional questionnaire to my husband—you would be amazed at the differences!" This was the single comment on the back of one respondent's returned survey. Although I did not send another questionnaire to this woman's husband (research protocol overpowered curiosity in this case), the request raises the possibility that real differences exist within smallholder families in terms of both what kind of work should be done on their minifarms and who should do it. In some cases these differences may lead to serious, and chronic, conflict. For most families, however, different perspectives on homestead work are likely incorporated into the pragmatic and flexible coping mechanisms that smallholders use to balance the competing demands of self-reliance, voluntary simplicity, and relaxed country living. The comments of a forty-year-old Washington father and smallholder represent this tolerant approach to the back-to-the-land division of labor: "We bought this place to get out of town and eventually made a paying farm out of it. We are slowly getting the soil built up and a crop started. I am the farmer, my wife the gentleperson farmer, my sixteen-year-old daughter is a horse nut, and my eleven-year-old son is a motorcycle and bike person. We don't all pull together or like the same things, but we get along after a fashion."

This toleration can entail considerable sacrifice, since one has to defer long-term homestead dreams, subjecting them to the contingencies of family relationships. A woman in her thirties from Washington wrote, "I've been looking forward to moving to my island property as soon as I had it paid for, and living out my life there in a back-to-the-land style. Now I've paid for the land, but two years ago I met an irresistible man with his own house and a business in this little town. So the land waits. And I bide my time and continue to dream and work my mischief to get us all out there some day. We grow lots of flowers, but no goats yet." Following this same theme, a Missouri homemaker-artist adds, "Sometimes my ideals don't match up with the lifestyle I have chosen. That's because I'm married to a wonderful man whose opinions are not always the same as mine. We compromise a lot."

Although it is hard to imagine a marriage where conflict is absent, many respondents reported relatively harmonious relationships. A mid-sixties male from California wrote, "We try to live a partnership of equals, both producing income and sharing or alternating household tasks. I (the husband) do over half the cooking because I enjoy it, and all the dishwashing because my wife doesn't enjoy it. I pay some bills, she pays others. She takes care of our five cats because I would rather not have pets at all. But I should be more alert to help with housecleaning without her having to ask me." A forty-year-old woman smallholder, also from California, expressed similar sentiments, "We are best friends and partners and consider our home a place of equal responsibility. We share the work and chores of keeping the house up and garden and animals going. We do it all fairly equally, even the boring stuff! Some tasks suit one or the other better—I love to cook and he loves to hunt and fish. I'm better at finances; he's better at striking deals, bargaining or trading. It works out."

Struggling toward a common goal is the source of much of the cooperation between back-to-the-land partners. A *Countryside* respondent in her early thirties from Minnesota compared her dreams with her current reality in the following way: "Life is great in the country, but hard. My husband and I both have jobs forty miles away. I do the morning chores (5 A.M. to 7 A.M.) and then go to work; my husband does the evening chores

(4 P.M. to 6 P.M.). Soon we will both be home full-time, and then life will be perfect!"

But life for a minority of the smallholders is far from perfect. They find themselves in marriages where there is little shared purpose. The conflict in these marriages often arises over smallholding itself, with one spouse committed to the back-to-the-land way of life and the other alienated from it. In extreme cases this conflict means separation and divorce. "I feel my answers on the questionnaire don't reflect the way I'd like things to be," wrote a twenty-seven-year-old Idaho homesteader; "and the reason is because my husband and I are having marital problems—because I want a natural life and he doesn't. There are all sorts of things I'd like to do but can't. Also we may be separating in the near future. Self-sufficiency and natural living are very important to me—it's a beautiful way of life." This kind of loyalty to country life was also evident in the response from another woman facing up to the possibility of divorce. "At the present moment my husband and I are considering a divorce, and that colors some of my answers. But if we do split, the farm stays with me. At the moment it's why I stay."

Conflict over country living, however, does not have to destroy a marriage. If the nonfarming partner can acquiesce to his or her spouse's homesteading eccentricities, there is still a chance that the relationship will survive, if not always thrive. "My husband has no interest in farming," wrote a survey respondent in her forties from Missouri, and then elaborated on her relationship with her husband, "He said, when I wanted to get chickens, 'The only time I want to have anything to do with them is when they're on my plate!' And he's stuck to that—he won't even feed them when I'm out of town. However, I can do as I please in the yard—no 'permission discussion.' It's my interest. He doesn't mind living in the country, as long as he doesn't have to commute too far to work."

The kinds of tensions described above by the Missouri smallholder can at times be blunted by a sense of humor, one that can accommodate both pain and irony. A middle-aged college instructor from Minnesota explained his predicament in the following way: "Prior to moving closer to town four years ago, we lived on a two-hundred-acre farm for twelve years. We really tried living off the land—wood heat, milk goats, and growing all of our own food. The children felt isolated. They actually hated living so far out. The family wanted more of the 'comforts' of civilization. We now live a 'mid-ground' type of life. Would I move back? In a second! Would my wife? No way! *The yuppies in us have won!*"

Stoic endurance, however, with or without irony, is the fate of at least a few back-to-the-landers whose conflicts with their spouses remain unresolved, with minimum accommodation for smallholder interests. "This was a dream we planned together that went sour," wrote a sixty-two-year-old *Countryside* respondent on the back of her questionnaire. "My husband really didn't have a realistic idea what farm life was all about. *I am enjoying it,* but need help in doing things, although I certainly am trying— oh boy!" For at least the time being this smallholder is staying on her farmstead, and with her marriage. Others, however, are ready to leave their homestead dreams behind, and keep their marriages intact. A woman in her sixties from Washington represents this kind of painful compromise: "My husband's sentiments about farm life stem from an unhappy experience in the dustbowl years of the 1930s, when his family farm was lost to mortgage foreclosure and crop failure. My own enthusiasm over the years has been slowly eroded due to his negative attitudes, and as I get older and more tired, I may find it easier to 'switch' than 'fight' for my beloved little minifarm."

These responses on the back of the *Countryside* questionnaire provide an insight into the range of emotions smallholders go through in trying to plan their ideal homesteads and work out an accommodation with their spouses. But to see how typical are their strategies for dividing up the farmstead chores, from cooperation to conflict, it is necessary to turn to the specific questions of the *Countryside* survey. In the questionnaire I presented the respondents with a list of common small-farm and household tasks, from taking care of the animals to washing the dishes, and I asked them who most frequently did the particular work in question: usually the wife, wife and husband about the same, or usually the husband.[22] In Table 13, I have summarized the *Countryside* readers' responses to three common homestead chores: (1) gardening, (2) animal care, and (3) repair work.

Table 13.   Three homestead tasks: *Countryside* respondents' division of labor

Task	Usually the Wife (%)	Both About the Same (%)	Usually the Husband (%)
Gardening	42	22	36
Animal care	32	27	41
Repair work	8	13	79

Note: Total number of respondents = 565 (actual responses numbered from 525 to 535, since not all respondents answered each question and since respondents living alone have not been included).

One of the pieces of information that jumps out of Table 13 is the sharp division of labor on these three tasks; men and women share equal responsibility only about a quarter of the time on gardening and animal care (22 percent and 27 percent respectively). On these two tasks, however, there is a symmetrical division of work responsibilities, with women being a little more likely to take responsibility for gardening than men, and men taking more responsibility for animal care. But when it comes to repair work around the farmstead, there is a dramatic shift toward male responsibility, with 79 percent of the respondents reporting that husbands usually took care of homestead and household repairs. This same pattern also holds true for woodcutting, which I have not included in Table 13. The respondents report that 90 percent of the husbands on their homesteads usually cut wood, with only 4 percent of the wives usually doing so. Evidently, working together as partners in a homestead enterprise, for most smallholder spouses, does not necessarily mean working side by side.

To see how this pattern, a definite division of responsibility along traditional gender lines, carries over to routine household tasks, I asked the *Countryside* respondents how they divided up the jobs of preparing meals, washing the dishes, and cleaning the house. In Table 14 I list the survey respondents' answers to the household division of labor questions.

Table 14.   Three household tasks: *Countryside* respondents' division of labor

Task	Usually the Wife (%)	Both About the Same (%)	Usually the Husband (%)
Preparing meals	76	13	11
Washing dishes	74	16	10
Housecleaning	80	14	6

Note: Total number of respondents = 565 (actual responses numbered from 533 to 535, since not all respondents answered each question and since respondents living alone have not been included).

Table 14 shows that with basic household tasks the burdens fall heavily on female smallholders. Just one out of ten males usually prepares the meals or washes the dishes (11 percent and 10 percent), and these low percentages drop almost in half when it comes to back-to-the-land men usually doing the housecleaning (6 percent). This gender-based division of labor is intriguing in light of many of the smallholder's original intentions in moving back to the country. In many of my interviews back-to-the-landers told me that in moving to the country, they wanted to start over,

with a much more egalitarian sharing of homestead and household responsibilities. But these same interviewees admitted their plans rarely
matched their performance. Homestead males, as weekenders, were often
the ones who ended up working full-time away from home, leaving their
wives to care for both farm and household. The coming of children often
reinforced the skewed division of responsibilities, with mothers usually
staying home to care for the children. While these smallholders were
clearly disappointed at their inability to put their idealism into practice,
most accepted with at least a degree of equanimity what they felt were the
realities of a back-to-the-country move. As one *Countryside* female respondent put it, "It looks like I do all the work around here, and that's not so.
Most of the heavy work falls on my husband's shoulders. I feel quite good
about the division of chores as I'm the one who gets the most enjoyment
out of the garden and animals."

This smallholder's comment raises the question of how the back-to-the-
landers cope with what for many of them is a less-than-ideal division of
labor. Do they harbor chronic frustration? Or do they more typically, as
my interviews suggest, reconcile themselves, not without aggravation, to
the contingencies of their new lives in the country? To be able to answer
these kinds of questions, I asked the *Countryside* questionnaire respondents how satisfied they were, for each of the homestead and household
tasks, with their family's division of labor, giving them four choices from
not at all satisfied to very satisfied. On at least initial review, the survey
respondents appear to be generally satisfied with the way dividing up the
chores has worked out for them. Except for how they feel about sharing
responsibility for cleaning their homes, the survey respondents report dissatisfaction levels (those who are either not at all or fairly unsatisfied) of
13 percent or under—from the 13 percent who feel dissatisfied about the
division of dishwashing responsibilities to the 9 percent who feel the same
way about homestead repair work.

But the nearly one-quarter (23 percent) of the *Countryside* respondents
who report being dissatisfied with the choice of who ends up having to
clean the house makes one wonder if there is not a genuine resentment,
even if below the surface, over having to do the work on a smallholding.
Since the task of cleaning falls disproportionately, by far, on women, the
next natural question is whether they show higher levels of dissatisfaction,
not only with cleaning the house but with the other homestead tasks as
well. As expected, on the issue of household cleaning, women are twice as
likely to report being dissatisfied as are men, 31 percent to 15 percent.

This ratio, slightly more than two to one, also carries over to all the other household and homestead tasks, though the overall dissatisfaction percentages are lower.

Identifying the reasons for women being more dissatisfied with the homestead divisions of labor is elementary. Even though men and women roughly share gardening and animal care, and though men take the responsibility for repair work and cutting wood, women are left with the constant challenges of preparing meals, washing dishes, and cleaning house. In addition, women carry the primary responsibility for taking care of the children; in the *Countryside* survey they were on average more than several times more likely than men to put children to bed, to tell them what chores to do, and to discipline them.

The frustration from this unequal burden showed up not only in the specific questions on the division of smallholding labor but also in the comments on the last page of the questionnaire. One woman put the matter simply and matter-of-factly: "We would both be more satisfied if my husband did not work full-time and if homesteading work could be shared and experienced together." More specifically, and without evident emotion, another smallholder wrote, "My answers to the questions reflect that we are just establishing a farm, and my husband works full-time and more at his job. So, most things fall on me. This spring I must build a buck barn, a sheep shelter, a pig enclosure and shelter, get the gardens going and keep up the landscape for the wildlife we are trying to encourage to come back to the property." But then a final comment shows that this kind of commitment can wear thin. "My husband is gone *far* more than he is home, so a great deal of the responsibility falls on me. Very little has turned out like we planned. I am alone most of the time. Everything could be so much better if my husband could be home, and have the time we need to do things!" Given the nature of the homesteading experience, with its prevalence of weekenders who do not devote the time to smallholding that either they or their spouses would like, it is remarkable that the *Countryside* respondents do not express even higher levels of dissatisfaction with the division of labor. For all their differences, most back-to-the-land couples are likely united by a common attachment to the ideals of country living, which compensates for the aggravations of the often snail-like pace toward their homestead dreams. One piece of evidence in support of the idea that homesteading couples share a commonality of purpose is the *Countryside* respondents' very low levels of dissatisfaction with their relationships either with their spouses or with their families (5 percent and 4 percent respectively). And women respondents were just as likely as men to evaluate these relationships positively. Apparently, the dissatisfaction women feel about the unequal burdens they carry does not necessarily contaminate their relationships with either their husbands or their families.[23]

This accommodation to the less-than-ideal circumstances in which most back-to-the-landers find themselves was not restricted to traditional family relationships. While heterosexual unions were predominant among the *Countryside* respondents, a small number of same-sex oriented couples identified themselves on the questionnaire, and they also expressed frustration at the search for an untroubled division of homestead labor. Typical of their comments is the following reflection of a retired teacher in his early fifties: "There are many contradictions in the way I live—at times I feel I may be just escaping. Basically I live as an individual and depend principally upon myself to do all the work on the farm—my partner is a male who lives in his own apartment during the week to avoid a long commute to his job and because he is more social than I. His spiritual, emotional, and financial support are crucial to me."

Dividing up the farmstead chores, naturally, is not something that just takes place between husbands and wives or two adult partners. Children are also part of the homestead work equation. In fact, a very important motivation for many parents moving back-to-the-country is the ability to provide an environment for their children that includes meaningful work and reinforces values like responsibility, thrift, and self-reliance. "We moved to our farm from a large city to raise three young boys," reported a *Countryside* respondent from Minnesota, and then explained how the experiment turned out: "Our family has enjoyed all the good benefits of small-town country schools and the freedom of farm living. Over the past twenty years the boys have learned that hard work builds confidence and self-pride. Two of the boys have graduated from college and have good jobs, and the third is a junior at the University of Minnesota." A Texas respondent added his testimony on the worth of a small-farm life for raising children, including an unreserved endorsement of country living:

> After years of treadmill city living we went "back to the land." It's been tough starting over. Cutting out lots of "stuff" we used to eat, buy, do, pursue, live. We used to be fast-trackers—now we are committed to simpler living. We've cut our income by more than half. We home-school our kids; we try to live a life

we can be proud of. We want our kids to grow up ecology-minded, honest, hardworking people. Not hooked on TV or anything else. We milk our goats for the pure joy of it as much as the food value. We love our life, and wouldn't go back to the city for anything. My mom lives with us, we consider her a vital member of our family. (Why did large extended families go out of style?) We feel blessed each morning as we look out over our beautiful Texas Hill Country—no we *wouldn't* go back to the city. Give us the simple life!

"For about four years we had sheep, goats, pigs, and chickens, partly as projects for our teenage son." In trying to penetrate the reality of homestead life, one has to wonder whether this report from a Washington father represents a contrivance that many farmstead children see through. It is likely that many smallholding children find it difficult to make sense of having to milk cows or work in the garden when their families could easily buy milk and vegetables at the town supermarket. Nevertheless, a number of the survey respondents included comments on their returned questionnaires to the effect that their children's labor was genuinely needed on their homesteads. A woman in her late fifties from California wrote, "When we moved from the city to the country, our children thrived because we *needed* them to help repair this old house, *and* they knew it. Their former city friends, in many cases, got into trouble or drugs." Another woman simply affirmed, "Without our children's help we could not have done the many things we did." At least some of the farmstead children, then, as adults, can retrospectively see the value of their back-to-the-land labor. As a Minnesota mother explained, "We no longer have children at home, but they were very involved with the operation of our home and farm during childhood. They have since thanked us for teaching them the joy of self-discipline and personal achievement."

Not all smallholders, however, are ready to declare such unqualified success. A Missouri college professor and farmer wrote, "Our children are a mixed blessing in terms of homesteading. The small children contribute very little in the way of help; the older children contribute labor but are influenced by the 'yuppie' attitudes of their peers at school. One of our main challenges is the two-hour daily bus ride to and from a centralized public school system. We are seriously considering home schooling at least for our younger children." This Missouri back-to-the-lander, however, is not alone in his concern over what he considered alien values undermining the homestead ideals he was trying to pass on to his children.

There is the Minnesota smallholder who, in acknowledging his family's surrender to the commercialism of the world outside his homestead, declared, *"The yuppies in us have won!"* Then there is Dan Wright, the country romantic from Chapter 1, who was struggling with his two teenage sons, who in turn were experiencing pangs of cultural deprivation in the absence of appropriately labeled jeans.

It certainly stands to reason that impressionable, younger children, dependent on family relationships, will find homestead values and routine congenial to their own social and psychological needs. Teenagers, as they fight for independence, often by counteridentifying with their parents, are more likely to be swayed by the pressure of peers away from the relative austerity of smallholding life. Although this transition from an unaffected acceptance of small-farm living to a sometimes affected alienation from the smallholding is to some degree inevitable and a part of family life regardless of where one lives, it can still be very painful to back-to-the-land parents. They are part of a movement that runs counter to the mass culture of modern America, and, like close-knit ethnic and religious communities, they have an investment in passing their strongly held values on to their children.

One way of arriving at an idea of the extent to which children are integrated into a back-to-the-land way of life is to move beyond anecdotal accounts of their contribution to the farmstead division of labor and look at more precise measures of how much smallholding work children do. In the *Countryside* questionnaire I asked respondents how much their children helped (not very much, some, or a great deal) with the basic homestead and household chores. In Table 15, I have summarized the respondents' answers for their children's help in doing the gardening and the animal care.

Table 15.   The children's contribution: two homestead tasks from the *Countryside* survey

	Children's Contribution		
Task	Not Very Much (%)	Some (%)	A Great Deal (%)
Gardening	31	53	16
Animal care	21	49	30

Note: Total number of respondents = 565 (actual responses numbered from 303 to 305, since not all respondents answered each question and since responses were limited to those with children at home).

Table 15 shows that most of the *Countryside* respondents place their children's contribution to the homestead work into the broad middle category of some help. The children, however, are almost twice as likely to help a great deal with animals as with gardening (30 percent to 16 percent). Feeding and watering animals are the kinds of routine jobs even small children can handle independent of an adult presence. One smallholder added the following note to the side of the survey's question on children's contribution to farmstead animal care: "Wife actually supervises animal husbandry as children do most of the work." This back-to-the-lander had four children, two between the ages of twelve and eighteen and two between six and eleven. And for both the younger and older children farmyard animals like goats or sheep, and even chickens, can take on a petlike character.

Still, Table 15 shows the children's contributions on average to border on the marginal. But for many back-to-the-land parents the object of having homestead work for their children to do resides more in the realm of process than product. They seem to be interested in the educational value of the farmstead experience as much as or more than in any substantial accomplishment, especially in the case of young children. A Maine *Countryside* respondent explained her perspective on small children and homestead chores: "Our children are not old enough to help out much yet, but they love to be around me when I'm working. They're a *great* moral support." And another Maine respondent added, "Our son is fifteen months old so doesn't do much in the way of chores. He does like to feed our dog." It would be easy, of course, to discount these experiences by holding that they contain little more than sentimental value. Nevertheless, even in the simplest of homestead tasks there is the potential for a lasting impression. A Minnesota *Countryside* respondent was able to see what she considered a remarkable understanding in her small child: "My husband and I are both city kids with dreams of farm living, and we moved from Chicago to rural Minnesota a year ago when we bought our farm. We have a three-year-old daughter who shocks her city grandparents by telling them how milk gets to the store and how babies are born. She's a big help on our farm—eagerly helping with feeding and cleaning up after our livestock, even in the bitter cold. Her health has been a 100 percent better since our move."

While it is difficult to take all of this mother's report at face value, there is little doubt that a great number of children take pleasure being responsible for the care of farmstead animals. A number of other things, how-

ever, not as attractive as animal care, have to be done around a homestead. The more contentious tasks cluster around the household work,
which disproportionately falls to women homesteaders. In Table 16, I
have summarized the *Countryside* respondents' reports of how their children help with the three common household tasks: preparing meals,
washing dishes, and housecleaning.

Table 16.   The children's contribution: three household tasks from the
Countryside survey

	Children's Contribution		
Task	Not Very Much (%)	Some (%)	A Great Deal (%)
Preparing meals	42	47	11
Washing dishes	36	43	21
Housecleaning	30	51	19

Note: Total number of respondents = 565 (actual responses numbered from 300 to 301,
since not all respondents answered each question and since responses were limited to those
with children at home).

The overall pattern in Table 16 is much the same as it was for animal
care and gardening in Table 15: almost half the children (43 to 51 percent) give their parents at least some help with household work. But the
percentages contributing a great deal of help (11 to 21 percent) do not
match the 30 percent figure for animal care (Table 15). Consequently,
the mothers who do most of the housework can count on some, but not
substantial, help from their children. And these same mothers are four
times as likely as their husbands, according to the *Countryside* survey, to
tell their children what chores to do on their homesteads.

But the unequal division of labor on the back-to-the-land homesteads,
whether between mother and children or between husband and wife, appears for most smallholders to be more an irritant than a fatal infection,
and one that does not migrate to the sphere of personal and family relationships. As I have reported, women are just as likely as men to see the
relationship with their spouses and their families as positive, even though
they are twice as likely as men to be dissatisfied with the homestead division of labor. Apart from the obviously critical importance of commitment
to the back-to-the-land way of life, might it be possible that women are
able to tolerate the unequal burden because of the nature of the partnership relationships they have with their husbands? These relationships are

ones of mutual dependence. On the farmstead, women move away from either a dependency relationship on a husband and his income or a mutually independent relationship based on separate careers. Much more than in the suburban home, a woman's labor takes on a high profile: her contribution is essential to the success of a homesteading endeavor. The male's outside income and weekender labor, of course, are not to be discounted. The point is, however, that in a situation, such as on a back-to-the-land homestead, where an exchange of responsibilities is sharply defined in relation to tangible goals, one partner is likely to tolerate short-term injustices, such as a disproportionate share of farmstead work, and in the process carry a sense of accomplishment as a more-than-equal partner.[24]

This characterization of the female back-to-the-lander as supplying the muscle power to keep home and homestead operational redefines the idyllic picture of the smallholder family working shoulder-to-shoulder to complete the farmstead chores. Much of the homestead labor comes by way of individual efforts. The individual contributions are nevertheless coordinated and blended toward the goal of a productive homestead. Family members do at times work side by side, but jobs and school get in the way of a family's working together, at the same time and at a common task. But as time and inclination allow, overlapping schedules serve the construction of homestead dreams. While reality and the dreams usually bear only a superficial resemblance to each other, the smallholders transcend the ragged edges of their country lives with remarkably positive assessments of their marital and family relationships. As with so many other aspects of their lives, the new pioneers' ability to tolerate the less-than-ideal division of homestead work allows them to persevere as country survivors, to wait out a change in fortune or circumstance.

The corporate-governmental research-and-development establishment for the most part has refused to acknowledge the existence of a soft-technology path, placing its bets instead with the hard path of biotechnology, petrochemicals, and microprocessors.[25] Nevertheless, smallholders like Anne Schwartz, with her weeder geese, continue to experiment with the design principles of an alternative, sustainable technology. Back-to-the-country practitioners have translated these design principles into working models that have provided the text and graphics for thousands of pages of back-to-the-land magazines and books over the past two and half decades. Although researchers are only now beginning to explore the biological design principles that can make life both convenient and sustainable, there already exists sufficient knowledge and experience of soft technology to build at least the foundation for a sustainable future.[26]

The critical importance of the soft path for a sustainable future does not, however, mean that it necessarily has to replace hard technology in a steady-state economy. Paul Hawken, for example, suggests that to meet Donella Meadows and her coauthors' guideline of an 80 percent reduction in nonrenewable energy use and a 90 percent decrease in pollution by the mid–twenty-first century, goods will have to last twice as long and be built with half the resources they now require. Consequently, an efficient hard technology will certainly be part of any future sustainability solution. But since a growing worldwide population will demand ever increasing quantities of industrial production, hard technology will just as certainly have to be coupled with a soft technology that draws on the renewable energy sources of solar, wind, and muscle power.[27]

This preoccupation with efficiency, however, has the potential to remove what is arguably the most important variable in the sustainability equation: the reduction of demand. Soft technology is not only a package of techniques, it is also a worldview. One can, of course, abstract the techniques from the soft-technology belief system and apply them in service of a more rational exploitation of the earth's resources. But in the process the ideology of growth and accumulation and of the domination of nature is reinforced rather than replaced by the principles of frugality and voluntary simplicity and the desire to live in harmony with the natural world. The reduction of demand as a crucial factor in the struggle for a sustainable existence requires that social energy be directed away from the society-wide obsession with economic growth and toward the welfare of community and family relationships and the relationship of families and communities with the natural world. Soft technology, therefore, is a complex of beliefs and practices that contributes to sustainability both directly and subtly. On the one hand, soft technology rises to the challenge of providing its practitioners a comfortable material existence by the application of biological design principles. But on the other, by its very nature as applied technology it encourages restraint and, in the process, redirects human potential toward relationships that enhance life on earth rather than degrade it.[28]

Paradoxically, one important reason why back-to-the-land homesteads are only economy-model versions of the sustainable farmstead ideal is that smallholders tend to embrace soft technology as a way of life rather than as technical achievement. As was evident in the last chapter's examination of back-to-the-country values, smallholders, in order to enjoy the simple pleasures of country living, including relationships with family and friends, back off from an obsessive pursuit of self-reliance and voluntary simplicity. "Real self-sufficiency is a twenty-four-hour-a-day job" was the way the Washington State smallholder I quoted in Chapter 3 characterized the soft-technology dream. She went on to say, "I like to read a lot, [I] have a part-time job, and I want to spend my evenings with our kids . . . and having animals has been a real love affair. We love our lifestyle even if it is not self-reliant." To the extent that these sentiments channel an individual's or a society's energy away from material accumulation, they contribute to sustainability, even if at the same time they postpone a smallholder's soft-technology implementation schedule.

Regardless of the long-term cultural prerequisites for the adoption of a sustainable technology, there still remain the immediate and pressing problems of resource use and pollution—problems for which soft technology constitutes a potential solution. What, then, do the back-to-the-land experiments with soft technology mean for a much wider application of biological design principles? As I concluded earlier in the chapter, it is not realistic to expect that individual smallholders will be able to pull together the separate pieces of soft technology into integrated farmsteads without public policies that reward their efforts. Sustainability through individually executed soft-technology projects is an unlikely outcome in a complex, interdependent society that does not itself take sustainability seriously.

But as important as government intervention may be, I also believe that a sustainable future requires more than government policies and programs that support individual smallholders. Might it be that the essential characteristics of soft technology, particularly in its labor intensity, predispose it toward one kind of community technology or another?[29] If soft technology requires a certain level of cooperative behavior to be effective, then the next question becomes whether the back-to-the-landers themselves are predisposed toward the kind of collective action their technology of choice demands. The issue of the smallholders' cooperative inclinations, alongside the parallel question of back-to-the-land activism, I explore in Chapter 6, "Organizing for Change: New Pioneers as Activists." But before turning to the activist side of the homestead experience, I want to direct my attention in the next chapter to the potential smallholders who get left behind in the city, either by choice or by necessity. I am interested not only in recounting their experiences and their attempts to escape to the country but in trying to understand the extent to which back-to-the-land values and soft-technology design principles can be applied in an urban setting.

5

URBAN PIONEERS

 "Is homesteading a matter of living in the country or a philosophy of how to live your life?" An urban *Countryside* respondent asked this question at the end of her comments on the last page of her returned questionnaire. The question provokes a series of other questions on the meaning of the back-to-the-land movement and its relationship to overall sustainability issues. But before dealing with these questions in an urban context, with potential smallholders planning their escape to the country, I want to quote the rest of the subscriber's comments, which, in describing her family's lifestyle, go some distance in answering her own question.

> We are not what you could call "real" homesteaders, as we live on approximately one-quarter acre in a small city in Silicon Valley, but we long for the country life. We stay here because of the ideal climate and a house we love, even though the ground keeps moving (earthquakes).
>
> Our only "farm" animal is a cinnamon rabbit named Hasenpfeffer (which he will never become) who is our pet HOUSE rabbit. No hutch or cage for him. He has the run of the house.

We have seven fruit trees. We grow our own vegetables all year long, mostly in containers. It is a joy to be able to have truly fresh vegetables.

In filling out your questionnaire, I stated that we are not involved in bartering, but, in a small way, we are. We supply tomatoes and peppers to friends in exchange for persimmons, which we don't grow. We make our own soap, salsa, cheese, pickles, and sauerkraut; bake our own bread; prepare our own homegrown horseradish and sausages; can or freeze the vegetables; and smoke fish, fowl, meat, and sausages. We choose to live a simpler life than our neighbors and friends who consider the things we do too much trouble for them to undertake.

In a technical sense one does have to live on country property in order to qualify as a neohomesteader, but back-to-the-land is more than living on a smallholding. It is also an interrelated complex of values ("a philosophy of how to live your life") that centers around the ideas of self-reliance, voluntary simplicity, and mindfulness and the use of sustainable, soft technologies. A back-to-the-land smallholding, naturally, is an ideal place for an individual or family to translate these sustainability principles into actual practice. Nevertheless, a back-to-the-land philosophy can still be applied in an urban setting, regardless of obvious limitations, as the California survey respondent's recounting of her lifestyle confirms. And since most people in North America will continue to live in cities, sustainability itself will depend on the adaptation of the biological design principles of back-to-the-land technology to an urban setting. Consequently, what I would like to do in this chapter is present a profile of the lives of people interested in country living (*Countryside* subscribers for the most part) who have either temporary or long-term commitments to their urban homes. While my initial interest in these "urban pioneers" is to describe the planning process for a move to the country and the frustrations of having to delay homestead dreams, I also want to see to what extent the prospective homesteaders are able to live out their back-to-the-land philosophy, however selectively, in an urban environment.

In using the term "urban pioneers" to describe urban residents interested in self-reliant living on back-to-the-land smallholdings, I do not necessarily want to imply that these prospective homesteaders possess heroic qualities. Like their counterparts, the rural new pioneers, they are ordinary people who struggle with the contradictions between their ideals and their behavior. At the same time, they are often able to make significant progress in their attempts to live sustainably in the city—practice that universally applied would make urban America a much different place.

Urban Pioneers: A Profile

Of the respondents to the *Countryside* survey 133 were not living on country property; they answered no to the question, "Do you live on property that is large enough (and has no zoning restrictions if in a small town or city) to keep at least some small farm animals?" The first thing I wanted to know about these urban respondents was what a magazine like *Countryside* meant to them. Does *Countryside* provide only fantasy reading for these urban subscribers, as they vicariously experiment with small-farm life through the magazine's pages? Or are they actively planning a country move? Then, if they dream of a life in the country but find themselves unable to leave the city, what are the obstacles holding them back?

The *Countryside* survey did not include specific questions for the urban reader. The handwritten notes on the back of the questionnaire, however, provide an indication how the urban *Countryside* respondents feel about city life and their plans for an escape to the country. Typical is the response of a mid-thirties male who runs a shoe-repair business: "I *would be* out of here and living a self-sufficient lifestyle if I could get out of debt and buy a piece of land. I won't feel satisfied until I do. I *hate* city life! I *hate* eight to five!" Similar sentiments, though not as emotionally charged, were expressed by a forty-year-old electrical engineer from California: "My work would be enjoyed more if I could come home to country property."

Closely related to these feelings of frustration is the respondents' sense of being trapped in the city and their need to escape from an externally imposed confinement. As a sixty-year-old Georgia male explained, "We are leaving our hectic urban life in two years—retiring to twenty-five acres that we are presently spending every spare minute preparing for our *escape*." A Texas respondent a few years younger expressed similar sentiments, "We live in a city, not by choice, but because this is where the jobs are. When I retire in a year or two, we plan to move to property we own in Arkansas, and live like human beings again!" In harmony with this escape rhetoric, a mid-fifties secretary from Minnesota reported, "We expect to retire to our five acres within the next three years. We're too old to aim for total self-sufficiency, but I do hope to grow most of our food and keep some chickens and rabbits. For the past four years I have been landscaping and planting fruit trees on half of our property, and the other half will be my farm. I hope I shall be fortunate enough to die with a shovel in one hand and a pitchfork in the other." Given this kind of emotional attachment to country living, it is not surprising to learn that some survey respondents make their escape from the city much earlier than they originally intended. On the back of her questionnaire a data-processing technician in her late forties from California outlined her family's sooner-than-anticipated move to a new rural home: "Although we currently live in a large city, we plan on moving to our country place in the not too distant future and building our dream home—a solar one. We will commute, a hundred-mile round-trip until we are able to retire. We've owned our country place eight years. It was originally intended as a weekend retreat and eventual retirement place. But as our love for the country grew, we've decided to make the move a permanent one much earlier than we thought we would."

The idea of a country move fulfilling a lifelong dream runs through much of the questionnaire commentary from the urban respondents. One unattached college professor in his thirties from Minnesota is in the process of translating this dream into reality: "I've lived my entire life in big cities (Los Angeles, San Francisco) and have long dreamed of a rural life. I have just started a job in this college town. Presently I'm renting an apartment within the city limits, but I am in the process of buying a house and barn outside the city limits. I plan on doing a great deal of gardening, perhaps raising animals on a small scale, cutting wood in the lot, and enjoying the space between me and my neighbors. I'm not antisocial, but I've spent too many years in apartments. The house and sixteen acres will fulfill a lifelong dream."

All but two of the *Countryside* readers whose comments I have used to this point owned country property, although at the time of responding to the survey their principal residences were urban. The dream of a life in the country is, of course, much closer to reality when one owns country property and can work on improving it on weekends and during vacations. The possession of a place in the country by at least some of the urban pioneers raises the question of how common such ownership is, that is, ownership by city dwellers who experience country life vicariously through magazines like *Countryside*. In the *Countryside* survey 46 percent of the urban respondents reported owning country property. But this country orientation of the urban readers was not restricted to the ownership of rural property alone. As a group the urban respondents, with or without country property, were in possession of the basic tools of a rural life. Sixty-two percent said they owned a truck, 61 percent had a chain saw, 39 percent a rototiller, and 31 percent a tractor.

The ownership of homestead tools and country property gives an impression of the urban *Countryside* reader as poised to make the move to a rural smallholding. A number of questionnaire respondents, however, had moved in just the opposite direction, from country to city, and not always by choice. "We lived on ten acres with a large garden, chickens, ducks, geese, sheep, cows, and pigs, but moved for the sake of a job. We do miss the good life," reported a high school English teacher from Georgia in explaining his urban residence. A Texas respondent reported the same kind of job predicament, though in this case the family was able to hold on to their farm. "We moved away from our farm six years ago because of a job transfer," she wrote, and then added, "Our farm was in southern Ohio, where we had every animal you mentioned in the survey. We did not sell, but plan to retire to our 124-year-old farm in about four or five years. We miss the farm. We had a wood cookstove and it heated plenty of cold winter mornings for us."

With such nostalgic and evocative descriptions of farm life, one has to wonder how urban *Countryside* readers are able to tolerate city life. As a woman from Washington State in her late twenties wrote, "Whenever the city gets me down, I picture in my mind what my house will look like, what I'll plant, and the calm inside I'll feel. Every time I stop and smell a rose, I think of the rosebush I'm going to plant outside my kitchen by the window, and I go on, my hope refreshed." But there are good reasons why some prospective smallholders' rosebushes fail to make the transition from the imagination to homestead flower bed. The most obvious reasons, naturally, are financial ones. One correspondent reluctantly, and simply, admitted, "I guess I realize that my lifelong desire to live in the country will never become a reality, due to its expense." A sixty-year-old California woman added, "My husband and I are going to relocate in northern Montana within the next four or five years. We find the congestion in the Bay Area just too much for us. We're looking for a quieter, simpler life. I know many people who would also leave if they could swing it financially."

Being financially able to leave the city for the country, however, is more complicated than simply having the assets to support a move; it is also a matter of being able to liquidate those assets. A mid-fifties machine operator from Minnesota expresses the frustration of having an unsold home come between him and his family's country dreams: "We have our city home on the market and have purchased our retirement property in the country. But we are having trouble selling our city property due to present economic conditions. We are very frustrated because we have been unable to sell. Interest rates are going to hell and everybody's being eaten alive with greed and overtaxation." But even if one can sell the city residence, buy country property, count on a job or a pension in addition to accumulated savings, one must still cover contingent expenses, and for most people those include adequate health insurance. For many potential smallholders the health insurance issue places a country move into an uncertain focus. As a California state employee in her mid-forties explained, "We currently live in a large city, working at high-paying, stressful jobs. We recently bought forty acres in the country, and are planning to move there within two years. We hope to change our lifestyle dramatically. But our biggest concern is health insurance."

One can, of course, lower a house's asking price or gamble on getting by without health insurance, but if one's spouse or partner is reluctant to make a country move, saving a relationship may well mean giving up the smallholding dream. Marriage partners, as the section on the division of farmstead labor in the last chapter reminds us, are not always equally devoted to homesteading ideals, and consequently one spouse at times endures a less-than-congenial environment in the countryside. Conversely, some urban homesteaders end up with gardens and fruit trees on a city lot, rather than goats and chickens on a country smallholding, in order to placate a spouse allergic to small-farm life. A sixty-five-year-old telephone company employee described his forgone dream in the following way: "I grew up in a small town and did orchard and field work as a teenager. But I married a city girl who didn't like the country or the mountains. I started a garden at home on a city lot to relieve job pressures. I like fixing things (I repair clocks as a hobby and semiprofessionally) and have been a *Countryside* reader for over twenty years. I enjoy the articles and live a rural life through others."

Although there are urban homesteaders, like the telephone company employee, who make major concessions to a relationship by living out their smallholding fantasies through the pages of back-to-the-land magazines, it would be a mistake to assume that these *Countryside* subscribers necessarily lead lives of quiet desperation. While a life in the country may be important to them, they are able to construct meaningful lives, rejecting any simple equation of the ideals of sustainability with the virtues of a back-to-the-land homestead. Curt Huber of Everett, Washington, just north of Seattle, represents this more expansive vision of an urban existence. I met Curt through a network of people in the Seattle area who are interested in sustainability issues. While in the best of all possible worlds Curt would be a full-time smallholder, he is able to take satisfaction from supporting his wife's career and receives pleasure from transforming his city-sized lot on the edge of a suburban development into a mini–animal sanctuary.

Curt buys his birdseed in fifty-pound sacks. He has a number of feeders strategically placed around his home and spends part of his leisure time identifying the birds who take advantage of his largesse, often in the company of his nine-year-old son, Daniel. The Hubers have seen more than twenty different species of animals venture onto their property, and Curt is particularly pleased that Daniel takes an interest in his nature conservation projects. He readily admits the limitations of parental influence when matched against the pressures of the youth culture to which Daniel will be all the more exposed when he enters junior high, but Curt takes consolation in the opportunity he has had to help Daniel become aware of the natural world around him.

It was his own experiences as an impressionable child visiting his grandparents' farm to which Curt attributes to his abiding interest in a sustainable way of life. He has vivid recollections of his grandfather doing his farmwork with horses, although the surrounding farms were all mechanical. Curt's subsequent connections to agricultural were more indirect as he supported himself through high school to a bachelor's degree in English by working in grocery stores. After college, with very few opportunities for English B.A.'s other than high school teaching jobs, Curt took an assistant store manager's position with a Seattle grocery chain. He soon became manager of a medium-sized central-city store that catered to a neighborhood of elderly and modest-income customers. While Curt's own income rose steadily, in line with his experience and increased responsibilities, he began to feel overwhelmed by the twelve-hour days required by a store with sixty employees and a clientele that demanded personal attention. And he began to think and read about the entire system of agricultural production and distribution in which he was playing a key role. After reading Wendell Berry's critique of the agro-industrial complex in *The Unsettling of America: Culture and Agriculture*,[1] Curt came to feel that the values formed by his childhood experiences on his grand-parents' farm were incompatible with his everyday work. Consequently, when a large produce distributor bought his employer's chain of stores and in the interest of increasing profit margins changed the neighbor-hood character of the store Curt managed, he decided it was time to leave the grocery business.

"I felt I got my life back" is the way Curt characterizes his exit from the factory side of agriculture. Though his current job scheduling audits at a large accounting firm in downtown Seattle is not even remotely con-nected to his concerns with sustainable agriculture, it does leave Curt with considerably more time and energy for family life and enhancing the min-iature nature conservatory he has built around his suburban home. And a more routine job makes it easier for Curt to support his wife, Karen, in her career. Karen worked as a nurse to help Curt through college. Once Curt was established in the grocery business and Daniel had been born, Karen went back to school at the University of Washington to work on a degree in chemical engineering. After graduation she found a challeng-ing position with the Seattle Water Treatment Department, where she now works.

Curt's commitment to Karen and her career transcends his interest in a back-to-the-land move. Perhaps if they could afford country property within commuting distance of Seattle, he might actively pursue an ideal smallholding. In the meantime Curt makes sure the supply of birdseed in the garage is not running low, and he continues to read and think about what constitutes a sustainable way of life and to attend the occasional weekend retreat with like-minded urban homesteaders.

Curt Huber's backyard projects raise the question about what other ur-ban pioneers, whether temporary or more rooted city dwellers, are doing to advance the cause of sustainable lifestyles. The *Countryside* survey ques-tions on employment of soft technologies can provide some insights into the urban respondents' contributions to sustainability. In terms of prosaic homestead technologies like gardens or fruit trees, the city respondents' implementation rates were not altogether dissimilar from their country counterparts. Eighty-one percent of the urban respondents reported hav-ing a garden, as did 95 percent of the rural respondents. But even though urban gardens were common, their effectiveness, as rated by the respon-dents, diverged sharply from that of the rural smallholders' gardens: 74 percent of the rural respondents rated their gardens as either very or fairly effective in providing their families with self-reliance, while only 39 percent of the urban respondents gave their gardens the same ratings. This same pattern holds in the case of fruit trees. Fifty-five percent of the urban subscribers have fruit trees, as do 78 percent of the rural *Countryside* readers, and 47 percent of the rural respondents see their fruit trees as very or fairly effective, while just 23 percent of the urban respondents rate their trees at the same level of effectiveness. But of the twenty-five soft technologies I inquired about in the *Countryside* survey, only fruit trees and gardens had any kind of currency among the urban pioneers.

It is understandable that the urban pioneers would be much less likely to have back-to-the-land technologies and that, when they did employ the few that were practical, they would be less effective than their rural counterparts. The significantly lower levels of alternative technological use on the part of the urban *Countryside* readers, however, do not have to mean that sustainable city living is impractical. Jeff Gage, a prospective smallholder from Seattle, in his approach to a temporary urban confinement, illustrates how a back-to-the-land sensibility has concrete applications in a metropolitan setting. Intriguingly, Jeff's connection to sustainability starts with an improbable substance—giraffe manure.

Giraffe manure is not something one automatically associates with the challenge of moving American cities closer to sustainability norms in the 1990s. Though far down on the list from chronic urban concerns like traffic congestion, air pollution, and hazardous-waste disposal, the excreta of zoo animals are nevertheless one of a multitude of small-scale irritants whose cumulative effects exhaust the imagination of city planners. The problem in this case is that the zoo animals are making just one more contribution to an exploding waste stream that is overwhelming metropolitan landfill sites.

While urban planners were massaging cost-benefit equations for transporting solid wastes to distant landfills or building incinerator plants to turn the garbage to ash, Jeff came up with a solution to the giraffe-dung dilemma. In harmony with the ecological design principles applied on back-to-the-land farmsteads, Jeff turned a problem into an asset. He sold the management of Seattle's Woodland Park Zoo on the idea of composting the animal waste and then selling it as fertilizer. Gardeners from upscale Seattle neighborhoods now come to the zoo to buy Zoo Doo at $10 a bag and thus help remove what was once an undesirable commodity.

The Zoo Doo project was not Jeff's first, nor last, encounter with urban refuse. He has made a career out of garbage, in one form or another. Even though garbage and career are two words that rarely find themselves

together in the same sentence, Jeff Gage has transformed the idea of
garbage from a contaminate to be avoided into a career opportunity that
is a natural outlet for his unique blend of idealism and pragmatism. After
starting up the Zoo Doo enterprise at the Woodland Park Zoo, Jeff found
his way to Land Recovery, Inc., a private landfill site just south of Seattle,
where he directs composting and recycling projects on a much grander
scale.

Working at a garbage dump, which is what Land Recovery, Inc., amounts
to, is not the kind of job to which most college graduates would aspire,
particularly those, like Jeff, who have technical training. But, as one might
expect, Jeff Gage is not a typical college graduate. He holds a Bachelor of
Science degree from Evergreen State College in Washington's capital of
Olympia. Evergreen State College is a post–Earth Day institution with innovative programs in the environmental sciences. Jeff's degree is in en-
ergy-systems engineering, and his education included courses in land-use
planning, environmental law, and community development. While many
of his fellow students used their degrees to pursue careers with government regulatory agencies or private-sector reclamation projects, Jeff took
the nonsinecured route of grassroots environmental activism in order to
apply both the theory and practice of the ecological design he studied at
Evergreen State.

Jeff's work at Land Recovery, Inc., appears not only incompatible with
his investment in higher education credentials but also out of harmony
with his upper-middle-class family background. Jeff's father is an electrical
engineer with his own defense contracting business. The Gage family was
dedicated to providing their children with the kind of cultural refinement
that their affluence permitted. Jeff and his sister took music lessons, and
he was a member of his high school orchestra—and football team as well.
Though Jeff's idealistic sensibilities at times collided with his workaholic
father's priorities, father and son nevertheless bonded through their common affection for the outdoors. While Jeff was growing up, his father
squeezed in time for scouting, including periodic camping trips. Even
though Jeff's sometimes precarious activist existence diverges sharply
from his father's establishment perspective, there has evolved a mutual
respect between father and son.

After high school Jeff enrolled in North Seattle Community College,
where he first gave full-scale expression to his ecological activism. After
staging a series of student demonstrations in support of a campuswide
conservation program, he was appointed coordinator of the college's recycling program. The position of recycling coordinator demanded of Jeff

both an educational and logistical juggling act. North Seattle's student body, faculty, and staff had to be encouraged to move away from throwing their refuse into all-purpose wastebaskets and toward sorting paper by color into different receptacles and separating aluminum cans from glass containers. But Jeff's perseverance paid off. When he graduated from North Seattle he left behind an institutionalized waste-recovery program and a neighborhood recycling station. In its first year of operation, the program removed fourteen tons of recyclable paper from the waste stream—the equivalent, in Jeff's calculations, of saving 222 trees, 30 cubic meters of landfill, and preventing 355 kilograms of air pollution.

Out of Evergreen State and while coordinating the Zoo Doo project, Jeff proposed a series of innovative recycling experiments to Seattle's municipal governments. When the programs were accepted, he would bid on the contracts, writing his services in at a rate close to minimum wage. In collaboration with Seattle Tilth, a volunteer community agency working for urban sustainability, Jeff developed a Master Composter program, which was designed to reduce substantially the one-quarter share of landfill space that yard wastes take up. Seattle had initiated a prorated garbage-collection fee based on volume, but it had little in the way of complimentary education programs to help suburban residents cut the waste flow from their yards. The Master Composter program offered Seattle residents a short course in yard recycling and composting techniques to the end of having both a reduced garbage-collection fee and enriched garden soil. After the successful completion of the course and demonstrated proficiency in applying its principles in one's own backyard, it was possible to receive certification as a Master Composter.

Seattle's metropolitan governments, however, were not always susceptible to gentle persuasion. A case in point followed Seattle's decision to construct a garbage-incineration plant as the answer to rapidly disappearing landfill space. As a member of Seattle's Recycling Action Coalition, Jeff was involved in organizing community sentiment against the "burn plant." The coalition's campaign was based on the idea that doing the right thing ecologically is also cost effective. A burn plant, Jeff and the Coalition argued, would add to the problem of air pollution (with the potential for indiscriminate discharge of toxic particles), and then the city would still be left with ash residue that is one-third the volume of the original garbage. Working on the premise that 65 percent of the urban waste stream can be recycled, with a judicious combination of incentives and education, the coalition insisted that if resources equal to the cost of incineration were devoted to recycling, the need for new landfill space would be reduced as much as or more than it would by using a burn plant, but without the toxic side effects. In the end the Recycling Action Coalition's arguments proved persuasive, and as a consequence Seattle has developed one of the most aggressive recycling programs operating in the United States.

But as involved as Jeff is in making a contribution to Seattle's sustainability, and notwithstanding his recycling and composting accomplishments, he and his wife, Holly, are quietly planning their own escape to the countryside. Jeff's grandparents own farm property in Idaho's panhandle, six hours away from Seattle, and Jeff and Holly see themselves only a few years away from being able to set up their own homestead on a corner of the grandparents' farm. It is hard to imagine, however, that Jeff will be content with an uninvolved country life, simply taking pleasure in the morning sunrises as he collects the day's eggs. Rural underdevelopment is the flip side of the kind of urban expansion that Jeff has tried to redirect. It is only natural, then, to expect that many of Jeff's new neighbors will first meet him at their doorsteps or at town hall meetings, as he helps define community sustainability issues and encourages fellow citizens to organize in order to preserve and promote the good life in the country.

In his dedication to sustainability ideals, whether in city or countryside, Jeff Gage is certainly unique. Most of the urban pioneers and rural homesteaders have much more modest goals. This case study of Jeff, however, is valuable not so much because of its exceptional character as because it illustrates a principle underlying both the back-to-the-land movement and its urban application. Jeff possesses, as do prospective and current smallholders, though admittedly in varying degrees, a commitment to a way of life that is foreign to the consumer culture of the late twentieth century. The stewardship values reflected in the back-to-the-land philosophy find a succinct expression in the idea of "right livelihood." In the next section I want to explore right livelihood through the lives of a number of urban residents who are attempting to earn a living in the city while maintaining a country sensibility, as well as planning their own moves to the country.

Searching for Right Livelihood

At its core the back-to-the-land movement is a search for right livelihood. The search for right livelihood is an inward journey to find one's own authentic self-expression, one's unique talents and abilities, which one then dedicates to the common welfare of both planet and community in the process of earning a livelihood. According to Marsha Sinetar, author of *Do What You Love, the Money Will Follow,* the idea of right livelihood "comes from the teaching of Buddha, who describes it as work consciously chosen, done with full awareness and care, and leading to enlightenment, [which] embodies self-expression, commitment, mindfulness, and conscious choice."[2] From the point of view of right livelihood there are no necessarily good or bad jobs, only work that is either right or wrong for a particular individual. One can, consequently, find opportunities for expression and service in the most menial of occupations, as well as meaninglessness in the most prestigious professions.

Becoming a smallholder is a good example of following the right-livelihood path. Rather than use their educational credentials to pursue high-paying, professional careers, back-to-the-landers choose what they hope will be a simple life on the land. It would of course be a perversion of the idea to suggest that in a mass migration back-to-the-countryside urban dwellers would necessarily find self-fulfillment. While many city folk could profit from letting go of their urban sinecures for close encounters with the natural order of things on a small farm, there is, from a right-livelihood perspective, much good, honorable, and sustainable work to be accomplished in the city.

Although one's right livelihood might well be in the high-profile urban professions, such as a medical specialist or a corporate accountant, many occupants of these positions find themselves unfulfilled, even though their work accords them high status and its remuneration permits material indulgence. Sinetar relates a classic account of the consequences of allowing others' expectations, rather than one's own heart, to dictate the direction of one's lifework. Sinetar's example involves a graduate student who took a job as a waitress at an upscale restaurant while working her way through school. "She found she liked the varied dimensions of the role: she liked cooking, serving people and playing 'hostess.' She enjoyed decorating the tables and lightly socializing." Nevertheless, she refused to consider a career in restaurant management or ownership, since it did not carry the status she coveted. As of Sinetar's writing, the woman is "in a corporate headquarters environment; she awaits a promotion that has never arrived because she is perceived as overly brittle, humorless and stressed." Organizational psychologist Sinetar then concludes her case study, observing, "My impression is that this woman lost a spontaneous,

lovely part of her self when she sided against her real vocational prefer-
ences in favor of what her logical, rational self told her was 'acceptable.' "[3]

In contrast to the misdirected career of the repressed restaurateur, Sinetar reports on the experience of a cabinetmaker who reflects upon his
work in the following way: "I get great satisfaction from making fine furniture—the process enriches me, makes me feel that I am somehow in each
piece." Sinetar also provides a case history of a tenured college professor
who left academia to become a potter. "I voted with my feet to leave a very
successful teaching career . . . which seemed like walking off a cliff," he
reported, and then went on to say, "I think back and see a person who
wanted to be totally creative . . . when I come to see myself [now], I see
there is some higher self, some spirit or way that has opened. The universe responded to allow this kind of activity, and I'm totally grateful every
day."[4]

These reports from those who have left corporate security to become
independent artisans possess a common thread: one gains the freedom to
be creative while providing a unique service or product. And if one were
looking for this kind of creativity and freedom, it is not likely one would
seek out employment with government bureaucracies, schools, or large-
scale business. Rather, one would be attracted to small-scale enterprises:
setting up a bakery, a bookstore, a bicycle-repair shop, a child-care center,
a used clothing store, or organic grocery. As a proprietor of a small business,[5] the owner-operator has the potential to control the pace of work,
permitting the kind of moment-to-moment involvement with one's craft
that encourages mindfulness. This kind of intimacy allows the seeker of
right livelihood to see the immediate consequences of his or her work,
much as a smallholder follows a crop from planting through harvesting.
And, like smallholders, independent proprietors often have the luxury of
refusing to do work they believe to be harmful or unsustainable.[6]

The space that urban pioneers want to put between themselves and
what they see as claustrophobic bureaucracies, whether of the public or
private sector, finds concrete expression in the life of Marianne Twyman,
a Master Composter whom I met through Jeff Gage. Marianne is a backyard farmer. In the backyard of her home a few blocks from the University
of Washington in Seattle, in collaboration with her business partner, Dean
Dalton, Marianne grows a collection of exotic salad greens and herbs in a
network of plastic tunnel greenhouses, calculated to keep the garden
growing in the cool, cloudy Novembers of the Pacific Northwest. Marianne's backyard is unexceptional, except for the greenhouse tunnels and

a few chickens who defy city ordinance to scavenge for morsels in and around Marianne and Dean's garden. Against the garage there are sturdy composting bins that accept yard wastes like leaves and cut grass, along with kitchen scraps. The composter, in the process of turning yard and household wastes into enriched soil, is the direct result of Marianne's involvement in the Seattle recycling program.

But Marianne's interest in her backyard goes far beyond composting. Marianne and Dean have a backyard business. Twice a week they harvest several buckets of the salad greens and herbs for delivery to a number of Seattle's upscale restaurants, where the kitchen staffs turn the greens into $7 side dishes, garnished by the house dressing. While the restaurant patrons, by secondhand report, appear to enjoy the exotic salads, they are not necessarily aware that they are eating pepper grass, edible chrysanthemum, and nasturtium leaves. Marianne and Dean sell the greens destined for the gourmet salads at $24 a pound, although they are trying to organize a growers cooperative that would present the restaurant owners with a united front of backyard salad growers whose asking price for salad greens and herbs would likely rise to $30 a pound. At the time I visited them, however, they were the only active members of the Seattle Salad Growers Co-op.

On the November day I spent with them, Marianne and Dean carefully harvested several pounds of greens. The cool November weather had begun to inhibit the produce's growth, though Marianne and Dean believe they can keep the garden going for all but two of the winter months. With the harvest in hand, we climbed into Marianne's ancient Toyota Corolla for a journey down Seattle's Route 99 to the Pike Street market, a journey whose speed had only an incidental connection to the posted limits along the limited-access highway to downtown. Our specific destination was the Place Pigalle French restaurant, which occupies a prominent location in the Pike Street market complex. Marianne prowled the streets just below the restaurant looking for a parking meter with enough time on it to allow us to make our delivery and run errands. Once inside the restaurant the two urban gardeners affected a disinterested posture toward the exclusive ambiance, and with payment for two pounds of greens in hand, they took a direct course toward the kind of establishment where they feel obvious comfort—a bakery where they exchanged part of their garden profits for chocolate macaroons and raspberry tarts—before returning to Marianne's Toyota just as the recycled meter time expired.

Marianne and Dean's twice weekly expeditions to downtown Seattle with their harvest of backyard greens bring each of them a gross income that fluctuates between $200 and $400 a month. While not a large sum, the income from their urban farming project does make a substantial contribution toward their portion of the rent for the houses they share with kindred spirits seeking their own versions of right livelihood. But a backyard garden can hardly be expected to be the sole source of one's support, even for assiduous practitioners of voluntary simplicity. In Dean's case, he has a yard-maintenance business in addition to his partnership with Marianne. Though Dean has a bachelor's degree in psychology from the University of Washington and taught at an alternative high school for a year, he says he finds fulfillment in the physical encounter with the urban landscape that his own business and the backyard farming bring him. This relaxed approach to right livelihood leaves him time for a variety of community volunteer projects.

Marianne's path to simple living in the city has been much more circuitous than the one taken by Dean, whose transition from student to urban gardener was relatively seamless. On the other hand, Marianne has portable, and prestigious, credentials that she has at least partially abandoned. After graduating from the University of Washington in the mid-1970s, she went to California to study medicine. She originally wanted to become a medical missionary but, after her internship, entered private practice. She later married and found herself in a high-consumption lifestyle at the end of the materialism-asceticism continuum opposite that where she now makes her spiritual home. In her words, "We spent big." Disenchantment with her medical practice and the tensions in her marriage led her to both divorce and an exit from what she saw as the cul-de-sac of general-practice medicine.

Marianne, however, has not completely severed her ties with medicine. She works with women's health groups in Seattle, doing secretarial work as well as counseling in, for example, hysterectomy workshops. She calculates that she can make more of an impact in focused counseling sessions than in private practice, where she would see a succession of sore throats and assorted aches and pains, many of them the product of middle-class anxieties. In contrast, the slower pace of the counseling work allows Marianne time to follow up on a number of issues, to which she allocates varying degrees of passion, including gay rights, the environment, and foreign policy. And in many ways one might justifiably conclude that Marianne and Dean's primary right livelihood is the variety of volunteer projects they devote their time to, rather than the itinerant gardening and landscaping.[7]

Marianne and Dean's approach to urban survival with a back-to-the-land flavor might strike the interested observer as more a spontaneous adventure than a pursuit of a livelihood.[8] While their work includes the essential elements of right livelihood, it does lack the commitment to an ongoing identifiable enterprise such as an organic grocery or a bicycle-repair shop. Consequently, I wanted, before ending my excursus into the real and the idealized worlds of sustainable city living, to interview a small businessperson with a service ethic, preferably one who had country dreams. My objective was to penetrate the veneer of right livelihood in order to discover the human-scale costs, as well as the benefits, of trying to make money and work for sustainability. I tried to find an appropriate subject for my examination of profit and service in Seattle, but my previously reliable networks failed to produce an appropriate and willing interviewee. Serendipity, however, intervened, and I found an ideal subject in my own backyard of Calgary, Alberta, a city American enough to be called the "51st State" and to serve as Metropolis for the filming of Superman III. Pat Evanoff, the one-time owner-operator of the Sproutz vegetarian restaurant, just off Calgary's downtown core, consented to talk to me about both her pursuit of right livelihood in the restaurant business and her plans for taking up smallholding on the family's country property.

Pat Evanoff's encounter with right livelihood came not so much from the necessity to make a living as from wanting to provide an important service, a service that came packaged with two of Pat's own existential projects. First, she wanted to help her daughter, Nadine, find meaningful work, doing something with more cosmic significance than selling real estate or sitting all day in front of a video-display terminal. And second, having had a brother who died of bowel cancer, and convinced that a diet high in saturated fats and refined sugars had had a lot to do with her brother's death, she felt that in founding and operating Sproutz she and her family together, in their own small way, could help to introduce others to the kind of food that might have added years to her brother's life. Though she is a reluctant evangelist, Pat will say, not without some prompting, "The way we eat is almost obscene."

Pat's husband, Steve, took early retirement from Calgary's oil industry, and he and Pat turned their attention to development of their ten-acre country property and to their two married daughters living in Calgary.

When they first started talking about the family's running a vegetarian restaurant, they thought in terms of a table or two and a few chairs in front of a delicatessen counter. But the Sproutz that finally materialized entered the world as a forty-seat restaurant, a much larger undertaking than Pat had ever imagined the family's right livelihood project would become. And as a unique restaurant in a city of three-quarters of a million inhabitants, it did not take long for Sproutz to develop a loyal clientele who made up part of a steady stream of traffic coming through its front doors.

While uniqueness in the restaurant business, or any other business, might well guarantee a customer base, being a one-of-a-kind establishment does have its downside. For a vegetarian restaurant, especially one that de-emphasizes dairy products and eggs, originality will likely entail rejection of those suppliers who specialize in the mass production of prepared or processed food. At the other end of the restaurant continuum from Sproutz is McDonald's, supplied by refrigerated trucks carrying potatoes in the form of frozen french fries and meat in the form of individually frozen patties, just one step away from fryer and grill.

But at Sproutz, of course, things were much more complicated. The Evanoffs' typical day in the restaurant business would start with shopping trips to five or six of Calgary's wholesale food outlets, to buy everything from tahini by the gallon at an organic grocery to bean sprouts at a Chinese distributor. Back at the restaurant by midmorning, Pat, who usually took the early shift, would begin chopping vegetables, making sauces, and assembling the ingredients for soups and stews. The destination of Pat's work was a repertoire of recipes that more often than not omitted cheese and eggs. While there is no shortage of vegetarian recipe books, there are few low-fat recipes with the proven ability to win over palates conditioned by the sweet and oily fare common to North American cuisine. Consequently, much of Pat's time at Sproutz was devoted to concocting experimental dishes such as a tofu-based carob cheesecake sweetened with apple juice concentrate.

The five- and six-day weeks Pat and the Evanoffs devoted to Sproutz were a considerable investment of time and energy for a family of independent financial means. But there were, of course, those existential projects. And Pat is a person who loves to work with her hands, whether chopping vegetables for an experimental entrée or working on landscaping at the family's country property. For Pat, however, as one of the proprietors of Sproutz, the restaurant business was much more complicated than long hours of hands-on work. While she took comfort in the anonymity of the kitchen, the sometimes intense nature of the people work involved in running a business was in conflict with Pat's reserved temperament. Having to fire a desultory waitress, for example, was a painful experience for Pat. Because of her private nature, she was inclined to come to work early, work alone in the kitchen, and then exit early in the afternoon, leaving the hosting chores to her daughter and a small coterie of waitresses. "I'm just not a group person," she says; "they can be really frustrating for me."

Sproutz lasted for two years and two months. A number of things finally caught up with Pat and the Evanoffs. They were unable to find partners to share the physical and emotional pressure of everyday proprietorship. Having a growing clientele enjoy the healthy fare coming out of her kitchen compensated less and less for the logistical battles they had to fight—not only coordinating a staff but keeping books, paying bills, and negotiating leases. And while Pat and Steve found themselves tied down with the day-to-day routine at Sproutz, moose were eating their way through the garden at the family's country property, where a fish pond remained in an unfinished state. Consequently, existential projects aside, after twenty-six months Pat knew it was time for the family to close down Sproutz and start working on all the nonexistential projects that had been accumulating over the past couple of years.

Pat Evanoff's adventure at Sproutz crystallizes the difficulties inherent in the application of right livelihood. Right livelihood in the case of Sproutz came as a package, whose separate parts resisted Pat's efforts to disentangle them. In her unassuming way Pat wanted to be an evangelist for good, healthy food, rather than carry the primary responsibility, with her family, for all the things that must be done to keep a restaurant open twelve hours a day. But Sproutz would not compromise. It sucked the Evanoffs in and demanded their time and attention as accountants, personnel managers, purchasers, hostesses, and dishwashers. Of course, in the end it was all too much, and they had to leave.

Since Pat and her family were not financially tied to Sproutz, they could walk away. But what if Sproutz had been, in addition to Pat Evanoff's right livelihood, her only source of income? Without question she would have carried with her a sense of fulfillment as she left work at the end of each day. Still, the sense of accomplishment would have been purchased at a significant cost—having to do any number of things she did not much enjoy. Pat's frustrations are a commentary both on her personal approach to right livelihood and on the quality of the support for individual right-livelihood projects in urban North America. After all, being a proprietor of a vegetarian restaurant is not precisely Pat Evanoff's right livelihood. Part-time chef would have been more congenial to Pat's temperament. But Pat's exit from Sproutz was not a simple matter of her inability to align her personality with the demands of running a restaurant. There is here as well the issue of the kinds of cultural capital and institutional assistance that cities can and do offer to people like Pat. The requisite support is not necessarily formal government help but a network of individuals and businesses that provides the moral sustenance and human resources to keep enterprises like Sproutz alive and to allow the Pat Evanoffs of this world the kind of strategic retreat that permits them to keep their dreams operational. These kinds of resources, however, are all but absent from an urban landscape dominated by monocultural transnational franchises.[9]

But it should not be forgotten that Sproutz was a financially successful venture, even in an urban environment hostile to the fundamental premises of right livelihood. This acknowledgment raises the question how both public policies and private perspectives might be transformed to encourage right livelihood in the countryside as well as in the city. Example, however virtuous, is not sufficient. More to the point, it is hard to imagine that a change of consciousness and a change of policy will ever emerge without long-term focused organizing campaigns on the part of those committed to sustainability principles and the value of right livelihood. This issue of smallholder activism has been incubating throughout my report on the back-to-the-land movement, and it is the subject to which I turn in the following chapter. But one has to wonder how people like Pat Evanoff could possibly have the time or energy to do more than attempt to practice sustainable lifestyles, much less promote them. Circumstances, however, may at times conspire, as I explain in Chapter 6, to push reluctant homesteaders into activism's front lines.[10]

6

ORGANIZING FOR CHANGE

New Pioneers as Activists

 The question whether new pioneers are disposed to act as agents for change is one I have raised on occasion over the course of this report. The circumstantial evidence to this point does not leave a picture of smallholders who go back to the country with the primary objective of organizing the local populace to resist corporate designs on rural wealth. The motivations of back-to-the-landers are much more modest and private. They covet the peace that comes from working their own land. And more than half hold full-time jobs, on or off their smallholdings, leaving few hours from a round of off-farmwork, commuting, and homesteading for activism.[1] Circumstances, if not predisposition, however, can turn a country pacifist into a back-to-the-land activist.

The story of Barry Rosenberg, a refugee from the suburbs of Maple-wood, New Jersey, is an example of situational activism. Barry's collision with the bureaucratic machinery of the U.S. Forest Service pushed him out of the reclusive world of his forty-acre northern Idaho homestead and into the public life of community organizing. But Barry Rosenberg is exceptional. Few new pioneers find themselves the direct victims of circumstance, and only about one out of ten devotes significant amounts of time and energy to advocacy groups. Nevertheless, in this chapter I want to examine the experiences of those back-to-the-landers who do associate a sustainable future in the countryside with actively working for social change. My objective in dissecting country activism is not simply to provide a record of the back-to-the-landers' experiences with community development; I want as well to probe the limits of community action, both the limits the new pioneers place on themselves and the limits organizers run up against in their battle against the rural status quo. And Barry Rosenberg's experience is an illuminating point of departure for this discussion and analysis of rural activism. Barry is a spiritual descendant of the eighteenth-century yeomen whose banners carried the motto "Don't Tread on Me!"

Rosenberg's Mountain

The directions to Barry and Cathe Rosenberg's Idaho homestead would challenge an experienced car-rally navigator. "Go through 'wire-gap' gate and across a perilous-looking log bridge. Drive rough road across meadow (road follows creek) and into the woods. At T make a left. Go through blue steel-tube gate. Continue and go through green steel gate. Continue on up hill, past garden, and down to house." These are the directions to the last three-quarters-of-a-mile journey to the Rosenberg farmstead; the other twenty-seven miles from Priest River, Idaho, take the Rosenberg visitors on a route of multiple turns, stop signs, and directional land marks, over paved, gravel, and logging roads.

Reacting to the circuitous journey to the Rosenberg's home, one could easily draw the conclusion that Barry and Cathe have deliberately chosen a place to live so isolated that no one could ever find them to disturb their private enjoyment of their own small section of paradise. Appearances are of course deceiving. The Rosenbergs are not shy about giving printed directions to their home to family and friends—and even to professional curiosity seekers who carry the labels journalist, sociologist, or environmentalist. Still, in seclusion, with controlled access to their property, Barry and Cathe have found that it is very difficult to escape completely the unwelcome intrusions from the outside world, as their adventure with the U.S. Forest Service attests.

The Rosenbergs had five years of tranquillity on their Idaho homestead before trouble started. When the Rosenbergs originally set up their farmstead, in the mid-1970s, one of the first problems they had to solve was finding a reliable source of drinking water. On top of a small mountain just behind and above their homestead clearing runs a crystal clear stream. The side of the mountain belongs to the Rosenbergs, but the stream bed lies on Forest Service land. Since the Forest Service land is in the public domain, Barry approached the local ranger station about the possibility of drawing water from the stream through a series of pipes that would run down the side of the mountain and connect into their household plumbing, an ideal gravity-fed water-pressure system. The Forest Service routinely granted Barry access to the stream, and for a yearly fee, starting at $25, the Rosenbergs had a secure supply of pure drinking water.

Circumstances began to catch up to Barry when the Forest Service decided to carry out a timber sale on the land above his house. The timber sale meant that a logging company could buy a concession to build roads up the other side of the mountain and then clear-cut the timber on the sale land. A clear-cut with logging roads would set in motion erosion, and consequently the siltation of the stream that supplied the Rosenbergs' drinking water. If the timber sale were to proceed, Barry and Cathe's drinking water would turn from clear to muddy, and they would have to start a search for another source. As an independent homesteader, Barry could not accept having to buy bottled water from a Priest River grocery store.

Under the general provisions of the National Environmental Protection Act (NEPA) signed into law by President Richard Nixon in 1970 and the specific guidelines of the National Forest Management Act, the U.S. Forest Service is required, as are all federal agencies, to prepare environmental assessments on the consequences of its activities and programs and to consider alternatives when ecological damage is likely to occur. In addition, federal law requires the Forest Service to make public notification of its intended activities, like a timber sale, in order to allow concerned individuals or groups time to file appeals, appeals that could be based on the environmental considerations of the NEPA.

In the case of the timber sale above the Rosenbergs' land, the Forest Service did not provide the requisite public notice, nor did they inform the Rosenbergs directly. Barry and Cathe, as adjacent property holders and the possessors of a water permit, were legally due formal notice of the sale. The Rosenberg's case, however, was not unique. The Forest Service routinely ignored the legalities of the notification process. Consequently, appeals were rare. The checkerboard consequences of clear-cutting have become a taken-for-granted part of Pacific Northwest vistas. And Barry himself worked as a part-time logger. But when a neighbor who worked for the local ranger district let him know about the sale, Barry immediately delivered a letter of protest to the Forest Service, just two days before the expiration of the appeal deadline.

Barry's encounter with the local Forest Service rangers over the potential damage to his drinking water left him both alarmed and angry. He found them condescending as well as cavalier. After he made his case for the environmental damage to his own drinking water and to the entire drainage area, the rangers dismissed his concerns as trivial and blithely assured him that his drinking water would eventually start to clear up, after a few years. In addition, they told him, contrary to the provisions of the NEPA, that he had no right of appeal.[2] Barry came away from his first confrontation with the Forest Service with one very clear impression from the rangers: "Don't mess with our woods!"

The Forest Service functionaries would come to regret that they were not more conciliatory. Years later they conceded that their lives would have been much less complicated if they had just canceled the timber sale and moved it over to the top of the next mountain. As Barry allows: "When I start something, I have to finish it."

The Rosenbergs found a lawyer with experience in environmental law and retained him for a $500 fee, a considerable amount of money in 1981 for two country romantics. When the Rosenbergs' counsel saw Barry's documentation of the clear-cut's potential damage and learned that they had been paying a fee to the Forest Service for access to their drinking water, he smiled and said, "We've got 'em."

The timber-sale episode awakened passions in Barry that had lain dormant over his Idaho homesteading years, and it stretched his talents in uncharted directions. The collision with the Forest Service also revealed a constant of Barry's character: an indomitable spirit. He and Cathe came to their Idaho homestead when it was little more than natural forest and the slash left from selective logging. They spent their first summer in a tent while they put up their first building, a small cabin; and during that summer Barry had to shoot a marauding bear to protect himself, Cathe, and Thomas, Cathe's son and Barry's stepson. Today, in place of the cabin is a rustic two-story house whose power supply comes from photovoltaic cells. The large terraced garden is Cathe's project. Personal sanitation comes by way of an ample outhouse with a southern exposure. A set of coiled hoses twenty feet in diameter takes advantage of solar gain to turn mountain water warm for the open-air shower just off the Rosenberg's front driveway.

The Rosenberg homestead is concrete evidence that Cathe and Barry find pleasure in the physical encounter with the natural world. And their accomplishments stand as testimony to their perseverance. But they are not by any means one-dimensional individuals. Cathe attended Wellesley and then graduated from the University of Pennsylvania with a degree in fine arts. Barry is an English major from Temple who did substitute school teaching in inner-city Philadelphia. The challenge to document the potential damage to his drinking water pulled Barry back into academia, this time to the disciplines of hydrology, wildlife biology, and forestry management, disciplines that were to prove no less intoxicating than the study of good literature. Then, when it came to applying his research, Barry found himself venturing into community activism, an endeavor foreign to a semirecluse who had studiously avoided organizational compromise to his independence.

Over the winter, after his encounter with the Forest Service, Barry took his first steps toward becoming an uncredentialed hydrologist. His determination is hidden by a natural affability with a tendency toward shyness, and he easily made friends with Forest Service specialists in not only hydrology but also fisheries, plant pathology, and wildlife biology. Many of these men and women were chronically frustrated by the Forest Service's manipulation of their expertise. Through them Barry came to the conclusion that the Forest Service functioned more as an agency of logging corporations than as steward of forest resources. The rangers who supervised timber sales discouraged environmental impact statements that hinted at more than a minimum of ecological degradation. Working to protect their own jobs, the Forest Service technicians produced reports that qualified the impact of logging through the use of scientific modeling whose assumptions contained generous concessions to corporate interests. For Barry, scientific infallibility began to evaporate as he learned how a sedimentation equation, for example, could produce widely varying results, depending on the estimates and sampling techniques employed—procedures subject to political influence as well as technical considerations. This demystification process was facilitated not only by his personal contacts with the Forest Service technical staff but also by an examination of Forest Service documents, documents that often contained handwritten notes testifying to the elasticity of the practitioners' models. Later, as Barry organized timber-sale appeals across the region, the government's working documents were sanitized in order not to leave the impression of scientific imprecision or the notes to tutor neophyte skeptics.

After his winter apprenticeship, armed with technical documentation, Barry filed a successful appeal against the timber sale and clear-cut that threatened his drinking water. This victory, however, did not return Barry to the comfort of his forty acres; instead, he became a progressively more active opponent of Forest Service policy. To understand Barry's transformation one has to appreciate that the idea of integrity is the cornerstone of his view of the world. And in his judgment, integrity is exactly what most Forest Service officials do not have; the few who resist the logging companies' eased access to public land are often forced to resign. Barry's discovery of a Forest Service that, from his experience, did not respect either serious scientific research or the ideals of sustainable resource management started for him something much more than the protection of his own drinking water, and he could only finish this personal odyssey by a crusade against what he saw as Forest Service malevolence.

Barry's successful appeal of the timber sale brought notoriety and set in motion a sequence of events that would take him from part-time logger and tree planter to full-time community organizer. Other northern Idaho residents whose land or water was threatened by Forest Service–sanctioned clear-cuts started to come to Barry for advice, and he helped them draft appeals based on his successful model. After he and his fellow petitioners forced the Forest Service to submit revised plans for several timber sales, Barry met John Osborn of the Inland Empire Public Lands Council, based in Spokane, Washington. Osborn, a physician who works at Spokane's Veterans Administration hospital, dedicates his free time to forest preservation. He founded the Inland Empire Public Lands Council as a coalition of sports enthusiasts and environmentalists who devote their energies to lobbying and public education on behalf of natural-resource preservation in the Columbia River Basin, which takes in eastern Washington, northern Idaho, and western Montana. Osborn, who often worked on a macropolicy level, was attracted to Barry's more immediate approach to problems of resource depletion. While Osborn was working for long-term remediation through legislation, Barry was using federal law to slow down the Forest Service machinery.

The incongruous collaboration between back-to-the-lander and physician would eventually result in the Forest Watch program, an integral part of the Inland Empire Public Lands Council's activities. Forest Watch systematized Barry's ad hoc consulting on timber-sale appeals. Hired at a school teacher's salary by Osborn's group, Barry travels the region's back roads to set up Forest Watch groups that monitor Forest Service activities and launch timber-sale appeals. He coaches local groups in the mechanics and strategies of the appeal process. Into the early 1990s he had been a party to fourteen appeals, of which thirteen had been granted. Barry credits the Forest Watch success not only to his own technical expertise and his partners' hard work but also to Forest Service incompetence. As Barry sees it, when the primary objective of the Forest Service is to fulfill timber-cutting quotas on behalf of logging companies, it is virtually impossible for them to avoid environmental sabotage.

Barry's success as a community organizer, however, has jeopardized his standing as an independent homesteader. Taking the position of Forest Watch director has changed him from country romantic to weekender, and Barry has to wonder, with the all-consuming nature of social activism, whether he even qualifies as a weekender. He still has his forty acres, and the regular income from his position with the Inland Empire Public Lands Council makes his tenure more secure. But time to enjoy the pre-timber-sale solitude of smallholding is now an elusive commodity.

One of the intriguing aspects of Barry's transition from homesteader to activist is that it constituted a sharp break not only with his previous Idaho experience but with the entire trajectory of his life up to the point of the Forest Service's threat to his drinking water. Like so many other back-to-the-landers, independence and privacy are the principles on which his character operates. If these characteristics did not always express themselves in an absolute aversion to organizational entanglements (after all, Barry did graduate from Temple), they were the correlates of a natural aloofness that kept him emotionally uncontaminated by the political ferment of the 1960s, which he passed through on the way to his Idaho smallholding.

Barry, Cathe, and Thomas moved from the east coast to California and the San Francisco Bay area during a time of cultural and political agitation: Berkeley's Free Speech Movement and the Haight-Ashbury counterculture. The Rosenbergs, however, did not become emotionally involved in the social ferment that swirled around them. Barry would regularly pass Mario Savio's speeches at Berkeley, reacting to the demonstrations as only part of the taken-for-granted local scenery.

By the early 1970s the Rosenbergs had migrated three hundred miles north of San Francisco to Petrolia, California, where they bought a small house on three-quarters of an acre. For several years they enjoyed a modified version of the back-to-the-country life, but it did not take long for other urban refugees to discover the advantages of the Rosenbergs' adopted community. As the developers invaded and land prices escalated to the point where they lost hope of expanding their minihomestead, Barry and Cathe began to feel progressively claustrophobic. As the suburbs surrounded them, serendipity intervened in the form of a hitchhiker Cathe picked up on a rainy winter evening. The traveler was from northern Idaho and had friends with land for sale. The Rosenbergs followed him back home, then found and bought their forty-acre farmstead and part of a mountain on a handshake, never seeing the earth itself, since it was covered by six feet of snow. They went back to California, sold their property, and quit their jobs in time to return to Idaho for their first summer of camping, clearing land, and building their cabin.

In the mid 1990s, more than a decade and a half after that first summer, Barry's circumstances diverge radically from what he imagined life in Idaho would be like, in fact, what it was like for the first several years. He passed through the crosscurrents of Berkeley politics for years with little more interest than detached amusement. Now he finds himself in a consuming battle with the Forest Service. Rather than recover by the side of a warm stove in the evening after a day working in his fields and in the woods, Barry sits at a desk piled with government reports, tweaking a siltation model on his portable computer.

Barry does have the consolation of Cathe's dedication to the arts and sciences of smallholding. Cathe is a weaver and keeps their garden in full production. Still, Barry is plagued by a list of abandoned projects. He feels the chronic need for a vacation, but wonders if organizational tactics and sedimentation equations would ever stop racing across his mind. He remembers when he had the time to spend half an hour in the morning in contemplation and reading motorcycle magazines, as the warm sun streamed through his substantial, though doorless, outhouse. Then, there are the cows in the pasture across from his property. As he races to his next meeting, he pauses long enough to express his envy. They graze, massaging their cuds, for all appearances perfectly content. "Blissed out," Barry says. "That's just how I want to be—blissed out."

But Barry keeps going, guiding his Mazda subcompact up past Cathe's garden and then down over the "perilous-looking log bridge" and on to his next strategy session. He started something with the Forest Service, and he does not intend to stop until he finishes it. Maybe, if he can pass enough of what he knows on to the Forest Watch groups, they will become self-sustaining, and he can take some time off. Maybe.[3]

The last time I saw Barry he was on stage at the Okanogan Earth Song Festival. Zumak, the Wild Bioregional Band, had just finished one of its paeans to the natural order of things. Using the photovoltaically powered microphone, and in his best Mario Savio imitation, Barry energetically, but still politely, gave his stump speech: "We need to do more than just feel good about the earth! We've got to do something, become active! They've put on five new timber sales just for us. I guarantee you! We'll shut 'em down!"

New Pioneers: The Activist Profile

Working from the assumption that many parts of rural America often serve as "sacrifice zones" of resource extraction and toxic-waste storage to feed and care for the machinery of an urban-industrial culture, I held the conviction, from the first interview, that any account of back-to-the-land life should address the question of smallholder activism. If a group like the back-to-the-landers wanted to claim the status as new pioneers, on the edge of a cultural frontier, I did not believe they could simply escape to their homesteads and ask the rest of us to follow their example, all while the wealth from their adopted communities continued to flow toward metropolitan centers.

With an introduction and five chapters as background, and from the perspective of rural communities in various degrees of underdevelopment, the time has arrived to start the final inquiry into the back-to-the-landers' search for a sustainable future: the general question of their community-mindedness and the specific issue of their disposition toward social activism to defend and promote rural well-being. But with the discussion of activism only a few sentences away, a degree of perspective is needed to make sense of the numbers. If the countryside does indeed face multiple environmental, social, and economic crises, then it might reasonably be expected that any one person or group, like the back-to-the-landers, committed to the principles of sustainability, would dedicate much of their energy to the cause of community and planetary survival. "Crisis," however, is only a word, and one much depreciated through its inevitable overuse in contemporary public discourse. In the rock-solid, taken-for-granted reality of everyday life, the commentators' crises possess a distant quality, even if acknowledged as genuine. Only occasionally do circumstances conspire to grant immediacy to these crises, as was the case for Barry Rosenberg and his drinking water. Given, then, the abstract nature of many social-ecological problems, is it reasonable to expect that most smallholders will devote other than a contingent portion of their discretionary time to activism? A preoccupation with organized resistance to rural underdevelopment would obviously divert them, as it has Barry Rosenberg, from practicing sustainable stewardship on the land, the passion that brought them back to the country in the first place.

In addition to the absence of an immediate threat to the smallholders' rural way of life, there is another, more global factor that accounts for potential back-to-the-land pacifism—sanity. Onetime activist and present-day back-to-the-land college professor Noel Perrin makes the following observations on the apathy he found infuriating during the years of protest against the Vietnam War. His point of reference is a "peace walk" he participated in at Dartmouth in 1961. He begins by writing, "Except for a little group of fanatics who started it [the war], and another little group of fanatics who tried in vain to prevent it, everyone else was watching baseball [during the peace walk, and symbolically in the rest of the country as well]." He then adds, "With twenty years of perspective, I see the matter differently, see that apathy is by no means always bad. If everyone were 'involved' or 'concerned' all the time, the insanity rate would be up around 80 percent. There are so many causes and needs and injustices in the world that to let oneself care about even all the urgent ones would lead most of us to instant emotional bankruptcy."[4]

But even acknowledging the validity of Perrin's observation that each of us possesses a finite amount of psychic energy to invest in a seemingly infinite number of worthy causes, there is still the question of the back-to-the-landers' activism in defense of their immediate self-interests in their properties and their communities. In contextualizing this kind of small-holder activism, it stands to reason that most, or even a majority, of back-to-the-landers do not have to be country activists for the movement itself to posses an activist quality. Nevertheless, it is still important to have a point of reference for an informed judgment on smallholder activism in defense of sustainability in their adopted communities. One candidate for a point of reference comes by way a of a Sierra Club survey that was used to identify potential recruits for membership in environmental organizations. According to the survey, advocacy groups like the Sierra Club, Friends of the Earth, and the Audubon Society are all competing for the 8 percent of the general population sympathetic enough with the idea of environmental activism to make at least a pledge of membership.[5] Another point of comparison, and a more optimistic one, comes from long-time environmental movement chronicler Kirkpatrick Sale. Sale suggests one in seven adults actually belongs to a major environmental organization.[6] With these 8 percent and 14 percent figures as approximate indicators of a predisposition to environmental activism among the population in general, it is possible to place the *Countryside* survey results into a comparative context—one that compares back-to-the-landers with the general population. In the survey I asked the respondents a series of questions about their involvement with "community or regional groups working to solve environmental, social, or economic problems." In Table 17, I present a summary of the *Countryside* respondents' answers to the questions on activism.

Table 17. Profile of *Countryside* respondents' activist orientation and behavior (in percentages)

Sympathize with activist groups	93[a]
See the need for activist groups	68[b]
Financially support activist groups	47[b]
Belong to at least one activist group	41
Hold leadership positions in activist groups	15
Spend quite a bit or a great deal of time working with activist groups	10

Note: Total number of respondents = 565 (actual responses numbered from 542 to 546, since not all respondents answered each question).
[a]Includes the first three responses on a four-item sequence.
[b]Includes the first two responses on a four-item sequence.

In light of the earlier characterizations of back-to-the-landers as time-constrained homesteaders whose first priorities are the private pleasures of smallholding, Table 17 contains some unanticipated results. The *Countryside* figure of 41 percent of back-to-the-landers who belong to at least one advocacy group is approximately three to five times the national average. And just over half (51 percent) of those who do belong to an activist organization hold membership in two or more groups. And when it comes to financial contributions, the support level moves even higher, with 47 percent of the respondents reporting that they give either some or a great deal of financial support to reform-oriented groups. Just less than a third (31 percent) said they made no financial contributions to these organizations. On the other hand, Sale reports that half the population at large makes no financial contributions to environmental organizations.[7]

Absence of membership in or financial support for environmental organizations does not necessarily mean that one is not sympathetic to activism. Only 7 percent of the *Countryside* back-to-the-landers said they were not at all sympathetic to social change organizations—with the remaining 93 percent very much, definitely, or to a certain extent sympathetic to the goals of activist groups. In addition, *in their own areas,* 68 percent of the respondents saw either a definite or great deal of need for organized citizens groups, with only 9 percent seeing no need for these organizations. But the break point in the support for advocacy organizations naturally comes down to time, the smallholders' least elastic resource. A little less than one in six (15 percent) respondents reports holding leadership positions in activist organizations, and just 10 percent say they spend either quite a bit or a great deal of time working with social change–oriented groups. Nearly two-thirds (64 percent) claim they spend very little or no time with activist organizations, while 26 percent said they spent some time.

Although the responses to the issues of activism on the part of the smallholders, as summarized in Table 17, would not permit one to conclude that activism is a defining characteristic of the back-to-the-land movement, an observer could nevertheless safely say that the movement possesses an activist dimension. More back-to-the-landers sympathize with activist groups (93 percent) than report that growing their own food is either important or very important to them personally (89 percent; see Table 18). Of course, 95 percent of the smallholders actually do have gardens (see Table 9, Chapter 4), while only 15 percent hold leadership positions in activist groups. And while only one in ten of the *Countryside* homesteaders spends either quite a bit or a great deal of time in community or environmental organizing, this relatively low percentage translates into very large absolute numbers on a base of a million or more back-to-the-landers. If the *Countryside* survey can be generalized to the entire back-to-the-country population, there could be from 100,000 to 150,000 new pioneer activists across North America working to protect the integrity of rural ecosystems. Then, given the back-to-the-landers' overall sympathy for activism, the potential always exists, contingent on local and individual circumstances, for several hundred thousand additional smallholders to join the activist ranks.

It is difficult to know just how many of the back-to-the-country activists, like Barry Rosenberg, have been drawn into community organizing by the force of necessity. The majority, however, likely gravitate much more gently into activism, motivated by general concerns rather than by the immediacy of an impending disaster. If back-to-the-land activism does flow from a raised consciousness regarding the preservation of rural America's wealth, then it should be a relatively simple matter to detect this sensitivity through a series of questions on a survey. In the *Countryside* questionnaire I attempted to capture the smallholders' basic values on environmental concerns by presenting them with a list of statements and then having them tell me how important each statement was to them on a four-point scale from not at all important to very important. In Table 18, I have summarized the *Countryside* respondents' reactions to eight value statements, from ordinary homestead concerns through contentious ecological issues to mundane household purchases.

Table 18.   *Countryside* respondents: a value profile

Statement	% Responding Quite or Very Important
Growing my own food	89
Providing habitat for endangered species	84
Preserving old-growth forests	83
Reducing energy consumption	83
Population control	75
Expansion of wilderness areas	74
Human rights in the Third World	72
Having a microwave oven	29
Having a computer	24

Note: Total number of respondents = 565 (actual responses numbered from 541 to 557, since not all respondents answered each question).

In Table 18, I have included one back-to-the-country ideal ("growing my own food") and two consumer-oriented statements ("having a microwave oven" and "having a computer") as points of comparison with the other five statements that reflect activist concerns. As expected, "growing my own food" is either very or quite important to almost nine out of ten (89 percent) of the questionnaire respondents, while possessing the two admittedly useful but hardly essential consumer-society items is seen as important by only about one out of four respondents, 29 percent and 24 percent respectively for the microwave oven and the computer.

Of the ecologically oriented statements, several compete in the small-holders universe of values with that of growing one's own food. Providing habitat for endangered species has an 84 percent importance rating, and preserving old-growth forests and reducing energy consumption (a more generalized ecological concern) each have ratings of 83 percent. In this series I also included two issues that have activist implications but more indirect environmental relevance: population control and human rights in the Third World. These two statements also ranked high in the back-to-the-landers hierarchy of values, with ratings of 75 percent and 72 percent respectively. And it is interesting to note that the *preservation* of old-growth forests has a nine-percentage-point advantage over the more instrumental ideal of the *expansion* of wilderness areas (83 percent to 74 percent).

These high percentages of support for basic environmental values in Table 18 are certainly compatible with the relatively strong expressions of support for activism found in Table 17. Naturally, the activist behavior is lower than activist sentiment, demonstrating the difficulty of translating conviction to action. But considering the smallholders' values, in conjunction with their advocacy work, there seems to be sufficient evidence to say that one of the back-to-the-land movement's characteristics, at least in a secondary, if not primary sense, is a progressive, concerned approach to the problems of protecting the rural environment. The smallholding movement is not one that has completely retreated from organized attempts at passing on a sustainable future to the next generation, even though the majority of its members are more supportive than confrontational when it comes to matters of community and environmental activism. But at the same time, the movement's sympathies appear to be sufficiently tilted toward activism that circumstances could transform its members from spectators to participants.

An additional window through which to take a measure of the back-to-the-landers' disposition toward activism is the issue of political party involvement, as well as political philosophy. The question is whether smallholders are active in the political process or feel alienated from it. To probe this question, I asked the *Countryside* survey respondents if they identified with a political party, and, if so, which party. Just over half (53 percent) of the respondents said they did not identify with a party; among those who opted to indicate a party preference, Democrats (46 percent) roughly equaled Republicans (43 percent), with the remaining 11 percent choosing third or independent parties (primarily Ross Perot's United We Stand movement). But perhaps even more revealing on the matter of back-to-the-country activism than political affiliation is the question of political philosophy. In response to the question of which broad political positions back-to-the-landers felt most comfortable with (capitalism, socialism, or anarchism), an even 50 percent chose capitalism, with only 7 percent selecting socialism, and 1 percent anarchism. Thirty-four percent said they were not comfortable with any identifiable political philosophy, and 8 percent checked the "other" category and listed an eclectic set of possibilities from Christian fundamentalism to one combination or another of socialism and capitalism. The responses by the back-to-the-landers on questions of political orientation and philosophy reveal once again their conventional side and demonstrate as well an abiding apolitical predisposition. There are here, then, very few of the ideological resources that might be exploited in favor of an activist agenda.

In concluding this activist profile of the back-to-the-landers, I do not want to leave the impression that the smallholders' involvement in their communities need or ought to be limited to supporting and working with change-oriented organizations or functioning as political operatives. Many of them are members of volunteer fire departments or serve as village or town councilors. As one middle-aged male full-time machinist from Maine put it, "I usually do not agree with the goals and/or methods of environmental, social, or economic groups. I am, however, involved in the community. Currently, I am on the town planning board, the volunteer fire department, and am the code enforcement officer." And as a school teacher from Minnesota explains, "Small-town life forces me to become involved in the local community, ensuring that it will function. Township boards, town meetings, fire department fund raisers, church-oriented socializing are all part of our lives—community is the 'forum' by which we function."

The question of community adds another dimension to the investigation of back-to-the-land activism. Running through the movement is a definite sentiment in favor of preserving the countryside's natural resources, but there is in addition the issue of cultivating the human resources of rural America. To what extent, then, do smallholders become part of their adopted communities? Are they more likely to retreat to the privacy of their homesteads, only joining with members of their local communities when their collective way of life is threatened? In answering these questions, I want, in the next section, to draw a profile of back-to-the-landers as members of rural communities and, in the process, examine their neighborliness and the extent to which they feel comfortable in small-town America. There is no necessary implication here, however, that activism presupposes community or that active membership in the communities of rural America guarantees mobilization in defense of small-town resources. At the same time, however, it is hard to imagine reclusive smallholders devoting sufficient time and energy to building the personal and community networks that are prerequisites for effective activism.

New Pioneers: The Question of Community

In order to draw an accurate picture of the back-to-the-landers' feelings about neighborliness and community, I want to start with the question of communal living, which for them is a radical prospect. Wanting to live communally, or even being sympathetic to communes, does not necessarily constitute part of the criteria for measuring one's community-mindedness. But knowing how the back-to-the-landers feel about the limitless compromises that flow from sharing the same living and working space with a variety of other adults and children permits insight into the extent to which the smallholder is a gregarious species or one that possesses a reclusive strain. Even ambiguous sentiments about communal arrangements signal a sympathy for close, even if circumscribed, working relationships with others. There are, of course, trade-offs that come packaged with relationships of any kind of intensity and duration. One surrenders personal freedom to a relationship in exchange for a sense of belonging. A survey respondent, a former kibbutz member on a leave of absence, expressed the tensions between individual freedom and a sense of community in the following way:

> My husband was born and raised on an Israeli kibbutz. We were married and lived there for ten years. We loved it—for ourselves and our kids. But the problem was very little privacy, very little personal room. Still, the opportunities for personal development were phenomenal.
>
> We moved back to the States three years ago, looking for some room—the ability to be free to make our own decisions without communal approval.

We are here essentially on a three-year leave. We now have to make a decision. We're leaning back toward the kibbutz. With all of its community, which can sometimes strangle, it nevertheless has a great many pluses—and socialized medicine is a big plus.

These kinds of ambivalent sentiments about communal living are, however, difficult to detect among the back-to-the-landers. They possess an unequivocal aversion to the communal-living enterprise. Only two of the 565 *Countryside* respondents said they were living communally at the time of the survey, and just 4 percent report that living communally is either quite or very important to them (see Table 19). Forty-five (8 percent) of the respondents have had experience with a communal living arrangement, but only sixteen (36 percent) of these former communards would consider living communally again.

One of those who would entertain the possibility of returning to commune living wrote the following nostalgic comments at the end of his returned questionnaire: "I lived on a commune for three years in the mid-'70s. We raised milk goats primarily, but had chickens and turkeys and a small garden too. Thinking back, it was a real joy working hand in hand with others—even though it was often from sunup to well after dark. Petty concerns disappeared, and the sense of community was ever present. I left to develop my 'financial self,' and have not regretted it. But a piece of me remains—tied close with the earth." There is the implication here that one's exit from the rural and communal experience may be attributable not only to the immediate threats to one's individuality but also to the absence on back-to-the-land communes of opportunities for long-term personal (in this case, financial) development, as defined by the mainstream society.

Most objections to communal living, including the above desire for individual financial independence, are obvious rather than obscure. Compromises to one's individuality and personal freedom are central to a reflexive protest against intimate encounters in groups larger than families. Though the smallholders value personal freedom, as their self-reliant way of life attests, it was the elevation of privacy in my interviews and in the comments on their returned questionnaires that dominated their rationales for a noncommunal approach to country life. "I am very excited being outdoors and being around animals, but I have the opposite feeling for being anywhere that a number of people might be gathered, say over five or six," reported one *Countryside* respondent, reacting to the prospect

of any kind of collective compromise. A thirty-year-old Minnesota homesteader did say that she and her husband would "like to get to know the
neighbors better," but then added, "Getting to know the neighbors will
come in time, and besides, . . . if we wanted to hang around in a crowd all
day—we would have stayed in town." In this same spirit, a woman respondent from Montana elaborated on the drive toward privacy: "My main
reason for living in the rural area I live in is to have an independence that
is not available in the city. I have a need to limit my interactions with
others—I do not have any great need to be privy to the latest gossip or
intimate detail of others' lives. I am not an unfriendly woman, but I do
have a sense of privacy. I also like rearing my children away from town
and its values. I am, however, active in school affairs and am a member of
our local school board (a thankless task!). Perhaps I live out here because
I am a reserved person and this is the only place where I have the privi-
lege of my reserve."

As valuable as these comments from the survey respondents are in providing an insight into the smallholders' social worldview, they still carry an
incomplete, anecdotal quality. In order to come to a more systematic understanding of the private-public dimensions of the way the new pioneers
see their life space, I want to turn again to a comparative examination of
the back-to-the-landers' values. In Table 19, I have added several statements that relate to the issues of communal living and privacy, and I have
included as points of reference three statements from Table 18 (those on
growing one's own food, providing habitat for endangered species, and
having a computer).

Table 19. A profile of the *Countryside* respondents' community and
individual values

Value Statement	% Responding Very or Quite Important
A sense of privacy	98
Having time by yourself	91
Growing your own food	89
Providing habitat for endangered species	84
A sense of community	60
Having a computer	24
Living communally	4

Note: Total number of respondents = 565 (actual responses numbered from 546 to 557,
since not all respondents answered each question).

The figures from Table 19 confirm the smallholders' passion for privacy, a value evidently more important than their gardens; a sense of privacy and "having time by yourself" are seen as either very or quite important by 98 percent and 91 percent of the *Countryside* respondents, while 89 percent feel the same way about "growing your own food." At the same time, a sense of community is still important to these new pioneers, with three out of five of them (60 percent) rating it as very or quite important. A sense of community, however, rates 24 percentage points less in importance than providing habitat for endangered species—for the *non*human residents of the planet. Still, a sense of community, at 60 percent, is ranked far ahead of communal living, at only 4 percent. Even having a computer is 20 percentage points ahead of communal living. But their placing communal living at the bottom of their hierarchy of values does not necessarily mean that smallholders are not neighborly; 60 percent do feel that a sense of community is important. And it is certainly possible to value sociability, while at the same time trying to create private space in one's life. "We are both lovers of solitude, and are each other's best friend" was the way a fifty-year-old California homesteader described his relationship with his wife, and then went on to say, "Most of our time (work and leisure) is spent on our property. We seldom go out socially; however, friends often come over."

While it is not difficult to understand the back-to-the-landers' resistance to communal living or to appreciate their embrace of privacy, one may still speculate that they could fall somewhere on the broad middle ground of neighborliness, which is not necessarily incompatible with their preference for solitude. One way to take a measure of neighborliness is to ask whether these latter-day homesteaders visit and help their neighbors. Or does their attachment to privacy translate into a reclusiveness that means they seldom venture from the homestead gate? In response to the question, "How often do you help your neighbors with work on their property?" almost half (43 percent) of the *Countryside* respondents answered "rarely" or "never," thus admitting to a certain unneighborliness. But slightly more than one in ten (11 percent) did say they worked with their neighbors frequently. And almost another half (46 percent) said they occasionally helped their neighbors.

The picture that seems to be developing here shows back-to-the-landers in their communities as individuals who invest their time and energy in country life in order to carve out refuges of privacy in rural America. Self-reliant homesteads, apart from their connection to nature and the pleasures of manual labor, make a substantial contribution to the small-holder's privacy project. Deriving a good share of one's necessities and much of one's recreation from one's own property means minimal com-promise of privacy, a compromise that ordinarily comes through routine business transactions and social entanglements. But it would be inaccu-rate to apply a reclusive label to the back-to-the-landers as a group, though it is safe enough to say that a solitary strain runs through the center of the movement. Almost half of them report helping their neigh-bors occasionally, and more than half see a sense of community as impor-tant. One in ten does help neighbors frequently or invests considerable time in working with activist groups (Table 17). With these qualifications to the new pioneers' reclusive predispositions, perhaps it could be said that smallholders are a group of people who covet privacy but still value community—especially if they are able to define neighborliness on their own terms in order to limit the extent of their social relationships.

To measure this ability, to assess whether back-to-the-landers felt at ease in their communities, I asked the questionnaire respondents the extent to which they felt from their local communities approval for their lifestyle and ideals. This question not only generated revealing statistics but also prompted a range of reactions on the comment page of the question-naire. One extreme reaction, and very much of a minority position, as will be evident, was that of a Maine smallholder, who explained, "Country life is just life in the country. My neighbors drink a lot, screw each other's wives, drive big pickup trucks, and think we should have nuked Vietnam." On a more moderate note, a Georgia homesteader wrote, "Here we have typical southern rural institutions plus a large contingent of mostly very conventional middle-class retirees who try to perpetuate their former sub-urban lifestyle. We have enough contact to keep the wheels greased with neighbors, but otherwise we have superficial relationships with them." And then a final comment more on the positive side: "We love our new house and community—it's so nice to go to a store and know the folks and chat with them. Our main disappointment has been the schools, but, otherwise, we love it here!"

If this range of positive to negative perceptions is the filter through which back-to-the-landers see their local communities, what does this say about the smallholders' perceptions of the approval and acceptance they receive from their local communities? Though they tend to be private and outsiders, the new pioneers as "conventional radicals" sense very little negative reaction from their adopted communities. Just 2 percent of them report feeling disapproval from their local communities, and more than a third (35 percent) say they feel tolerated—neither approval nor disapproval. The rest, more than three out of five (63 percent) say they sense from their immediate communities either approval or a great deal of approval for their ideals and behavior.

For all their aloofness the back-to-the-landers still fit comfortably within the rural communities they have chosen for their homes. Ninety-four percent of them are either very or fairly satisfied with the area where they live, and 89 percent feel the same way about their relationships with their neighbors. When the back-to-the-landers do show their reclusive side, it may not always be in the interest of personal privacy. Their isolationist tendencies can at times be driven by what they perceive as a threat to their way of life, a way of life that might be jeopardized, they believe, by exposure or publicity. During my early interviews, I ran up against this kind of "social" privacy. One of my potential interviewees declined to talk to me, and then elaborated on her refusal in a letter to the *Smallholder*, the magazine from whose subscription list I was drawing my sample:

Dear Smallholders:

I received a letter from Mr. Jacob requesting an interview concerning self-sufficient smallholders. After a great deal of thought, I am refusing to participate in this study, and I question the *Smallholder*'s cooperation in this matter.

I cannot see what possible benefit this study could be to the so-called self-reliant sector of our society. On the other hand, I can see possible use for government, higher education, and big business, a use which could easily be harmful to our struggle.

We are living in a capitalist society. A capitalist society will survive only as long as the masses work for wages, pay taxes, consume enormous quantities of material goods, and produce a great number of little consumers to keep the ball rolling. The only class that actually profits from this is the top echelon—government, corporations, and educational facilities.

We, the self-sufficiency advocates, are the flies in the ointment. What would happen if half the population decided to "live lightly on the land?" Wow!

The average person is expected to (1) work as a wage earner in industry, (2) pay half his wages in income tax, (3) use large amounts of new goods and rely on outside services, (4) raise at least 2 children for future economic profit.

We are barely tolerated by the big boys. I will use myself as an example. I have (1) never made more than $1000 a year, (2) never paid income tax, (3) always tried to provide my own needs, bought secondhand where possible, and used a minimum of outside services, (4) not produced children.

Recognition from the "boss" sounds great at first, but I wonder what the final results will be. Whenever anyone in power shows interest in me, I get worried.

For hundreds of years milk could be sold wherever there was a need. Now it is illegal to sell milk except under government regulation. How long will it be before other products follow—eggs, meat, wool, vegetables . . . ?

This study sounds harmless and pleasant, but again I ask: What benefit will it show to us? Statistics mean nothing to the average person, but professionals thrive on them. We have a lot of ways to obtain necessary information on self-sufficiency. Family, acquaintances, work, books, workshops, and magazines all provide.

Perhaps you think me churlish to refuse, overly critical, paranoid, and unrealistic. As for being paranoid, I would like to say the *real* world is out here, not behind a university desk.[8]

While I regret not being able to interview this smallholder, I do appreciate her writing a letter to the *Smallholder* to express her reservations about my study, even though in the process I come out as representing BIG-HOLDER. It is not likely that the writer's views reflect, in a precise way, the prevailing opinion of most back-to-the-landers on the world of government and business. But the letter does, in a general way, mirror the alienation of smallholders from what they see as the centers of corporate power. They are on occasion frustrated by marketing regulations that restrict the selling of their produce, and they do worry about the Internal Revenue Service intruding on their barter relationships.

As victims of alienation, back-to-the-landers often feel that there is very little they can do directly to change a system, an entire civilization, that is at the heart of the sustainability predicaments. While they are sympathetic to activist causes and are at times drawn into direct confrontation with the machinery of rural underdevelopment, for the most part they direct their moral indignation inward, in an attempt to change themselves rather than the outside world. Deciding where to channel their idealism, however, is a matter of delicate moral balance. Haru Kanemitsu, a former member of the *Smallholder* editorial collective, in response to a *Smallholder* correspondent who was struggling with the private and political dilemmas of working for social change, offered the following perspective based on her own experience:

> When I was 21, I wanted to change the world. It took me a long time to realize that I must first change myself, step by step. I've still got a long way to go, but it's comforting to see that many are walking with me—many who have decided for themselves to live a simple life that is rich and full . . .
>
> So, . . . we need not be organized for social change. We can each do what we are capable of doing within our circumstances. It does help to get moral support from groups, but more important is the daily personal involvement in our homes, work and relationships.[9]

But waiting for the rest of the world to follow one's example, without trying to proselytize the ecologically deviant, is a moral position with its own ethical fault lines. It is a stand vulnerable to charges of escapism. One of the *Countryside* survey respondents, however, was able adroitly to defend escapism by recourse to the power of personal example. After ruminating about why a back-to-the-land questionnaire might include a question on human rights in the Third World, a California smallholder wrestled with the problem of how to work for a better world while at the same time retreating to the country:

> My approach to a solution [to human rights abuses, government corruption, etc.], however, is entirely different than most, I'm afraid. The biggest, most basic problem that trickles up and down the scale to virtually everything is people refusing to accept *responsibility* for themselves, their lives, their families, and their actions. From the highest and most powerful to the most poverty stricken, if *all* accepted responsibility for themselves and their actions, I think there would be a major revolution of thought that would ensure human rights worldwide.
>
> *In my small way,* I'm doing that—accepting responsibility and being self-sufficient and independent—and hoping someone, somewhere, will see my example and follow suit. Then someone will see their examples and someone will see theirs, and it spreads into peaceful coexistence, respect, and understanding

worldwide. Would mega-giant corporations knowingly dump
hazardous wastes if they took responsibility for their actions
and grew into awareness? Would rapists, child molesters, or the
Husseins of this world continue their hideous acts if they could
grow into an awareness of taking responsibility for their actions? I don't think so.

So mine is a small voice out here in the forest, but it will be
heard someday, nonetheless. Love and Light!

Love and Light. The power of example. For a good share of the back-
to-the-landers, going to all the trouble to find their place in the country
may not be an unadorned act of escapism, one of solitude and privacy.
There is the refuge of a fundamental idealism here, one that attempts to
transcend mere rationalization. In the move back to the country, the potential vices privacy and escapism are transformed into public virtues by
way of self-reliance, voluntary simplicity, and right livelihood. Even if the
majority of smallholders are not actively organizing for change, they can
still take consolation from the sense that they are standing on the moral
high ground of their own examples.

The problem, of course, is getting everybody else to pay attention to
their examples and, particularly, helping those who dump hazardous
wastes into the water and air and clear-cut forests to come to a sense of
their responsibility. But how does one go about getting their attention?
For the 10 percent to 15 percent of the new pioneers who are of an
activist persuasion the answer lies in organizing for change—either to
promote their vision of the good life or to stop its destruction. Organizing
for change, however, is almost always a matter of becoming part of group.
But how do back-to-the-landers function in the close encounters of the
organizational kind? What kind of organizations are the products of their
efforts? And what kind of resources can they count on in their struggles
for change? In the next section I answer these questions by examining the
precarious world of back-to-the-land organizing.

Promoting the Vision, Organizing for Change

These pages reflect my curiosity about the back-to-the-land movement
across a variety of subjects and issues, from small-town life to soft technol-

ogy. In pursuing new pioneers down the back roads of rural America, I have been fortunate to find smallholders who represent the broad range of experiences the movement encompasses. When the serendipity of networking my way to interviews did not pay off, Jd and Diane Belanger's *Countryside* subscription list systematically extended my inquiry. But a lingering frustration has distressed me from the beginning of my investigation. This vexation has been my inability to get inside a back-to-the-land advocacy group, to see firsthand and over time how smallholders work with each other to promote their vision for a sustainable society.

This discontinuity in my fieldwork is the result not only of my unrealistic expectations for becoming an organization voyeur but also of the character of the back-to-the-land organizations themselves. They often possess a phantom quality. I would read in a book, a magazine, or a newsletter enthusiastic accounts of the current activities and plans of organizations with impressive names like the Permaculture Institute of North America, Friends of the Trees, or the Chinook Learning Center. But on making a call to an organization's office, I more than once encountered a disconnected phone, and letters of inquiry came back stamped "Forwarding address unknown."[10]

In characterizing new pioneer organizations as carrying a phantom quality, I do not want to imply that I was chasing institutional apparitions. Nor am I trying to say that the kinds of organizations smallholders build and support have short life spans. But I do want to make a point about the permeable nature of these organizations. Not long after it disconnected its phone at its headquarters on Whidby Island near Seattle, the Permaculture Institute of North America reinstitutionalized itself in Hawaii, though much more as a one-person operation than as a collectivity. And Friends of the Trees moved from central Washington to the north end of the state's Okanogan Valley, the new address for its persistent, if not always periodic, newsletter.

Since these organizations rely much more on their founders' dreams than on their dollars, their operations are more contingent than permanent. Farmhouses become headquarters; children answer the phone and fasten address labels on outgoing newsletters. Volunteers give full-time service until the money runs out from their part-time jobs.

The precarious nature of back-to-the-land organizations is an obvious detriment to their missions of evangelizing their versions of sustainable living. There is, however, a certain virtue in these organizations' perilous existence. Advocacy groups as voluntary organizations, from the Sierra

Club to the latest blueprints for action that have yet to leave the kitchen table, are all suspended in a state of chronic dependency. If their supporters withdraw either their money or their time, institutional bankruptcy is the inevitable result. Activist groups that grow to the point where they are able to hire cadres of specialists with support staffs are particularly vulnerable to their contributors' whims. Recessionary times and miscalculated priorities mean salaried staff have to migrate in search of more comfortable niches in somebody else's hierarchy. In the sometimes affluent environmental establishment, organizations naturally become as much or more concerned with financial solvency as with ecosystem survival. David Brower, onetime president of the Sierra Club and founder of Friends of the Earth, complained that "there is too much movement now away from the ideals and too much emphasis on bottom lines. The MBAs are taking over from the people who have the dreams. Do MBAs dream?"[11]

Brower's frustrations reflect one of life's enduring paradoxes: organizations can keep dreams alive, but they also can, and do, strangle them. Paraphrasing an axiom from the sociology of religion, what religion (and an environmental organization) needs most, and suffers most from, is institutionalization. The back-to-the-landers' elusive kitchen-table variety of organizations, however, rarely have to worry about institutional suffocation. The dreams endure, but not because of organizational permanence; rather, through the tenacity of small groups of believers, the organizations continually reinvent themselves. Organizational effectiveness is not so much the issue as is the survival of idealism. What survives, however, might be more accurately labeled nodes in a network of relationships, rather than a formal organization. Kirkpatrick Sale, chronicler of the environmental movement, estimates that there are twelve thousand grassroots groups across America, with one variety of a sustainability agenda or another, in contrast to 150 nationwide organizations.[12]

As grassroots organizations, typical back-to-the-land groups do not have to worry about the conflicts between the immediate concerns of local chapters and the priorities set by headquarters in San Francisco or Washington, conflicts that plague the environmental establishment. For smallholders there are no hierarchies of local and national chapters, just small and independent grassroots groups putting out newsletters and organizing gatherings of the clan like the earth song festivals and the barter fairs. Activist back-to-the-landers do, however, cultivate networks of relationships with like-minded individuals and groups across the United States and Canada. These networks are more like confederations of independent social actors than closely coordinated advocates of a narrow range of objectives. Though the purpose of all activist organizations may ultimately be to animate their members, these networks do so primarily by reminding their members that they are not alone in the struggle to spread the message of sustainable living rather than by directing well-coordinated and focused campaigns.

My outline here of the characteristics of the free-form, networklike back-to-the-land organizations is part description of smallholder culture and part explanation for my initial difficulty in locating one of these elusive groups to observe firsthand. But after my frustrated attempts to reconstruct the anatomy of a back-to-the-land organization in the Pacific Northwest, I decided I would turn to that reliable source of alternative America, *The Whole Earth Catalog,* in order to find the most stable, well-known organization I could locate in its pages and then fill in the blank in my study with a description and analysis of the group in question. My search yielded one obvious choice: the New Alchemy Institute of Falmouth, Massachusetts. Since the early 1970s *The Whole Earth Catalog* compilers had consistently chronicled the virtues and the progress of the New Alchemy Institute, while organizations with similar ambitions regularly disappeared from the pages of subsequent editions.

In the fall of 1992 I prepared to make a pilgrimage across most of a continent to Cape Cod to see the New Alchemy Institute in action. A simple phone call was to set my research agenda in motion. But to my surprise and consternation, a disconnected phone once again came between me and my modest research goals. After confirming with directory assistance that there was indeed no listing in the Falmouth area for the New Alchemy Institute, I called *The Whole Earth Catalog* people to see why an organization whose geodesic domes and solar greenhouses were prominent features of their illustrated case histories of the alternative-technology movement had seemingly disappeared off the face of Cape Cod, if not the earth. At the offices of the *Whole Earth Review,* J. Baldwin, the soft-technology editor and a former "Alkie" (New Alchemist) himself, answered my inquiry. His simple answer was that New Alchemy had just shut down. He nevertheless suggested I might still want to make my trip, since many of the principals from the glory days of New Alchemy were still in the Cape Cod area, and he thought an archaeology of the remains could generate insight into why counterestablishment organizations have a hard time staying alive. To assist me in my reconstruction project, Baldwin gave me the name of Earle Barnhart, a longtime New Alchemy staffer and trustworthy guide to the evolution, and devolution, of the institute. I called Earle, and he agreed to an interview upon my arrival in Falmouth.

Before I turn, with Earle Barnhart's guidance, to the history of the New Alchemy Institute, I want to pause in order to pursue some conceptual housekeeping in reference to what I have loosely been calling back-to-the-land organizations. These organizations generally have one of two basic orientations, though over time they may shift from one orientation to the other. On the one hand, there are those organizations whose major objectives center around the preservation of the rural environment. In order to do so, they find themselves mobilizing resources to block the momentum of the industrial machinery intent on rearranging the countryside. The Inland Empire Public Lands Council and its Forest Watch program, which employs Barry Rosenberg, is one example of this approach.[13]

The second kind of organization that back-to-the-landers either staff or are attracted to is that which sees its objectives as primarily educational. These organizations dedicate themselves to promoting a sustainable way of life rather than directly confronting the corporate interests trying to exploit rural America's wealth. Since the organizations with educational missions are not marshaling defenders for what they might see as an immediate threat to a particular ecosystem (a clear-cut or open-pit mine, for example), they find it difficult to sustain over time a high level of commitment. They become, then, the nodes of a network—expanding and contracting and held together through the dedication of a small number of believers.

The New Alchemy Institute's organizational goals were essentially educational, rather than political and confrontational. But in spite of its educational orientation, the New Alchemy in the 1970s and 1980s, in comparison to its back-to-the-land cousins, was a high-profile research-and-development institute, often with a full-time staff of more than twenty and an equal number of volunteers and apprentices. Founded in 1969 by marine biologists John and Nancy Jack Todd, with fellow aquatic biologist and writer Bill McLarney, New Alchemy in 1971 rented a twelve-acre Cape Cod farm. Earle Barnhart, with a brand-new B.A. in ecological design and alternative technology from New College of Sarasota, Florida, joined the Todds and McLarney and their half-dozen itinerant staff in 1972. Over the next two decades, Earle, who became New Alchemy's education coordinator, as well as a member of its board of directors, watched the institute grow from a farmhouse with outbuildings to a multidisciplinary research laboratory with a budget of over $500,000 a year.

New Alchemy approached the problem of sustainability in a post-petroleum era through the marriage of biology and architecture. Earle and his research-and-design compatriots built and tested what they called bioshelters—Arks, which, as closed-loop systems, were to provide for the material needs of their inhabitants while transforming wastes into beneficial substances. Around the farmhouse, the staff built solar greenhouses, with massive southern exposures and windmills overhead, looking like "steeples of a solar age."[14] At the heart of the design concept were seven-hundred-gallon water-filled cylinders strategically located inside the Arks' greenhouses to absorb and store solar gain throughout the day and then radiate their heat back to the buildings during the night. The cylinders carried not only water but also fish and generous amounts of algae. The algae provided nutrients for the fish and served as an effective medium to trap the sun's heat. The cylinder's water, complete with fish fertilizer, was used to irrigate the Arks' vegetable gardens. According to design specifications, the bioshelters were to keep their crop and fish occupants warm and well fed through even the bitterest of New England winters, with at most occasional backup from a wood-burning stove.

Visionaries, whether they favor conventional technology or the alternative, soft varieties, are prone to living in the realms of the hypothetical. To bring the imaginative down to the level of the practical, Earle and his New Alchemy associates instituted a series of rigorous research protocols. They carefully monitored and measured the Arks' critical indicators, from fish weight and length to median temperatures, noting fluctuations as they experimented with the bioshelters' range of variables. Then, to communicate their findings, they published their own journals, the *New Alchemist Quarterly* and *Journal of the New Alchemists*. This scientific approach to alternative technology won the New Alchemists a series of major grants, from agencies and foundations as diverse as POINT (*The Whole Earth Catalog*s' philanthropic arm) and the National Science Foundation.

Earle found this cautious and systematic side of New Alchemy's experiments congenial to his own way of looking at the world. He grew up on a 130-acre diary farm in Ohio, predictably moving through the 4-H and Future Farmers of America programs. But rather than follow his siblings to college at Ohio State and to careers in teaching and agriculture, Earle accepted a scholarship at the definitely divergent New College in Florida. After joining New Alchemy, Earle's practical instincts started to reassert themselves. Of more than twenty staff, he was the only one with a farm background, and about one in four of the staff held a Ph.D. Though intrigued by flights of the speculative, Earle emphasized during his New Alchemy years the importance of painstakingly verifying the institute's innovations before the staff pontificated on them publicly.

Earle's two-decade tenure at New Alchemy became more than a unique career experience. Hilde Maingay, an artist and historian, was a New Alchemy organic vegetable gardener when Earle arrived at Cape Cod in the early 1970s. Hilde and Earle's relationship evolved over the years from a personal one to a formalized professional partnership. They are currently the proprietors of the Great Work, Inc., an ecological-design and landscape contracting firm operating out of Falmouth.

Earle and Hilde's entrepreneurial success in the late 1980s and the early 1990s was one sign of the declining fortunes of the New Alchemy Institute. Throughout the 1980s members of the New Alchemy staff were starting to channel their energies toward personal endeavors, away from collective ones. But it was not just that the staff in general started to lose focus; the key factor was John and Nancy Todd's own diffusion of interest. In retrospect, Earle believes that it was not realistic to expect that the institute could limit the Todds' inventiveness to a twelve-acre stretch of Cape Cod landscape. From the very beginning of New Alchemy, John and Nancy's imagination extended beyond the institute's farm. With support from the Canadian government, New Alchemy in 1976 opened a full-scale Ark on the east end of Prince Edward Island, complete with inaugural ceremonies presided over by Prime Minister Pierre Trudeau. Then, in the early 1980s, the Todds started Ocean Arks International and the Center for the Restoration and Protection of Waters, respectively not-for-profit and for-profit organizations designed to develop and promote the application of their solar aquatic design principles. Their energies are presently invested in the commercialization of a biologically driven water-purification process that involves running sewage through a series of increasingly complex life-form filters, from bacteria to fish, in order to transform it into drinking water.[15]

Without John Todd's ability to take the work of generalists, like that of Hilde, and the narrower interests of the Ph.D. staffers and integrate them into cutting-edge funding proposals, New Alchemy found it increasingly difficult to find research money in the environmentally hostile climate of the 1980s. In the Todds' absence the institute changed both directors and direction, drifting more toward an educational mission, while its research-and-development proposals became more pedestrian. In the meantime, the staff gravitated to other positions or, like Earle and Hilde, started up their own small businesses and consulting enterprises, leaving only part-time energy for New Alchemy. In July of 1992, the New Alchemy Institute's board of directors decided it was time to close down the dream.

It is one thing to close down an organization like New Alchemy, as difficult and painful as that might be, but the dream itself is much more resilient than the lines on an organizational flow chart that connect the directors of a board to members of a research staff. The New Alchemy Institute was nearly coterminous with the back-to-the-land movement of the past quarter century. Although the formal organization known as the New Alchemy Institute has ceased to function, its alumni have infiltrated a variety of governmental and nongovernmental organizations, from state departments of agriculture to university environmental studies programs, where they continue to do battle for the ideals of sustainable living. The institute's records, research data, and journals have been deposited in the American Archives of Agriculture at Iowa State University in Ames, but John and Nancy Jack Todd, back at Cape Cod, still preside over a small-scale publishing industry that reports their ongoing research with the principles of ecological design.[16] And Earle Barnhart and Hilde Maingay are keeping the windmills turning above the geodesic domes at New Alchemy's original twelve-acre farm site. They are part of a group transforming the institute into a cohousing village that will keep the physical artifacts of New Alchemy still functioning as the "tool and die company for the new age."[17]

With the New Alchemy Institute's demise, or, perhaps more accurately, its transformation, I missed the opportunity to share firsthand the organizational energy of back-to-the-landers promoting their vision of a sustainable future. Through my discussions with Earle Barnhart and my attempts to move beyond the disconnected phones and the unforwarded mail, I believe I have a good sense of the nature of back-to-the-land activism. Most back-to-the-landers, of course, make their sustainability statements by example and let others take their places on the picket or newsletter-collating lines. A minority of their compatriots become involved in a combination of educational projects and protest, alternately trying to tell everyone else how to start living the good life and attempting to keep the timber and mining companies from destroying what is left of it in rural America. But when to educate and when to stand in front of a bulldozer is a strategic decision, usually dictated more by circumstance than by calculation. In the next and concluding section of the chapter I want to turn to the experience of Susan Willis, whose predispositions led her in the direction of educational activism, an activism of the long-term, nurturing variety. In Susan's case, however, like that of Barry Rosenberg, events conspired to subvert her natural inclinations.

Save Roslyn Ridge

"What really got to me," Doug Johnson tells me, speaking softly but deliberately, "was that the Plum Creek people got paid to meet with us—it was part of their jobs. But for me to meet with them, I had to pay for a substitute or try to get a personal day off. Then we had to find a babysitter to look after the kids. And we paid for motels, food, and gas. It was really hard to take, really hard to believe." Doug Johnson is a high school math teacher. He is talking about the three years he and his wife, Susan Willis,[18] spent lobbying the Plum Creek Timber Company and the state of Washington to limit the rate of harvest to sustainable levels on timber companies' privately held lands. Doug and Susan, and their supporters, did not win all their public battles, but there were nevertheless important personal victories. Plum Creek still cuts away to supply a lucrative market for unfinished logs in Japan. For the Willis-Johnsons, however, the timber wars are not over; they have only changed direction.

The fight with Plum Creek exhausted the Willis-Johnsons' energies, and their family suffered. But the healing process is under way. And even though their battle with the timber interests and the state agencies that facilitate resource extraction was intense, they feel they have learned a great deal, about themselves and the forces that covet rural America's wealth.

The Willis-Johnsons' wanderings through the psychic territories of naïveté, resignation, and renewal started with a rumor. Doug and Susan and their family live in Roslyn, a small town of 850, twenty miles from the foot of the east side of the Cascades in central Washington. Interstate 90 runs a few miles to the south of Roslyn on its way over the Cascades to Seattle, eighty miles away. The rumor that caught the Willis-Johnsons' attention, and that of most of Roslyn, was that the Plum Creek Timber Company planned to clear-cut Roslyn Ridge.

Roslyn Ridge does not belong, in the legal sense of having title, to the town. It is on land owned by Plum Creek, though Roslyn's character as a place on this earth is bound up with the ridge of evergreen that flows down the Cascades on the town's north side. The ridge is a point of reference that defines where home is for those who live in Roslyn.

Given the sea of green that surrounds Roslyn, the ridge is more a subtle than a spectacular landmark. The casual visitor could, therefore, be excused for wondering why the town was alarmed by the possibility that a timber company might cut trees on its own land. To understand the town's deep concern at only a rumor, one has to appreciate just how much of an unnatural disaster a clear-cut is. If Plum Creek were to proceed with its cutting plans, the view from Roslyn would be of a moonscape, a gray-brown expanse of bare earth scarred by logging roads and littered with the slash of broken trees. For many in Roslyn the reassurance that comes from feeling a part of nature's magnificence would be replaced by melancholy at the sight of the cancer on their mountainside.

But for Susan, the clear-cutting of Roslyn was not a matter of simple aesthetics, just a question of the view from her home on the edge of town. In the decade before the timber wars Susan and her family not only enjoyed the sense of being surrounded by the forest, they also spent much of their free time exploring its contours along the mountains' back trails. Over time, the Willis-Johnsons became impressed with the forest's growing diversity as it recovered from the clear-cuts of the late 1890s. The wild flowers growing on the forest floor and beside and around the trees were, for Susan, harbingers of returning health for a once severely damaged ecosystem.

The possibility that Plum Creek was ready to cut down the ridge and destroy one hundred years of the Roslyn ecosystem's recovery set the town in motion. The chamber of commerce organized information and discussion sessions. Doug attended the first one, while Susan stayed home with the children, and then they took turns going to the subsequent meetings. The meetings were of the brainstorming variety, with small-group facilitators who captured the participants' discussions in point form with colored markers on large sheets of paper. The bottom line at the meetings was always "Save Roslyn Ridge," but the subject matter expanded from questions about what Plum Creek might, or might not, be doing to considerations of the meaning of sustainable development in a natural resource–based economy like that which supports Roslyn.

As he reflects back on the electricity of those first meetings and the intervening years of confrontation and negotiation, Doug Johnson thinks that he could have lived with Plum Creek's cutting down most of their own trees if they would have just agreed to leave the ridge alone. "Not me," counters Susan, without interrupting Doug, speaking more to a spot on the floor than to her interviewer, quietly yet intensely. And it was Susan who was to become the family activist. After the first several months of meetings, Doug slipped into a supportive role, while Susan's involvement deepened. She helped organize RIDGE, the community group that would carry the fight against Plum Creek, and then later served as RIDGE's representative to Washington State's Sustainable Forestry Roundtable.

Susan is one of those persons who has the gift, and perhaps the eventual disability, to experience deep concern for people and events in which she has no immediate self-interest. She worries about human rights in Honduras and famine in Somalia. In short, she is very much an idealist. And it was idealism that brought her to Roslyn. Her father was a military man, and consequently the family never lived anywhere long enough to become part of a community. To compensate for the transience of her childhood, Susan felt drawn toward the connectedness of small-town life. She wanted to build friendships with her neighbors, learn how local schools work, and become a part of her children's education.

In the mid-1970s Susan found herself as a single parent living in southern California. During her California sojourn she discovered the Sierra Nevada mountains. Susan's destination of the heart became a small town with mountain vistas. On a visit to a friend in Washington she was converted to the Cascades, and subsequently chose Roslyn as the kind of human-scale community where she could feel at home. While setting up residence in Roslyn, she took a job with the U.S. Forest Service, doing a variety of work, including measuring traffic flows over logging roads. Doug was also working for the Forest Service, taking a few years' break from small-town teaching. The Forest Service played unintentional broker to their relationship, and Doug, also a single parent, and Susan started their small-town life together with a ready-made family of two boys.

From the modest two-story house on a large lot next to the forest on the edge of Roslyn, Susan began to piece together an active small-town life from the evolving blueprint she had been drafting over the years. She and Doug had two children together, Laura and Dylan. Although it was important to Susan to be a full-time mother while her children were young, the dedication to motherhood did not preclude volunteer work at the local schools and working with a network of neighbors on a number of community projects. She helped form a peace-and-justice group that sponsored monthly meetings with guest speakers, as well as a walk for international peace.

Many small towns might have dismissed as an eccentric someone with Susan's passions. But Susan wanted to learn from the community just as much as she wanted to help Roslyn become a better place to live. Her neighbors taught her how to garden and when and where to pick huckleberries. Then Doug and Susan's aspirations were in line with those of their neighbors. They were content to live like the people around them; gentrifying their side of Roslyn would have been foreign to their natural inclinations.

Environmental activists, however agreeable, in a small town whose material well-being depends on natural-resource extraction, can still be seen as *agents provocateurs,* and consequently as a threat to community welfare. How did Susan manage to become part of the community while at the same time trying to change it? Susan believes she was accepted so easily, in part, because the town was dying. Coal was once the basis of Roslyn prosperity, but Burlington Resources shut the local Northwest Improvement Company mine in 1963, claiming that cheaper coal could be mined elsewhere. Burlington Resources is the holding company that includes the Burlington Northern Railroad; it created the Plum Creek Timber Company to harvest the timber on the land grants Burlington Northern received in the late nineteenth century for building the Great Lakes–Puget Sound link of the northern transcontinental railroad. There was a strong feeling in Roslyn that Burlington Resources was in the process of abandoning the town, cutting rail service, closing the coal mine, and then clear-cutting the forests that surround Roslyn. Since many of Roslyn's old-time residents still depended either directly or indirectly on what was left of Burlington's goodwill, they were reluctant to become personally involved in the confrontation with Plum Creek, but they were not shy in encouraging Susan and her fellow activists to step up the pressure on the company. "We're glad you're doing this; keep it up" is the kind of support Susan remembers.

The free-form town meetings evolved toward focused opposition to Plum Creek's cutting policies. The vanguard of the opposition was RIDGE. RIDGE held weekly meetings in front of the Roslyn Cafe on Sunday afternoons—parents with their children in tow educating themselves on the theoretical and practical dynamics of the forest industry. In reflecting back on those early meetings, Susan smiles, slowly shaking her head, and remembers, "We were so open, so incredibly naïve. Open hearts and open minds. How could we have been so innocent?"

RIDGE's first problem was information. The RIDGE members read and shared information on natural-resource law and the science of forestry. They invited lay experts and foresters to their meetings. Armed with technical insights and driven by their idealism, they soon came to an obvious conclusion: the answer to both the town's and Plum Creek's problems was a sustainable rate of harvest. Roslyn wanted to keep its ridge, and Plum Creek, presumably, wanted to stay in the timber business. If Plum Creek cut fewer trees and replanted those it did cut down, it could support logging and mill jobs in the Cascades indefinitely, while leaving Roslyn's scenic vistas and ecosystems intact. Since their conclusion logically followed from their uncluttered assumptions, the RIDGE activists felt that all they had to do was to explain the common sense of their position to the Plum Creek officials. "We would educate them," Susan says as she recalls the optimism of those early days. "We were going to touch and change their hearts. And then they would say, 'Oh, this is wrong. You're right—we can manage a sustainable harvest. We don't need to clear-cut.' "

The Plum Creek executives, however, were operating from a different set of assumptions. While they were willing to discuss RIDGE's concerns politely, they, not always patiently, explained that timber harvesting was a business and that in the competitive business of resource extraction their first responsibility had to be to their shareholders. They felt that they had been asleep to the value of their holdings, and now they had no choice but to take competitive advantage of their position in the global marketplace. Japan was paying premium prices for raw logs from the Roslyn forests. Sensitive to the boom and bust cycles of their industry, the Plum Creek people could see no alternative to harvesting and selling as much of their Cascade timber as possible while the prices were high. Once their Roslyn forest was cut, they planned to move on to their other holdings. Sustainability was a factor missing from their profit and loss equations.[19]

Since Plum Creek's position on the unsustainable rates of harvest on its own forest lands was uncompromising, RIDGE had to find a way other than appeals to sustainability logic to persuade Plum Creek to change its corporate behavior. As a first step, Susan and her RIDGE associates turned to public pressure. They took their case to the news media, eventually finding themselves on occasion in the pages of the *Seattle Times,* and the controversy they generated put Plum Creek, cast in a critical light, on the front page of the *Wall Street Journal.*[20] In addition to the media campaign, RIDGE began to lobby legislators on behalf of the Roslyn forests. Washington has a Forest Practices Act that regulates timber harvesting in the state. Although Plum Creek owns the Roslyn land on which it was cutting,

RIDGE believed that the company could be held accountable under sustainability implications of the act. Consequently, they took their case to the Forest Practices Board and the commissioner of public lands, as well as to the legislature. For the most part they received a sympathetic hearing; the bottom line, however, was talk and letter writing, but no action. Their one advocate in the legislature, incongruously from the inland prairie region of Moses Lake, died before he could press RIDGE's case on the floor of Washington's House of Representatives.[21]

Up to the time of the Roslyn Ridge controversy, Plum Creek cut and sold its logs in relative obscurity. But in the late 1980s it found itself at the vortex of claims and counterclaims surrounding sustainability issues. As curious bankers started to make indelicate inquiries regarding their reasons for clear-cutting entire mountainsides, Plum Creek officials found that they needed to draw on the art of public relations as well as the science of forestry management. RIDGE and Plum Creek agreed on an involved twenty-three-point set of ground rules for their continued discussions—including a provision that neither party would contact the media without prior notification. The talks continued, although RIDGE became chronically frustrated by Plum Creek's refusal to place rate of harvest on the bargaining table; the timber company would discuss technical issues like mill jobs and erosion but not sustainable rates of harvest. Susan discovered that one of the Plum Creek executives was from a European forestry family. When she asked him whether his family had used sustainable rates of harvest, he admitted they had. But he then went on to say that it was now a different time and a different place. The global marketplace had to be the final arbiter of what happened to the Roslyn forests. Once again Susan's passion for place collided with Plum Creek's global pragmatism.

While RIDGE talked, Plum Creek cut. The RIDGE people, however, believed they had a tacit understanding with Plum Creek to the effect that it would not work on land RIDGE considered sensitive. But on a fall morning in 1988, the abstractions of the timber economy were transformed into a painful reality. Several of the RIDGE members discovered loggers at work in an area behind the town that they thought was still under negotiation. They confronted the loggers and tried to persuade them to stop cutting. The loggers simply said that they had a contract to cut, there was no mistake, and there was no way they would stop cutting. RIDGE was devastated by what they considered betrayal. For the RIDGE members the clear-cut was like losing friends. They had come to recognize many of the trees, appreciating their individual characteristics and having their own favorites. Now they were gone. "She almost cried," Doug says, speaking of one of Susan's friends who witnessed the cutting firsthand. "She did cry," Susan echoes softly yet firmly.

After the clear-cut the RIDGE–Plum Creek relationship deteriorated. RIDGE went to the media with the story of the clear-cut. Plum Creek considered RIDGE's action a violation of their agreement on notification prior to media contact. But apart from the procedural details, Susan and her RIDGE partners could see that their asymmetrical negotiations with Plum Creek did little more than provide a grace period for the company's business-as-usual impulses. It became obvious that Plum Creek was only going to change when state or federal governments, through penalty or subsidy, made it change.

These conclusions made RIDGE's acceptance of an invitation to join Washington State's Sustainable Forestry Roundtable a logical extension of their advocacy work. And Susan was the natural choice for RIDGE's representative to the roundtable. The roundtable was a coalition of government, timber industry, and environmental groups organized in 1989 by the state government to come to an agreement on a set of guidelines that would govern forestry practice in Washington—ending years of contention with broad-based consensus.

For the next thirteen months, Susan, with the children either in the back seat or at baby-sitters, crisscrossed the state to meet with citizen groups, lobbyists, and public officials. The experience was often stimulating, but always tiring. In the end, however, the result was little more than the Plum Creek–RIDGE negotiations on a larger scale. The timber people were intransigent on the rate-of-harvest issue, while government officials supported compromises that were, in Susan's judgment, oblivious to the key sustainability issues. The roundtable finally fell apart when RIDGE and one other environmental group vetoed an agreement that, from their point of view, was so general and watered-down as to be meaningless.

The collapse of the roundtable discussions crystallized for Susan and her colleagues a fundamental dilemma. While they needed help from state and even federal regulators to put pressure on Plum Creek, their preoccupation with state and regional concerns undermined their attention to critical local issues. With RIDGE distracted from exclusive attention to the Roslyn Ridge problems, Plum Creek had more room to maneuver. The timber company was able to talk and keep cutting when RIDGE tried to negotiate on a local level, and when RIDGE turned to state agencies for help, Plum Creek's lobbyists stalled the reform movement.

The RIDGE–Plum Creek confrontation was a war between, on the one hand, a handful of local activists who were devoting their energies both to the principle of sustainability and to the needs of their own families and careers and, on the other hand, the transnational timber industry, which was able to pay for the full-time defense of its interests. The timber battles had little effect on Plum Creek other than diminishing its self-promoted image as a responsible corporate citizen. But for Susan Willis and Doug Johnson and their children, the struggle with Plum Creek had a profound impact. Susan's idealism extended not only to preservation of the Roslyn Ridge but also to the nurture of her own family. The barrage of meetings, phone calls, and letter writing preempted the close attention she wanted to give to her husband and children. The sound of the phone ringing began to make her ill. She would promise to talk for only a few minutes, but an hour and a half later she would still be deep in strategy sessions on the latest countermoves against Plum Creek. Laura asked, "Why do you have to go to so many stupid meetings," as Susan shifted her from one baby-sitter to another. Susan saw herself being transformed from the mother who would always be at school and community programs for her children to a distant parent who received secondhand accounts of her children's activities. She and Doug tried to compensate for the constant distractions by going camping, where they could find at least temporary seclusion, but the strain persisted. When Dylan told his mother, "Mom, it seems like you're not my own mom anymore," Susan knew that she had to let go of saving Roslyn's forests in favor of preserving her own family life.

After leaving the roundtable, Susan said she found herself "not responding, not initiating." "I would go to RIDGE meetings, but have to say, 'You guys, I'm getting really tired.' I wasn't following through. My energy was gone." It was time to let the healing begin. Letters went unanswered. Susan's clear, firm voice on RIDGE's answering machine summarizes her exit: "Susan Willis will not be taking RIDGE calls. RIDGE calls should not be directed to the Willis-Johnson residence."

"I don't have regrets," Susan says in retrospect, "There was a lot of pain in our family, but we've healed. It just got to the point where I had to stop. I had no alternative."

Susan's mental and emotional exhaustion from her fight to save Roslyn Ridge has not precluded her continued interest in and participation with

RIDGE activities. But now she limits herself to working as one member in the group rather than as a spokesperson for a vanguard of reformers. She feels deeply that education is the key force that will win the resource battles for the sustainability side. Susan and RIDGE started by trying to educate the Plum Creek executives on the advantages of a sustainability approach to forestry management; RIDGE wanted to keep timber jobs in Roslyn for the indefinite future, but the logic of short-term gains in the global market transformed the common sense of their arguments to unadorned romanticism. Then, as RIDGE's representative to the Sustainable Forestry Roundtable, Susan extended her role as educator to the state level, as she worked with environmental, governmental, and industry interests to come to a consensus on the sustainability issue. Again, business imperatives overwhelmed the conservation message. But Susan has not by any means given up on education. As a mother, a neighbor, and community activist, education is what defines her character. In the end she decided it was not so much that education itself had failed as that it had been directed at the wrong beneficiaries. She now believes the general public, rather than industry and government functionaries, has to be the target of the activist community's education campaigns. Change may not be the immediate product of the educational struggle, but when and if change does come, Susan is convinced that its effects will be deep-rooted.

While this kind of social transformation starts its own incubation period, Susan, enthusiasm renewed, is in the middle of her own personal education project. A nearby school board offered her, along with a colleague, a time-share contract to teach fifth grade at one of their elementary schools. She feels fortunate to be working at a school her children can also attend. It is with the elementary school children, with their open, inquiring minds, that Susan feels that she can make a difference. "The children need this information [on the timber controversies]; they need to be able to see all sides of the issues, to ask questions and make connections. This is where I can make my contribution."

As Susan devotes herself to education for the long term, there still remains the immediate problem of Roslyn Ridge. Due to the pressure that started with the Sunday afternoon meetings in front of the Roslyn Cafe, Plum Creek has yet to cut down the ridge. And the prospects for its preservation are better now than at any time in the recent past, though its survival can be attributed as much to serendipity as to the designs of the Roslyn activists. The producers of *Northern Exposure*, the thirty-something television situation drama, discovered Roslyn. Its weather-beaten main street, strategically decorated with moose antlers, was ideal for the re-creation of *Northern Exposure*'s Cicely, Alaska, and less than a two-hour drive away from the interior sets at a Seattle sound stage. On Saturday morning tourists line up for a table at the Roslyn Cafe, its exterior signs carrying an *'s*, transferring the synthetic of television to the nouveau authenticity of Roslyn's Cafe. With the town's notoriety, it is not likely that Plum Creek, with its born-again public relations sensitivity, will try to level Roslyn Ridge in the foreseeable future. But Plum Creek continues its clear-cutting ways, though out of sight of Roslyn's main-street tourists, while Susan Willis, survivor of the timber wars, invests her idealism in the education of Roslyn's children. Whether the ridge will still be standing when the children reach adulthood, or whether there will even be a community the children can consider becoming part of, are open questions. Susan may not have the answers to these kinds of questions, but asking them and trying to find answers to them is what she sees her work with the children to be all about, trusting that the process will be one more contribution to the survival of the small-town way of life she discovered in Roslyn.[22]

The apparent primordial instincts of new pioneers draw them back to the country for the solitary pleasures of subsistence agriculture on their secluded smallholdings. While privacy stands at the top of their hierarchy of values, the preservation of the ecological integrity of the countryside is also important to them. They are, as well, sympathetic to the goals of activist organizations fighting to solve the problems rural America faces. In addition, the smallholders' support for advocacy groups, including holding leadership positions, is as much as or more than what one would expect from the general population. Then, on occasion, back-to-the-landers like Susan Willis and Barry Rosenberg become swept into the vortex of environmental activism, paying the personal price of time away from their land and their families for the defense of their communities.

While most back-to-the-country people translate their concern over the threats to the rural way of life into a renewed dedication to live voluntary simplistic and self-reliant lifestyles, 10 to 15 percent of them nevertheless go to meetings and write letters, either to promote sustainability or to protect its precarious gains. This minority of new pioneers is part of the twelve thousand grassroots groups across America, according to Kirkpatrick Sale, that are trying to get the rest of us to support the causes of a revitalized countryside and greener, more self-sustaining cities. Over the past thirty years these groups, along with the 150 nationwide organizations, have made important contributions to raising the environmental awareness of the general public, to preserving particular ecosystems, and to establishing a body of environmental regulation. Yet, as environmentalist José Lutzenberger explains, "in the environmental movement, our defeats are always final, our victories always provisional. What you save today can still be destroyed tomorrow."[23]

The interminable battles yet to be fought in the war for a sustainable future are of such a proportion that it is only quixotic to believe that back-to-the-land organizations, usually centered around the dreams of one person and continually reinventing themselves, can do more than occasionally divert the ongoing extraction of the countryside's wealth. However well organized and coordinated all the disparate elements of the back-to-the-land and environmental movements may yet become, they face not only well-financed corporate interests with single-minded, insatiable appetites for rural resources, but also a mass culture whose defining core is material accumulation.

The struggle for a sustainable future, however, is not just between the environmental movement and a consumer society that sees no alternative to economic growth. There are other important players in this contest. The most obvious counterforce is, of course, government. In its attempts to protect rural communities, government will naturally continue to play a critical role in the legislative and enforcement arenas. But the introduction of government into the sustainability equation reflexively depresses the spirit of the discussion. The late twentieth century is a time when proposals for comprehensive government intervention to make the world a better place to live evoke images of ponderous, inefficient bureaucracies sucking out the life blood of spontaneous social and economic development. In spite of the disrepute into which government intervention has fallen, I still want, in my final chapter, to look at the possibility of explicit public policy encouragement of the back-to-the-land movement's sustainability goals.

The basic question here is whether back-to-the-land is an idiosyncratic movement, with a certain curiosity value, best left to follow its own internal dynamics, or whether it might be possible to use carefully focused public policy to expand its virtues and in the process take another step or two down the road toward a sustainable future. Apart from exploring policy options, however, I want to use the last chapter to assess the back-to-the-country movement in terms of the sustainability criteria I first developed in the Introduction. From a technical perspective, back-to-the-land smallholdings, with their gardens, fruit trees, and chickens, are anemic reflections of the ideal farmsteads from the pages of the *Mother Earth News,* and for the most part neohomesteaders are too busy, and too private, to channel very much of their energy into community development and environmental activism. But I still want to explore the possibility that at some deeper level the back-to-the-landers might nevertheless qualify as the new pioneers they initially set out to become.

7

BACK-TO-THE-LANDERS AS NEW PIONEERS

The Search for a Sustainable Future

 Can the back-to-the-landers in any serious sense be considered new pioneers? Or are they simply a group of people who escape to the country to enjoy the private pleasures of physical labor on their smallholdings? And to what extent does the back-to-the-country experience expand our appreciation of the prerequisites for a sustainable way of life? Finally, are there effective and efficient ways in which public policy can encourage the best instincts of the back-to-the-landers, and other like-minded individuals and groups, in their attempts to live within the earth's ecological limits?

One way to begin answering these questions is to remind ourselves what the requirements for a sustainable lifestyle are. From a technical point of view, as I argued in the Introduction, sustainability is the switch from non-renewable fossil fuels to the renewable energy of sun, wind, and muscle power. On this criterion the performance of the new pioneers is disappointing. One unsustainable characteristic of the neohomesteaders' approach to country living is obvious: their long-distance commuting habits negate the energy they save by growing about a third of the food they eat. Cultivating gardens, keeping fruit trees, raising chickens, and using wood heat, however, are about as far as the smallholders go in applying ecological design principles. The kinds of alternative technology that possess the greatest potential to move the sustainability project forward (solar heating and gray-water-recycling systems, for example) are resident on most back-to-the-land homesteads only in the pages of the *Mother Earth News* lying open on kitchen tables.

Sustainability, however, is more than a technical achievement. It is also a social product—neighbors working together to promote their common interests in the ecological integrity of their contiguous properties. But on the community dimensions of sustainability the back-to-the-landers as a group also struggle to qualify as new pioneers. While they value community, community-mindedness is not much above the midpoint on their hierarchy of good-life values. Privacy is what they covet: all but 2 percent of the *Countryside* survey respondents rate a sense of privacy as either quite or very important, compared to the 60 percent who feel the same way about a sense of community. The smallholders, however, not only crave privacy, they also appear to do little to inhibit their solitary instincts. Almost half of the survey respondents report that they never or rarely help their neighbors with homesteading projects. When the issue shifts from the experience of community to community and environmental activism, the pattern of low levels of involvement reappears. Only 10 percent of the *Countryside* respondents say they spend either quite a bit or a great deal of time working with activist groups. In addition, just over half of the respondents do not identify with a political party, and a third of them claim no identifiable political philosophy. These attitudinal and behavioral patterns, however, do need to be placed in perspective. In terms of alienation from the political system, the neohomesteaders are likely not much different from the typical citizen in the 1990s, and though their activism levels may be low in absolute terms, they are still above national averages.

As admitted country underachievers, are there still ways the reclusive, apolitical back-to-the-landers model the virtues of sustainability rather than simply subscribe to its principles? While it is not easy to rehabilitate smallholders as putative new pioneers, I do believe there are subtle and indirect criteria on which they have made significant progress toward living a sustainable life. One not particularly obvious way the back-to-the-landers exemplify sustainable practice is in their long-term residence patterns. On average the *Countryside* survey respondents report living about a decade and a half in the area where they now make their homes. This long-term commitment to a particular place has definite sustainability implications. Of all the simplifications that one could make in characterizing the unsustainable nature of the contemporary consumer culture, perhaps the most defensible is the claim that environmental degradation is directly linked to hypermobility—the sometimes extreme transience of individuals, families, and corporations. Without a sense of permanence, the motivation to ensure the long-term viability of one's residence and community is absent. One can always escape contamination or resource exhaustion by moving on. Intergenerational residence in a particular place encourages the kind of discipline for which ethical considerations and regulatory legislation are at best second-class substitutes.[1]

Back-to-the-land activism, if and when it does come, is often connected to the defense of a particular place, rather than directed toward distant, generalized, or global problems. One last example of smallholder activism demonstrates the tenacity with which long-term residents will fight for the welfare of their communities. On the back of his returned questionnaire, a South Texas sixty-five-year-old, who identified himself as a Republican, made the following statement:

> I am president of the Citizens' Action Committee fighting the toxic chemical, nuke dump at Spofford, Texas, only thirty miles upstream from Eagle Pass. Texcore Inc. is trying to force this upon the citizens of this area. I feel that we are fighting our own tax money with private funds. We have appeared on local TV, and I have written a letter to the President concerning this situation. We are and will be fighting this situation tooth and nail to the end.
>
> Sincerely
>
> W.O. Robinson, Jr.
> President, Citizen's Action Committee
> Retired Teacher
> Full-Time Employee of Wal-Mart

Few back-to-the-landers have circumstances conspire to cast them in activists' roles, but there is at least one other, though paradoxical, way in which they demonstrate the potential to support sustainable practice. This is their ability to tolerate their own poor performance on the sustainability criteria. This tolerance can of course lead to complacency, as the years go by and the root cellar and greenhouse never exit from the realms of homestead dreams. But tolerance can also engender perseverance. Since the individual and collective journeys yet to be made in the direction of a sustainable future will consist of many more detours than unobstructed highways, perseverance at least keeps the possibility open that some of the travelers will eventually arrive at their destinations.

Although the back-to-the-landers' progress toward their homestead dreams has to be measured in years, perhaps decades, rather than weeks and months, they do nevertheless have a vision of the good life that they are pursuing. The arrival of my questionnaire in the mail was for many of the *Countryside* readers an unwelcome reminder of the considerable distance between their ideals and their accomplishments. More than a few respondents protested the absence of a section in the questionnaire where they could check off soft-technology projects at the planning stage, or space were they could at least acknowledge work in progress. This kind of idealism extends as well to the ways in which they intend to go about completing their homestead projects. Just over a third of the *Countryside* respondents are sufficiently committed to sustainability ideals that they feel it is important to use hand tools rather than power tools in their farmstead work, and more than two out of five feel the same way about human or animal muscle power rather than petro-chemical or electrical power.

The issue of smallholder idealism raises one of the fundamental questions that inspired my investigation of the back-to-the-land experience in the first place: How far can a group of highly motivated, well-educated individuals go, *by themselves,* in constructing sustainable lifestyles? The evidence from the preceding pages and the current discussion is that the neohomesteaders' progress toward the practice of sustainability lies more in the realm of potential, rather than actual, performance, and the reasons are obvious. Back-to-the-landers are typically overcommitted and underfunded. The time-money dilemma I initially discussed in Chapter 2 pushes them, on the one hand, toward working full-time off their properties to purchase homesteading's soft-technology accessories but then having little time to implement their plans or, on the other hand, spending more time on their farmsteads but without the funds to buy the paraphernalia necessary for a productive smallholding. Given these compelling constraints, perhaps my characterization of smallholders as country underachievers is harsh. Rather than review the neohomesteaders' obvious deficiencies, my analysis might become more productive if it were to shift its emphasis to the back-to-the-landers' good intentions and to the kinds of public policy necessary to translate dreams into practice.

Public Policies for a Sustainable Future: A Preliminary Exploration

When a group or individuals with a worthy objective, like that of sustainability, come to a point where their own efforts seem only marginally to advance their cause, the reflexive course of action is to ask for government assistance. On the surface the case for government support of the back-to-the-landers appears transparent. It is not a matter of government having to coerce reluctant smallholders into environmentally responsible behavior; rather, it is a question of how to go about encouraging their already well-developed sense of ecological rectitude. But the precise character of government policy in aid of the neohomesteader is an issue that is more opaque than obvious.

The initial policy dilemma here is a conceptual one. Since the smallholders constitute anything but a homogeneous group, it is difficult to formulate a set of coherent policies that apply to all of them. Consequently, in the discussion that follows, I want to make a distinction between the back-to-the-landers who are primarily consumers of soft technologies, like solar water heaters and photovoltaic cells, but who are likely to continue their semisubsistence habits, and those who either are or who would like to be serious producers and make all or a substantial part of their living from their farmsteads. In order to sketch out policy options and strategies that apply to each of these two groups, I want to use as a point of departure the suggestions and complaints of two *Countryside* survey respondents who used the last page of their questionnaires to outline briefly the ways that government policy could either ease the burden of their attempts to practice sustainable lifestyles or help them become independent microproducers. The first comments come from a California woman in her mid-thirties and address themselves to the consumer-semisubsistence side of smallholding. "I would like to express my frustration at all the barriers government and society set up to make a low-consumption, self-sufficient lifestyle difficult and often more expensive; e.g., I would dearly love to walk and ride my bicycle much more than I do, but the roads and fast drivers in my area make that very dangerous. We would love to have solar power, but it is extremely expensive, and tax laws encourage debt and overconsumption; and I could give many, many more examples."

The absence of urban amenities like walking and bicycle paths paralleling the typical two-lane country blacktops demonstrates the underdeveloped character of much of rural America, but regardless of their conservation virtues, bike pathways have likely not even made the low priority lists of most county boards of supervisors.[2] The solar power on the California homesteader's wish list, however, is far from an impractical request. Tax breaks and low-interest loans are probably the best candidates for providing the assistance and the incentives for back-to-the-landers to move ahead with long-delayed kitchen-table projects, and in the process removing the "extremely expensive" label from most soft technologies. If the neohomesteaders were to receive investment credits or deductions against their incomes for the costs of buying and installing gray-water-recycling systems, composting toilets, photovoltaic cells, and retrofitted superinsulation, a resurvey of the *Countryside* readers within a few years would almost certainly find significant increases in their soft-technology adoption scores. This conjecture, however, is not entirely speculative. The Carter administration's policy of giving tax incentives for the installation of energy-conserving technologies serves as a precedent. Barry Rosenberg, for example, has a bank of photovoltaic cells lashed to the top of a thirty-foot poplar tree to the side of his and Cathe's house. The cells, purchased and installed with assistance from the Carter programs, provide the Rosenberg residence with its only source of electricity.

Subsidizing the purchase and installation costs for a variety of farmstead improvement projects is about as far as most back-to-the-landers would expect the government to go in supporting their individual versions of smallholding. Even if the earth were to move beneath the feet of the agricultural establishment and small-scale producers were to find themselves with the opportunity to earn a living, most back-to-the-landers would likely be content to continue their semisubsistent ways, bartering blueberries for eggs and commuting to city jobs. At the same time, however, it would not be surprising to see significant percentages of each of the smallholder types gravitate toward the microfarmer way of making a country living if they had the opportunity to do so. After all, many neohomesteaders tolerate less-than-ideal jobs so they can spend their off-hours working on their properties. If the opportunity were to arise for smallholders to spend most of their time on their properties, making their living by growing a cash crop with a stable market value (and, as I noted in Chapter 1, most would be happy to do so), many back-to-the-landers might see a definite advantage in moving, for example, from country romantics or weekenders to microfarmers.

A precondition, however, for back-to-the-landers becoming serious farmers would be a fundamental restructuring of the agricultural commodities markets. Few back-to-the-landers are attracted by the frenetic work schedules of microfarmers who grow a variety of specialty crops that they aggressively market to prospective buyers. If, however, the agricultural marketplace were structured in such a way that the large-scale corporate farmers were no longer able to take advantage of economies of scale, microfarmers practicing sustainable agriculture could more casually enter the marketplace with their smaller harvests and still receive a fair return. Since this scenario has factory farmers and smallholders playing on a level playing field, the immediate question is, What kinds of policy can even up the odds between large- and small-scale producers? A starting point for answering this question comes from comments written by a forty-three-year-old male homesteader from Missouri on the last page of his returned *Countryside* questionnaire: "We need less government regulation of small farms. We need tax breaks for small farms to encourage people to leave unproductive cities and return to small farms. We need more widely disseminated information about sustainable agriculture. We need *effective* research in coordinated diversification for small farms. Availability of information is a critical need."

Before I begin to draw out the implications of the Missouri homesteader's policy prescriptions, I want more clearly to identify whom I am intending as the beneficiaries of a restructured marketplace. In the following analysis I use small farmer, smallholder, and microfarmer interchangeably. In an agricultural marketplace where corporate growers lose their traditional advantages, microproducers and small farmers are likely to find they have much in common in their commitment to stewardship principles. As a consequence, any change in agricultural policy that encourages sustainable practice will tend to make natural allies of small farmers from the alternative-agriculture movement and back-to-the-land microfarmers,[3] even though the small farmers' properties may extend up to 160 acres, while the microproducers work on only a few acres. These diverse groups of small-scale producers would, however, share a common policy objective: having farm owner-operators make a comfortable living on their own properties through the use of sustainable farming practices.

The Missouri back-to-the-lander does not specify what he means by "less regulation of small farms." A reasonable inference, however, is that he is saying that, as things stand, small-scale producers have to play by the same rules as industrial farmers and that, in the process, government regulation either prohibits them from selling their produce directly to consumers or raises the costs of production to the point where they are unable to make a living. For example, an ordinance common to many localities across North America forbids farmers to sell raw or unpasteurized milk to individual buyers. Capital-intensive dairy farmers are naturally not interested in selling milk one gallon at a time, since they make their money delivering large quantities of unprocessed milk to commercial dairies that pasteurize, homogenize, and package it for home and store purchase. The large-scale producers and processors have adapted to the regulatory environment by building the costs of regulation into their selling prices, while the regulations intended to protect consumers effectively lock marginal producers out of the marketplace.

Exempting small farmers from the regulations that apply to agribusinesses would certainly open a window of opportunity for microproducers. Nevertheless, the ability to cope with government regulation is only one very small benefit from a rather lengthy list of advantages that corporate agriculture has over the small farmer. Many of these benefits take the form of tax policies that favor large growers. These tax breaks include depreciation allowances and investment tax credits. In general, government tax policy subsidizes the farmer who relies on high-cost machinery and expensive breeding stock, rather than the labor-intensive microfarmer who practices sustainable agriculture. Consequently, it comes as no surprise that the Missouri back-to-the-lander wants "tax breaks for small farms to encourage people to leave unproductive cities and return to small farms." While the "unproductive cities" part of the smallholder's prescription maybe be problematic, it stands to reason that if factory farmers lost their tax breaks and were even penalized for their unsustainable farming practices, and if in the process the lost benefits were transferred to small farmers, then the tilt of the marketplace would start to move in the direction of sustainable smallholders.

In what precise ways, however, might agricultural policy directly support the small, sustainable producer? Perhaps one approach would be to turn agricultural policy completely on its head. The logic that drives current policy is the goal of increased production through energy- and capital-intensive farming.[4] To compensate factory farmers for their investment expenses, as well as for low commodity prices attributable to overproduction, government offers a series of tax breaks and subsidies. These policy mechanisms place microfarmers at a disadvantage, since they rely more on muscle power than on petrochemical energy—they are not likely to have large tractors on which to claim deductions. But if farm policy can underwrite capital investment, it can also credit labor, since the substitution of renewable solar, wind, and muscle power for nonrenewable fossil-fuel energy is a policy objective (sustainability) government would presumably want to pursue. One could forecast a situation where a microfarmer, for example, grows $50,000 worth of produce on a labor-intensive smallholding. Against the labor investment in growing the farmstead crop, the smallholder could be allowed to deduct a certain percentage, perhaps 20 percent of gross income, as part of a net income calculation. Smallholders would have no invoice to show an Internal Revenue Service auditor, as they would from the purchase of capital equipment, but the labor-intensive quality of small farms could be verified in much the same way that many states now certify organic producers.

Transferring the tax advantages of fossil-fuel-intensive corporate agriculture to labor-intensive small farmers is one significant step toward the policy objective of sustainable agriculture. But, as the Missouri smallholder would surely agree, tax breaks are of no value unless one has an income from which to make a deduction. Public policy for a sustainable agriculture, therefore, has to be directed toward ensuring a fair and secure income for the microfarmers who subscribe to a conservation ethic. One reason why small producers have historically found it difficult to earn a sustaining income in the agricultural marketplace is chronic overproduction on the part of industrial farmers, a surplus encouraged by current agricultural policy. This overproduction drives down commodity prices to the point where vulnerable small farmers cannot meet the cost of production, while government subsidies and tax breaks protect the corporate growers from the logic of the marketplace. A prerequisite, then, for raising the income of small-scale producers is the regulation of production.

In order to calculate the effect of production controls, one does not have to rely on the hypotheticals of computer modeling. Precedent for regulating production to support the small producer already exists. Since the 1930s the federal government, through the Department of Agriculture, has kept alive the small-farm tradition for at least one group of growers. Intriguingly, the group in question is tobacco farmers, whose receipt of benevolence dates back to New Deal planners' attempts to keep farmers on the land by enacting legislation as a counterweight to the power of the tobacco cartels. Although the tobacco programs are currently threatened by tobacco companies' use of more and cheaper foreign leaf, they provide a policy framework that can be applied to other crops and to the objective of raising small-farm income. Eric Bates, the investigative editor of *Southern Exposure*, succinctly summarizes the basic elements of the tobacco-support programs:

> First, the U.S. Department of Agriculture restricts the number of farmers who can grow tobacco by handing out quotas—in effect an exclusive federal license to raise the crop. Second the U.S.D.A. restricts how much tobacco farmers may grow each year based on how much tobacco companies say they will buy, and it provides loans to process and store any surplus leaf. Limiting tobacco supplies artificially raises prices, eliminating the need for direct government subsidies. In addition to protecting prices, the government also grades the leaf, collects and analyzes market information and provides funds for research and education. It's centralized planning on a remarkable scale, it guarantees tobacco farmers prices well above what they receive for other crops.[5]

While the tobacco support programs have been effective in keeping small farmers on the land, it is still an open question whether the tobacco farmers are necessarily sustainable producers, or as sustainable as they could be. Since they farm on a relatively small scale and on their own land, one has to presume that their methods of operation are much more environmentally friendly than those of corporate producers who operate as absentee farmers. Still, production controls by themselves provide no guarantees that their beneficiaries will be model growers. There is, however, a policy option that gives producers a direct incentive to practice sustainable agriculture, while at the same time it complements the production-control objective of pushing commodity prices high enough to keep small-scale producers on the land. The policy instrument is full-cost pricing, and it is based on the distinction between a product's price and its cost.[6]

Application of the price-cost distinction to late-twentieth-century agriculture leads to the conclusion that North Americans eat relatively cheap food that comes at a very high cost, and that the actual costs of low-priced food are not paid at the checkout counter. These costs start with the cafeteria of benefits made available to corporate farmers. There are as well the costs of environmental degradation that come from highly mechanized, energy-intensive monoculture: topsoil loss, salinization of irrigated farmland, aquifer depletion, the destruction of wetlands, and groundwater contamination from pesticide, herbicide, and fertilizer residues. Groundwater contamination, for example, as well as indiscriminate chemical farming, takes its toll in rising health-care costs for farmers and farm laborers. Then, at the distribution end, there are the transportation costs: highway maintenance to keep trucks, many of them refrigerated, moving over the nation's interstates. The fuel bill to move food is a substantial one; it takes three times as much energy or more to transport, process, and package food than to grow it.[7] And these costs do not take into account the social costs of corporate agriculture: the spiral of farm foreclosures that leads to the abandonment of small towns and sends displaced farmers to metropolitan areas in search of jobs that may have migrated to Mexico, all placing increasing burdens on mental health, welfare, and employment services.

Orthodox economists are by no means unaware of the price-cost distinction, though, in order not to inhibit either their theoretical models or the everyday functioning of the marketplace, they label the costs not internalized in prices "externalities." The essence of full-cost pricing, then, is to use government as an activist mediator in the marketplace in order to force producers to internalize the costs that have been treated as externalities. The critical questions, of course, are how to go about estimating the costs of corporate agriculture and where in the cost chain to impose the impact fees or green taxes that complete the full-cost equation. Many of the costs of factory farming are, unfortunately, inestimable. How does one place a price on the lives of Mexican farm laborers who die each year from pesticide poisoning while harvesting tomatoes destined for midwinter Minneapolis salads?[8] Nevertheless, it is possible to calculate expenses involved in any number of reclamation projects, from wetlands restoration to topsoil regeneration, and estimates can be made as well on the contribution of petrochemical farming to health-care costs. The dollar value of rebuilding communities damaged by corporate agriculture can also be factored into the full-cost equations.

But the question remains how to find an uncluttered, parsimonious way to pass these costs back to producers. Assigning to specific corporate actors degrees of responsibility for pollution and then billing them for the damage could be a cumbersome and contentious process, with lawyers on both sides the chief beneficiaries. If, however, the government agency charged with recovering the quantifiable costs of factory farming were to levy impact fees in the form of green taxes directly on the petrochemicals that make large-scale farming possible and that are the easily identifiable causes of environmental degradation, then full-cost pricing could have a chance to become an effective policy instrument. Full-cost pricing, naturally, would mean a sharp increase in taxes on gasoline and diesel fuels, pesticides, herbicides, fungicides, and synthetic fertilizers. These taxes on agricultural inputs in turn would have the effect of sharply raising the costs of production for factory farmers. Corporate producers, of course, would have little choice but to pass their increased costs on to consumers. As a consequence, the prices on supermarket shelves would go up proportionately, to reflect the actual costs of production.

It is at this point that back-to-the-land microfarmers and other small-scale producers reenter the discussion. Since small farmers employ labor-intensive soft technologies rather than energy-intensive hard technologies, they would have the advantage over the factory farmers in a restructured agricultural marketplace. Whether at farmers' markets or in supermarket coolers, the price for microfarmers' produce should consistently undercut those of corporate farmers, since the microfarmers' taxes would be lower. Of course green taxes would give corporate producers every incentive to cut their costs by switching away from fossil fuels. Their primary alternative, however, is muscle power in the form of human or animal labor. The relatively high cost of labor in the North American market would likely guarantee that smallholders working their property with their families would continue to be more efficient agriculturists than their corporate counterparts.

Full-cost pricing has the potential to demonstrate that government can make far-reaching and progressive changes without reflexively falling back on the paternalistic and inefficient programs that characterize command-style bureaucracies—programs like the well-intentioned work of the New Deal's Division of Subsistence Homesteads I briefly discussed in the Introduction, which failed in its attempt to establish back-to-the-land communities in the 1930s. But, as with any major social change, green taxes on agriculture would set in motion a series of dislocations that require corresponding policy adjustments. The most immediate and serious repercussions from green taxes would be a rise in food prices—an ecologically correct policy change, though anything but a politically correct one with regard to a populace accustomed to low food prices. The increased food costs would be particularly difficult for low-income families who spend a relatively high percentage of their disposable incomes on food. Consequently, it would be critical to counterbalance the rise in food costs with corresponding reductions in income taxes specifically targeted to provide relief to the working poor. Increased revenues through the green taxes in turn would compensate for the reduced revenue from low-income earners and the increased costs of food stamps and income maintenance for those unable to work away from their homes. Since middle classes as well would demand relief from higher food prices, it would be advisable to phase the green taxes in over a period of perhaps ten to twenty years in order to give both producers and consumers time to experiment and align their behavior more closely with sustainability principles. Then, as both consuming and producing habits evolved, the green taxes would naturally have to be recalibrated to maintain revenue flows. The purpose of the impact fees, however, is not so much to raise tax revenue as it is to encourage sustainable behavior. In the process, however, those households that were serious about sustainability would be rewarded with increased amounts of disposable income.

One threat to the plausibility of full-cost pricing, however, is critical. With the globalization of agriculture, the ultimate control over food production and distribution resides not at the national, but at the transnational, level. Low-priced grain, fruits and vegetables, and meat from all over the world could flood North American markets and destroy smallholder agriculture. In anticipation of this potential challenge to sustainable agriculture, Paul Hawken suggests replacing the Most Favored Nation tariff status, which the United States reserves for its preferred trading partners, with a Most Sustainable Nation tariff status.[9] A trading partner, then, that was willing to ensure that its producers followed sustainable agricultural practices (environmentally friendly technologies, reasonable farm-labor wages, and respect for human rights) would have access to U.S. markets. Since the practice of sustainable agriculture, along with long-distance shipping costs, would raise the price of foreign produce substantially, North American smallholders should be able to maintain their competitiveness. To the extent that the Most Sustainable Nation tariffs were seen to violate the free-trade provisions of international treaties like

GATT and NAFTA, the United States and Canada, in order to maintain their commitments to sustainability, would have to justify their noncompliance in terms of compelling national interests, as well as the welfare of the planet.

It is possible that the Most Sustainable Nation tariffs could remove the profitability from a Third World agriculture that relies on the application of chemicals banned in North America and wages calculated to do no more than reproduce a subservient labor force. If, however, sustainability requirements in the North were to cripple export agriculture in the underdeveloped South, the beneficiaries would be the masses of rural and urban Third World poor. With the dissolution of plantation-style agriculture, peasants would be free to turn their attention to growing basic grains in order to address the long-standing caloric deficit from which they and the urban poor suffer, rather than producing luxury crops for First World consumers. In addition, without the power and wealth that come from the ownership of cash-crop export operations, Third World elites would no longer have automatic access to the resources of oppression (paramilitary death squads, cooperation from armed forces, and extensive lines of credit). Consequently, in underdeveloped countries whose economies are heavily dependent on export agriculture, the loss of North American and Western European markets could create an opening for democratic movements, movements that in the past have been routinely crushed by the planter class.

The policy analysis here has come some distance, as it has moved from the Missouri back-to-the-lander's call for tax breaks for small farmers to the possibility of Third World revolutions linked to the demise of cash-crop, export agriculture. Agricultural policy is obviously a complex, multifaceted subject, but my intent here is a modest one: to make a contribution to the discussion on policies for a sustainable agriculture rather than to offer a definitive prescription. The organizational details of policy proposals are not as important as the clarity of their objectives. In this case it is critical that the objectives do not deviate from the goal of giving small-scale producers the ability to support themselves and their families on their own land, with every incentive to practice sustainable agriculture.

This discussion of the policy prerequisites for keeping sustainable producers on the land has not exhausted all of the Missouri smallholder's demands on government for support of the smallholding movement. His

remaining concerns are dissemination of information and effective research on sustainable agriculture. Working through government contracts
and land-grant universities, agricultural researchers over the past century
have been almost totally preoccupied with increasing production on en-
ergy- and capital-intensive farms. At the same time, research and development on low-input sustainable agriculture has had to survive within the
crevices of the agricultural research establishment. While the accomplishments of sustainable agricultural research are far from inconsiderable, its
resources are dwarfed by those devoted to corporate agriculture. Magazines like *Countryside* attempt to fill this resource gap by serving as information exchanges in which small producers can share anecdotal information about their homestead projects. But *Countryside* cannot completely
substitute for scientific journals that publish systematic studies of experiments in sustainable agriculture. If elements of production controls and
full-cost pricing policies ever worked their way through the legislative process and became law, one would expect a concomitant shift in research
priorities from large-scale to small farming. Without a fundamental restructuring of North American agriculture, however, the Missouri smallholder would be wise to keep his *Countryside* subscription, since *Countryside,* the *Mother Earth News,* and *Organic Gardening* remain the primary
sources of readily available information on alternative agriculture.

This brief excursion into the world of policy analysis has shown, perhaps
more than anything else, that government policy can have well-defined
and predictable outcomes. In this sense, a case can be made that agricultural policy over the past half century has been very effective—though
its effectiveness has been perverse. Government policy directs research-
and-development monies, investment credits, and infrastructure subsidies
all toward the goal of increasing production. In spite of periodic attempts
to control production, these policies have not only increased production
but have created a chronic overproduction problem. The costs of overproduction based on capital-intensive, petrochemical farming are obvious:
an unsustainable agriculture that is exhausting the natural capital on
which the earth's communities depend for long-term health and prosperity. There is, however, in this disheartening conclusion one very small
thread of optimism that can be tied to the prospect of sustainable agriculture and sustainable rural communities. If current agricultural policy can
be such a powerful force, though not always by intention, in the creation

of unsustainable farming practices, then there is reason to believe that an optimum mix of incentives and controls can create the necessary conditions for the regeneration of the countryside.

In the meantime, while the smallholders wait for action from Washington or from a state capital, they will continue to enjoy country life and, when time and money allow, make incremental improvements on their working versions of the sustainable homestead. But there are no policy incentives to keep them on the land; rather, back-the-landers work against a number of disincentives just to stay where they are. Going further by trying to practice self-reliance only complicates their lives. As the California survey respondent complained, "I would like to express my frustration at all the barriers government and society set up to make a low-consumption, self-sufficient lifestyle difficult and more expensive." And W. O. Robinson, president of the citizen's action committee trying to keep a toxic waste dump out of its Texas community, reaffirmed the California homesteader's sentiments when he wrote on the back of his returned questionnaire, "I feel we are fighting our own tax money with private funds."

Public policies are built around incentives and disincentives directed toward predefined behavioral objectives. By the very fact of their going back to the land, the neohomesteaders demonstrate their imperviousness to prevailing public policy. It is obvious that something other than raw economic interest motivates the back-to-the-landers. The commitment to a particular quality of life that involves country living and the pursuit of a sustainable lifestyle, however elusive, appears to be the best candidate for the primary force that drives smallholder behavior. In this chapter's, and the book's, concluding section, I want to examine more closely the less tangible aspects of the neohomesteaders' lives and draw out of the analysis a final commentary on the back-to-the-landers as new pioneers.

The Quality of Back-to-the-Country Life: A Perspective on the Search for a Sustainable Future

From an outsider's vantage point, and from a point of view that emphasizes the technical dimension of sustainability, a sympathetic observer would need little justification to raise concerns about the quality of back-to-the-land life. Chronic frustration is as much a part of smallholding as chickens and gardening. Most neohomesteaders simply do not have the resources to implement their self-reliant ideals. They are caught in the time-money dilemma that either leaves them without the funds to purchase the solar collectors and purebred goats absent from their farmsteads or ties them to a full-time job that does not give them the time to install and maintain the collectors or care for the goats. For the majority of the back-to-the-landers there are few short-term solutions to their time-money predicaments. And though the public policy prescriptions designed to encourage sustainable behavior may possess compelling logic and generous quantities of common sense, the neohomesteaders know their mortgages will almost certainly be paid off before Congress gets around to rewarding their potential contributions to the nation's welfare. But in addition to these generalized frustrations are the particular aggravations of personal and family relationships that sidetrack them from the pursuit of their homestead dreams. The following comments on the back of a *Countryside* questionnaire by a survey respondent in her late twenties and a year into a new marriage illustrate how at least in one case multiple pressures conspired to undermine the potential satisfaction of the homesteading experience:

> Before we were married my then future spouse shared in the responsibilities of the work at home and caring for the animals—and he made a promise to continue doing so. The *week* after we married, all help stopped. He expects me to earn as much money as I can possibly squeeze out of my company, which means putting in ten to twelve hours a day *plus* keep house, care for animals, garden, etc. I constantly feel exhausted and pressured to do more. I should have known better than to marry a city boy.
>
> I would *like* to be completely self-sufficient, but my current situation prevents that. When the land is paid for and marital problems resolved, I could work toward that goal, but currently I simply do not have the *time* that being self-sufficient requires.

Even though the *Countryside* reader laments the distance between her performance and her expectations, she has achieved a remarkable degree of self-reliance. On her ten-acre farmstead she has, in addition to a garden and chickens, a fish pond, goats, pigs, sheep, fruit trees, and workhorses. She reports that her property produces 75 percent of the food that she and her husband eat. Yet, in the survey, she chooses "fairly unsatisfied" as her response to the "progress toward self-reliant living" question, as well as checking the "not too happy" category for the general-happiness question. Naturally, much of her discontent can be traced to her relationship with her husband, which she characterizes as fairly unsatisfactory.

While this *Countryside* reader's comments do reflect how personal relationships and job constraints can come between smallholders and the image of the good life to which they attach themselves, the respondent's reaction to the obstacles in her life is definitely atypical of the overall satisfaction profile from the *Countryside* survey. Generally, the *Countryside* respondents report high levels of personal happiness and satisfaction, in spite of underachieving on their sustainability goals. More than nine out of ten (94 percent) reported being either very or pretty happy and either very or fairly satisfied with their family life, the area where they live, and their current housing (96 to 91 percent).

Paradoxically, the unhappy but relatively overachieving *Countryside* subscriber provides insight into why the rest of the survey respondents are positive about their lives even though their farmsteads remain incomplete versions of their homestead dreams. It is the dream itself, rather than the imperfect reality, that appears to animate this back-to-the-lander, as well as her fellow travelers. The *Countryside* respondent offers here no hint of compromise. Predictable counsel from an advice columnist would suggest she at least partially withdraw from her homesteading obsessions and that she could receive total relief with a complete exit from country life. But though her current distress is directly related to her commitment to smallholding, it is in the realization of her ideals that she eventually expects to find the kind of fulfillment that most of the *Countryside* respondents report that they presently experience. Marriage, time, and money all conspire to undermine her peace of mind, but there is in the respondent's comments no deviation from the belief that the ultimate source of her future satisfaction will be found with a life back on the land.

The kind of gratification that this back-to-the-lander expects to receive from homesteading and that now comes to her in insufficient quantities is reflected in the thoughts written by another survey respondent at the end of his returned questionnaire. His remarks confirm that it is not so much that a life in the country is free from pain as it is that the experience of mindful back-to-the-land living can counterbalance episodes of turmoil. In this particular case, the *Countryside* reader explains how events far removed from his smallholding and with no immediate personal effect can still challenge his peace of mind.

> The 1992 presidential campaign has been very disillusioning. We have become a nation that spends nine months trashing the candidates—constant exposure to examples of lying, cheating, etc., and then one of them becomes our leader.
>
> It makes those times when I am in my garden watching a cold front move in, or in the goat pasture watching a full moon rise, the only times when the world seems pure.

The outside world may contrive to sabotage their tranquillity, leaving them alienated from its impenetrable processes, but the back-to-the-landers can always take consolation in returning to the concrete reality of their farmsteads. Whether the frustrations in their lives are immediate (unhealed relationships like the precarious marriage of the smallholder and her "city boy" husband) or the aggravations are distant (a political system immune from common decency, for example), a mindful apprehension of the bounded world of their smallholdings is potentially available to the neohomesteaders simply by stepping out their backdoors and leaving the television news or a recalcitrant husband behind.

While not discounting their regenerative power, it is tempting to characterize these mindfulness interludes as episodes of escapism, confirmation of the reclusive strain that runs through the center of the back-to-the-land movement. The physical encounter with the feel, the odor, the sight, the sound of a smallholding does seem to transport the back-to-the-landers onto a different frequency from that on which the rest of us operate. But these experiences by themselves are not so much evidence of atavistic behavior as they are what inspire the neohomesteaders to go back to the land in the first place, and then help them stay there. It is here, on the issue of motivation, that I want to reconnect the smallholders to the issue of sustainability and to raise the question of the back-to-the-landers' status as new pioneers one last time.

Sustainability is both a technical and a spiritual enterprise—using "spiritual" in its broadest sense. On the one hand, it is a matter of attaining relative self-reliance through the application of soft technologies. It is in the technical dimension that the back-to-the-landers have difficulty qualifying as new pioneers. Sustainability, however, is a state of mind as much as or more than a matter of practice. What, however, are the defining characteristics of a sustainable attitude? The most obvious trait of a sustainable style of life is commitment to the ideal of reducing economic demand and to a related sense of "enoughness."[10] By extension, then, if one does not receive one's primary sources of gratification from material accumulation, one is presumably redirecting personal energy into areas that are at a minimum environmentally benign. Here is where the back-to-the-landers move from underachievers to potential new pioneers. An uncomplicated life on the land, not the acquisition of status, power, or wealth, is what inspires them. Furthermore, the very activity, smallholding, that leads to their sense of fulfillment, also makes a positive, direct contribution to the sustainability project itself.

The back-to-the-landers of course are not paragons of sustainability virtues. They practice anything but lives of pastoral asceticism, as they accumulate a collection of consumer-society accessories from microwave ovens to chain saws. In addition, to the extent that their behavior actually reflects sustainability norms, they lead decidedly unbalanced lives. At its most general level sustainability entails a shift in the direction of one's personal energy not only away from a preoccupation with material consumption but also toward the development of a wide range of relationships, from personal, family, neighborhood, and community relationships to relationships with nature, and the supernatural, and with ideas (the life of the mind). While smallholders do possess an extraordinary sense of pragmatism (as I reported in Chapters 2 and 3) as they balance the multiple demands on a finite amount of time against their commitment to self-reliance and voluntary simplicity, their primary source of gratification remains the private pleasure of enjoying nature on their individual homesteads. But in their relative neglect of community relationships they ignore potential sources of solidarity for the defense and promotion of their chosen way of life. Nevertheless, in spite of its reclusive character, latter-day homesteading does constitute a break, however partial and imperfect, from the mainstream consumer culture. If a prerequisite for a sustainable future is a fundamental, society-wide change in consciousness, regardless of how narrow, the back-to-the-landers have traveled at least partway down that road.

Any discussion of the preconditions for a sustainable future almost inevitably returns to quality-of-life issues. The tenor of these discussions is rarely dispassionate. The residual fears that sustainability could mean a decline in the overall quality of life are difficult to suppress. These anxieties in turn raise fundamental questions about what constitutes a satisfying quality of life. Fortunately, it is at this point that the analysis can at least temporarily move from the speculative to a base of solid social science research. Few aspects of social life over the past several decades have been studied more than personal happiness and satisfaction. Armed with questionnaire and interview schedules, sociologists, psychologists, anthropologists, and even economists have tracked down prospective respondents from all walks of life, every income level, and a variety of cultures in order to ask variations on one basic question: How happy are you?

Interestingly, the results of the separate studies manifest a rough consensus in their core findings. Overall, income and material accumulation are at best marginal predictors of happiness. It is not so much that the affluent are not happy, just that on average they are likely to have no more than a very small chance of being happier than the poor; and among the smallholders themselves, as I reported in Chapter 2, there is an inverse relationship between personal happiness and income. In predicting those individuals and groups who will have higher scores on quality-of-life indicators, however, the kinds of relationships that reinforce sustainability (in the neohomesteaders' case, the solitary enjoyment of the natural world on their smallholdings) are the best predictors of personal happiness and satisfaction.[11] If, then, these kinds of relationships are what predict happiness, independent of one's purchasing power, then practicing sustainable behavior, whether on a smallholding or in sustainable cities, has a chance not only to preserve life on the planet but to enhance it as well.

Going back-to-the-land is only one path on the journey to a sustainable society. The neohomesteaders, however, do demonstrate that a large and diverse group of families and individuals can make at least a partial break with the prevailing commercial culture and then find fulfillment by commitment to ideals like voluntary simplicity and right livelihood and trying to live up to them. Their failures can be attributed not only to their own humanity but also to the absence of public policies calculated to encourage their good intentions. In the final analysis, the study of the back-to-the-landers suggests that if and when we or our children arrive at some approximation of a sustainable future, it will be the creation of two interacting forces: (1) a wide cross section of the general population discovering that both their immediate and ultimate well-being depends on the quality of their relationships rather than the quantity of their possessions, and (2) government policy makers (a) enacting legislation that withdraws subsidies from those whose behavior jeopardizes sustainability and (b) rewarding and facilitating the idealism of citizens, like the back-to-the-landers, who commit themselves to a provident way of life.

NOTES

Introduction

1. The estimate of one million back-to-the-landers comes from Terry A. Simmons, "But We Must Cultivate Our Garden: Twentieth-Century Pioneering in Rural British Columbia" (Ph.D. diss., University of Minnesota, 1979). The demographic shifts affecting both rural and urban America are covered in Lorraine Garkovich, *Population and Community in Rural America* (Westport, Conn.: Greenwood Press, 1989). In Chapter 1, "Conventional Radicals: Back-to-the-Land Profiles," I treat the ebbs and flows of the movement back to the country-side in more detail.

2. The *Mother Earth News* quotations, in the noted paragraph and that which follows, are from John Shuttleworth, "The Plowboy Interview," *Mother Earth News*, no. 2 (March 1970): 6–7. John Shuttleworth's publishing venture was inspired in part by the appearance of the *Whole Earth Catalog*s in 1968. Though the *Whole Earth Catalog*s were early supporters of the *Mother Earth News*, their enthusiasm soon waned. As *Whole Earth Catalog* editor Steward Brand explained ("*The Mother Earth News*," in *The Next Whole Earth Catalog*, ed. Stewart Brand [New York: Point/Random House, 1980], 295):

> As the beginnings of the magazine are somewhat connected with *Whole Earth*'s early success, I have a mix of feelings about it that might be better expressed by frankness than by faint praise. No one we know that actually lives in the country uses the thing . . . Trust wilts amid the overwhelming ad space and uncritically enthusiastic articles ("Recycled Floor Mats!") and corpone language (energy writer Wilson Clark still winces about an article of his that *Mother Earth News* "translated into babytalk").
>
> On the other hand, founder John Shuttleworth's heart is mostly in the right place environmentally. The "Plowboy" interviews often are quite good and with non-celebrities of real interest. There's a conversational interaction that encourages readers to write and get published, often for the first time in their lives. Some of their ideas work. And there's that itchy audience. Solar designer Steve Baer noted, "When *Co-Evolution* [*Quarterly*, *Whole Earth Catalog*'s quarterly journal, now *Whole Earth Review*] publishes something about Zomeworks, all I get is a good feeling. When *Mother Earth News* does, I get a lot of orders.

While Brand's comments are not without merit, I would have to say, as an interested third party, that if the *Mother Earth News* discourse at times devolves into "baby talk," then there are also times when the *Whole Earth Review* struggles to escape adolescent pranksterism—with theme issues and articles like "Flying Saucers in San Francisco" (July 1985), "The Fringes of Reason: Strange Mythologies Beyond the Edge of Science" (Fall 1986), and "Waking Up the Monkey: The Dawn of Recreative Tree Climbing" (Summer 1994). In the *Whole Earth Re-*

view's twenty-fifth-anniversary issue (Summer 1993), an inside-cover picture of a graying editor Brand carried the following cutline: "Brand in 1993; post-maturely juvenile." Nevertheless, from my point of view, both publications provide useful, and even fascinating, information and ideas, though both can lapse into silliness.

3. Ron Eyerman and Andrew Jamison, in *Social Movements: A Cognitive Approach* (University Park: Pennsylvania State University Press, 1991), emphasize the critical role of intellectuals in social movements. The back-to-the-land movement has a well-developed intellectual tradition, with periodicals and a wide range of first-person accounts of the homesteading experience. In their advocacy of a back-to-the-land way of life, the movement's intellectuals perform, in Eyerman and Jamison's characterization, a role common to social movement intellectuals in general: "a challenge to the dominant assumptions of the social order, making problematic the self-image of societies" (165).

4. Social movements are far from monolithic entities. As they evolve, they typically split into factions and submovements, with overlapping interests and priorities. For a history of the environmental movement that recognizes the back-to-the-land movement as one of its many constitutive submovements, see Robert Gottlieb, *Forcing the Spring: The Transformation of the American Environmental Movement* (Washington, D.C.: Island Press, 1993), 98–105.

5. This phrase is from Martin Luther King Jr., cited in Mark Dowie, *Losing Ground: American Environmentalism at the Close of the Twentieth Century* (Cambridge: MIT Press, 1995), 254.

6. From Julian Bond, ed., *The Papers of Thomas Jefferson* (Princeton: Princeton University Press, 1950–), 11:682, cited in David E. Shi, *The Simple Life: Plain Living and High Thinking in American Culture* (New York: Oxford University Press, 1985), 77–78. For an overview of agrarian thought, see James A. Montmarquet, *The Idea of Agrarianism: From Hunter-Gatherer to Agrarian Radical in Western Culture* (Moscow: University of Idaho Press, 1989).

7. Shi, *The Simple Life*, 145.

8. The Berry quotations are from *The Gift of Good Land: Further Essays Cultural and Agricultural* (San Francisco: North Point Press, 1981), 116, 115, 105, 195. Berry's classic critique of American society is *The Unsettling of America: Culture and Agriculture*, 3d ed. (San Francisco: Sierra Club, 1996). Recent collections of Berry's essays are *What Are People For?* (San Francisco: North Point Press, 1990), *Sex, Economy, Freedom, and Community* (New York: Pantheon, 1993), and *Another Turn of the Crank* (Washington, D.C.: Counterpoint, 1995).

9. Garkovich, *Population and Community in Rural America*, 85.

10. My characterization here and in the following paragraphs of the country-life and back-to-the-land movements draws on Stanford J. Layton, *To No Privileged Class: The Rationalization of Homesteading and Rural Life in the Early Twentieth-Century American West* (Provo, Utah: Brigham Young University, Charles Redd Center for Western Studies, 1988).

11. See Layton, *To No Privileged Class*, for an extended treatment of the Country Life Commission. Though the Country Life Commission was concerned with the cartel-like quality of early-twentieth-century grain trading, there were 36 firms in 1921 accounting for 85 percent of U.S. wheat exports; by the late 1970s just six companies controlled the same percentage of exports. Vandana Shiva, "TNCs Threaten Third World Farmers and Health Through Free Trade," *Third World Resurgence*, April 1991, 16.

12. Arthur Markley Judy, "From the Study to the Farm: A Personal Experience," *Atlantic Monthly*, May 1915, 607–8, cited in Layton, *To No Privileged Class*, 52–53.

13. Layton, *To No Privileged Class*, 58–59.

14. *Congressional Record*, 64th Cong., 1st sess., 1130, cited in Layton, *To No Privileged Class*, 68.

15. U.S. Department of Agriculture, *Statement on Farm Population Trends*, prepared for the Bureau of Agricultural Economics by Conrad Taenber (Washington, D.C.: Government Printing Office, 1940), 6, cited in Layton, *To No Privileged Class*, 39.

16. The phrase "historic homesickness" comes from Thorstein Veblen, one of Tugwell's professors. Rexford Tugwell, *Political Science Quarterly* 75 (1960): 261, cited in Shi, *The Simple Life*, 234.

17. A description and analysis of the New Deal homestead program can be found in Paul K. Conkin, *Tomorrow a New World: The New Deal Community Programs* (Ithaca: Cornell University Press, 1959).

18. Jeremy Rifkin, in his book *The End of Work: The Decline of the Global Labor Force* (New York: J. P. Tarcher/Putnam, 1994), attributes most of the job loss to technological innovation—material advances that, theoretically, should make us all richer rather than poorer.

19. An overview of the Roper Organization survey can be found in Peter Stisser, "A Deeper Shade of Green," *American Demographics*, March 1994, 24–29.

20. Uwe Poerksen, *Plastic Words: The Tyranny of a Modular Language*, trans. Jutta Mason and David Cayley (University Park: Pennsylvania State University Press, 1995).

21. In David Cayley, "Plastic Words," Canadian Broadcasting Corporation IDEAS series transcript, February 4, 1993, 3.

22. World Commission on Environment and Development, *Our Common Future* (New York: Oxford University Press, 1987), 8.

23. Christopher Flavin and Nicholas Lenssen, *Power Surge: Guide to the Coming Energy Revolution* (New York: Norton, 1994), 40–41. Worldwide, fossil fuels supply 75 percent of total energy used. Flavin and Lenssen develop a scenario in which renewable sources provide 50 percent of energy needs by 2050. Using natural gas as a "bridge" fuel, they see a possible 73 percent reduction in coal use by 2025, along with a 20 percent reduction in the use of oil. This natural-gas transition period allows sufficient time for energy users to develop renewable-energy technologies, with the renewable-energy industry having, in 1993 dollars, revenues of $200 billion in 2025—twice the 1993 revenue of Exxon.

24. More precisely, the estimates for these necessary reductions are *per unit of industrial production*. Donella H. Meadows, Dennis L. Meadows, and Jorgen Randers, *Beyond the Limits: Confronting Global Collapse, Envisioning a Sustainable Future* (Post Mills, Vt.: Chelsea Green, 1992). Meadows and her coauthors' calculations raise the question of just how many people the earth can sustain, and at what level. In one effort to answer this question, Mathis Wackernagel and William Rees, in *Our Ecological Footprint: Reducing the Human Impact on the Earth* (Philadelphia: New Society, 1996), develop a methodological tool they call ecological footprint analysis. Rather than measure the carrying capacity of a particular ecosystem in relation to the impact of either actual or hypothetical populations, Wackernagel and Rees calculate how much land, in hectares, would be necessary to support one person, at various consumption levels. Translating this perspective into current worldwide aggregate demand on the earth's resources, the authors arrive at a required 9.5 billion hectares, considerably more than the 7.4 billion hectares of ecologically productive land actually available. The reason, of course, that the planet can tolerate a demand 30 percent over carrying capacity is the drawdown of nonrenewable resources. If, however, worldwide living standards were to rise to the level of those in North America (four to five hectares required per person), an additional two to three planets would be necessary to support the world's population. A population of eight to ten billion by the middle of the next century would naturally require "additional planets" if everyone were to receive his or her "fair share" of the earth's resources. If we are still limited to one planet in 2050, social and economic equity, as well as ecological sustainability, will require dramatically altered lifestyles—a reduction in demand by the rich of the Northern Hemisphere to enable the poor of the South to meet, and exceed, their basic minimum needs. Whether these changes will enhance or diminish the quality of life in the North is in part the subject matter of the pages that follow.

25. While I am confident that my definition of sustainability possesses generous quantities

of straightforward common sense, I must admit that in the popular and scholarly literature there exists little agreement on what sustainability actually means. The reason for this disagreement, however, is not that there are several sharply defined and competing definitions but that advocates of widely divergent ideological positions all express unqualified approval of the idea. Consequently, the conflict over the term's use is often subtle and a matter of divergent assumptions and working hypotheses. In the context of Third World development and underdevelopment, I have attempted to disentangle the contrary positions embedded in the plastic nature of sustainability. See Jeffrey C. Jacob and Beverley A. Suderman, "Alternative Visions of Progress: The Multiple Meanings of Sustainable Development," in *Sustainable Development in the Twenty-First-Century Americas: Alternative Visions of Progress,* ed. Beverley A. Suderman, Jeffrey C. Jacob, and Merlin Brinkerhoff (Calgary, Alberta: University of Calgary, Division of International Development, 1995), 2–10.

In addition to the previously referenced work of Meadows et al. and Wackernagel and Rees, my treatment of the sustainability question draws on David Orr, *Ecological Literacy, Education, and the Transition to a Postmodern World* (Albany: State University of New York Press, 1992), and Herman E. Daly and John B. Cobb Jr., *For the Common Good: Redirecting the Economy Toward Community, the Environment, and a Sustainable Future* (Boston: Beacon Press, 1989). In particular I am indebted to Alan Durning, *How Much Is Enough? The Consumer Society and the Future of the Earth* (New York: Norton, 1992), for the suggestion that the essence of sustainability is the redirection of human energy away from consumption and toward nonmaterial goals.

26. Though some of its data are almost ten years old, *Broken Heartland: The Rise of America's Rural Ghetto* (New York: Free Press, 1990), Osha Gray Davidson's overview of the contemporary state of rural America, including homelessness and food banks, still remains one of the best summaries available.

Chapter 1

1. Tom Gavin, *Denver Post,* October 18, 1978, 23.

2. This quotation and the following ones on the Rockwells come from Wilson Rockwell's published account of his family's experiences in their move from Denver and western Colorado to British Columbia. Wilson Rockwell, *We Hold These Truths* (Caldwell, Idaho: Caxton Printers, 1976), 14, 15, 79, 257.

3. Data for the productivity of the contemporary farmer comes from Don E. Albrecht and Steven H. Murdock, *The Sociology of U.S. Agriculture: An Ecological Approach* (Ames: Iowa State University Press, 1990), 95. In the course of researching U.S. agriculture, one comes across a number of different claims about the productivity of the American farmer, ranging from 50 to 150 urban residents for whom one farm laborer can produce sufficient food. I have used Albrecht and Murdock's figure as a conservative estimate.

4. For a discussion of the population movements over the last several decades, as well as a historical treatment of population streams from the colonial era to the present, see Lorraine Garkovich, *Population and Community in Rural America* (Westport, Conn.: Greenwood Press, 1989). More precisely, a metropolitan county, as defined by the Office of Management and Budget, has "either a city of 50,000 or more people, or a city and adjoining suburbs with a total population of 100,000 or more." Sharon O'Malley, "Country Gold," *American Demographics,* July 1992, 30.

5. The nonmetro counties' growth rate of 4 percent from 1990 to 1994 comes from an interview with Calvin Beale, senior demographer at the U.S. Department of Agriculture, in the *Baltimore Sun Magazine,* May 7, 1995, 9. For a comparison of metro and nonmetro growth

rates in the 1980s, see Kenneth M. Johnson and Calvin L. Beale, "The Recent Revival of Widespread Population Growth in Nonmetropolitan Areas of the United States," *Rural Sociology* 59, no. 4 (1994): 655–67.

6. A summary of the characteristics of edge city can be found in Joel Garreau, *Edge City: Life on the New Frontier* (New York: Doubleday, 1991). Garreau, who (according to *Whole Earth Catalog* founder Stewart Brand) "lives with his family on a Virginia homestead straight out of the early Whole Earth Catalogs" (*Whole Earth Review*, no. 88 [Winter 1995]: 64), takes a position on the relationship between edge cities and sustainability that is hard to categorize. On the one hand he acknowledges the unsustainable character of the automobile-produced and -maintained edge city, but on the other hand he celebrates the triumph of ordinary citizens' common sense over the planning industry's paternalism in the evolution of edge cities. And over the next several generations, Garreau sees the edge cities evolving toward at least some sustainable permutations. For more detail on Garreau's predictions for the future of edge city, see Joel Garreau, "Edgier Cities," *Wired*, September 1995, 158–63, 232–34.

7. The estimate of one million back-to-the-landers is from Terry A. Simmons, "But We Must Cultivate Our Garden: Twentieth-Century Pioneering in Rural British Columbia" (Ph.D. diss., University of Minnesota, 1979). Initial reports of the motivations for moving to the countryside during the migration turnaround can be found in James D. Williams and Andrew J. Sofranko, "Motivations for the Immigration Component of Population Turnaround in Non-Metropolitan Areas," *Demography* 16 (May 1979): 239–55; Tim B. Heaton, William B. Clifford, and Glenn V. Fuguitt, "Temporal Shifts in the Determinants of Young and Elderly Migration in Non-Metropolitan Areas," *Social Forces* 69 (September 1984): 41–60; and Rex R. Campbell and Lorraine Garkovich, "Turnaround Migration as an Episode in Collective Behavior," *Rural Sociology* 49 (Spring 1984): 89–105.

8. For the Stanford Research Institute's surveys, see Arnold Mitchell, *Nine American Lifestyles* (New York: Macmillan, 1983). The report on the survey for the preference of small-town living can be found in George Rebeck, "Saving America's Small Towns," *Utne Reader,* November/December 1991, 20–22. A summary of the Roper Organization survey is in Peter Stisser, "A Deeper Shade of Green," *American Demographics,* March 1994, 24–29. For the *Time* cover story, see Janice Castro, "The Simple Life Comes Back," *Time,* April 8, 1991, 50–53.

Michael Phillips, cofounder of Berkeley's Briarpatch network, has disputed the Stanford Research Institute's claims of a shift in values, both in terms of the number of people involved and what actually constitutes a simple style of life. Phillips ("SRI Is Wrong About Voluntary Simplicity," *Co-Evolution Quarterly*, no. 14 [Summer 1977]: 32–34) contends that SRI missed or glossed over voluntary simplicity's central characteristic, the desire to *reduce* income, and that it confused long-standing American values like frugality with value transformation. In addition to its superficial understanding of voluntary simplicity, Phillips claims SRI seriously overestimated the numbers of Americans practicing genuine simplicity—Phillips's estimate coming in at about one one-hundredth of the SRI figures. Phillips's criticisms provide a natural corrective to the enthusiastic predictions of a broad-based social movement toward simple living in the 1990s. At the same time, whether Americans are trying to recapture basic values by choice or out of necessity, the SRI surveys, the *Time* magazine article, and the Roper study do underline a renewed interest in alternative lifestyles like the back-to-the-land movement *and,* more important, confirm that there are, according to estimates ranging from conservative to generous, from a few million to perhaps fifty million North Americans sympathetic to the practice of simpler lifestyles.

9. The material in the following paragraphs, including quotations, is derived from Jd Belanger, "Autobiography of a Homesteader and the Recent History of *Countryside:* After 34 Years, the Circle Closes," *Countryside,* January/February 1991, 4–5, 57–61. Jd and Diane Belanger's *Countryside* should not be confused with the glossy, oversized *Countryside,* Hearst

Corporation's attempt to reach the upscale, country-estate-oriented consumer. Hearst, which also publishes *Cosmopolitan, Esquire,* and *Redbook,* had a press run of 250,000 for their first issue in March of 1990. On the grounds that the audiences for the two magazines were dramatically different, as were their contents ("Sumptuous Spring Picnics" is not the kind of article the Belangers run; "Why Hens Lay Soft-Shelled Eggs" is), the Hearst Corporation ignored Jd's protests of trademark infringement.

After reaching a press run of 400,000 copies, Hearst's *Countryside* was unable to match its operating expenses with advertising revenue, and it died in May of 1993 (*New York Times,* May 31, 1993, sec. 1, p. 41).

Just after the announcement of Hearst's *Countryside,* Jd Belanger wrote the following letter to *Advertising Age* (February 5, 1990, 28), under the headline "2nd 'Countryside' Heard From" (Jd likely was less than pleased with the second-place sequencing of his original *Countryside*):

> Your Jan. 15 edition notes that a magazine called *Countryside* is the brainchild of John Mack Carter [of Hearst Corporation]. That's interesting, because I fathered a magazine called *Countryside* in 1969 . . . and it's been published regularly ever since. *Countryside* has been devoted to the form of simple living and subsistence farming we call "home-steading." I can already hear irate readers of the real *Countryside,* after they see the Hearst version, telling me, "My God, you've sold out to Madison Avenue, just like *Mother Earth News* did." And you can imagine one of Mr. Carter's targeted upscale readers picking up a copy of the real *Countryside* only to find articles on butchering rabbits, milking goats and (gasp!) how to live without electricity and indoor plumbing. Maybe his slogan could be "This is not your father's *Countryside.*" After all, Hearst doesn't seem to be preoccupied with originality. This is the third start-up with this title in the past 10 years that I'm aware of.

10. Richard Nilsen, "Raising Small Meat Animals," in *The Next Whole Earth Catalog,* ed. Stewart Brand (New York: Point/Random House, 1980).

11. Survey researchers feel successful when they achieve a response rate over 50 percent, even with two or more mailings. I received a 48 percent response rate for the first mailing and then received only an additional 10 percent with the second mailing. This follows a pattern typical with most mail surveys. Mail survey researchers do not feel the return rate with more than two mailings justifies the time and financial investment of the additional mailings. It is very difficult, even with multiple mailings, to come up with a rate much over 70 percent. For mail survey researchers, then, there is always the uncomfortable question whether those who do not return a questionnaire are substantially different from those who do. It is extremely difficult to answer this question, since those who do not respond to the survey make themselves inaccessible. But having a large and varied number of respondents, as I do here, does give the researcher confidence that he or she is reaching a cross section of the targeted audience. And political opinion pollsters, who typically receive no more than a 50 percent response rate to their phone surveys, are often able to predict election results within a few percentage points of the final outcome.

12. James E. Strohauer, "From Urbanites to Countryfolk . . . in Just Eight Years," *Mother Earth News,* no. 88 (July/August 1984): 92–93.

13. Paul Nathanson makes this point in *Over the Rainbow: The Wizard of Oz as a Secular Myth of America* (Albany: State University of New York Press, 1991). Writer Osha Gray Davidson relates an incident that underscores small-town neighborliness, while parenthetically acknowledging that not all personal encounters in rural America are positive ones. He reports how one morning he had left clothes out to dry on the clothesline before going to his office, some distance from the small town where he was living, and had later felt helpless as an

afternoon thunderstorm swept through the area, assuredly drenching his just-dry clothing. "Thirty miles from the clothes I had hung out in the glow of bucolic bliss early that morning, I could do nothing but curse my stupidity. When I arrived home that evening I found the clothes not only dry but folded, sitting just inside my front door in a neighbor's laundry basket. It was just the first of many lessons about community (*not all so pleasant, of course*) that I learned during my stay." Osha Gray Davidson, "Those Little Town Blues," *Utne Reader,* May/June 1993, 111–12 (emphasis added).

Chapter 2

1. Rube Wrightsman, "Paradise Philosophy," *Mother Earth News,* November/December 1988, 81. The following two Wrightsman quotations are from the same source.

2. The unemployment rates belie the supposition by some social work professionals that back-to-the-landers might commonly apply for welfare or public assistance support and then count on their smallholding to stretch the meager welfare payments into a comfortable living. The unemployment rates from the *Countryside* sample are low compared with unemployment rates above 15 percent in rural America generally.

3. Helen Nearing and Scott Nearing, *Living the Good Life: How to Live Sanely and Simply in a Troubled World* (New York: Schocken, 1970), 97, 98.

4. Helen Nearing and Scott Nearing, *Continuing the Good Life: Half a Century of Homesteading* (New York: Schocken Books, 1979), 114.

5. Nearing and Nearing, *Living the Good Life,* 43.

6. Ibid., 187.

7. Haru Kanemitsu, "Continuing the Good Life," *Smallholder,* October 1979, 762.

8. Pat Stone, "Hope in the Heartland," *Mother Earth News,* special ed., Spring 1989, 72.

9. Ibid., 73.

10. Julia Lawlor, "Specialty Crops Feed Farm Income," *USA Today,* November 14, 1986, B1–2.

11. Booker T. Whatley and the Editors of *New Farm, Booker T. Whatley's Handbook on How to Make $100,000 Farming 25 Acres* (Emmaus, Pa.: Rodale, 1987).

12. Barbara Seeber, "The Producer," *Utne Reader,* October/November 1984, 100.

13. Booker T. Whatley, "The Men Behind 'The Ultimate Small Farm,'" *New Farm,* September/October 1987, 15.

14. An important variation on microfarmer agriculture is community-supported agriculture (CSA). In CSA urban residents buy shares in or subscribe to a farmer's harvest. Before the farmer breaks ground in the spring, he or she sells shares (typically numbering between twenty and a hundred and ranging in value from $150 to $600) in the farm's expected production. The urban shareholders support the farmer insofar as they share the risks, and the benefits, of the growing season. Robyn Van En, a cofounder of CSA in North America, explains how this works in terms of a disaster on her farm near Great Barrington, Massachusetts: "After a rainstorm dumped eight inches of rain in three hours, the winter baking squash had to be picked prematurely. Everybody froze, dried, and ate as much as they could, but it was basically a $35 loss to each share. That would have been a $3500 loss to an individual farmer" ("Eating for Your Community: Towards Agriculture Supported Community," *In Context,* no. 42 [Fall 1995]: 31). This incident shows the farmer under CSA breaking free of farming's normal contingencies to enjoy a much more stable income. In the process the urban consumer benefits from locally grown, fresh produce, usually delivered to a central locale, like a church parking lot, once a week and at a price calculated to approximate the supermarket shopper's normal produce bill. If the microfarmer has sufficient space in a root

cellar or comparable storage space, then the delivery of produce can continue through the winter.

Community-supported agriculture is a popular alternative to agro-industrial farming and has been growing each year since its founding in 1985, with five hundred operations in 1995 (Van En, "Eating for Your Community," 30), a national headquarters (818 Connecticut Avenue NW, Suite 800, Washington, D.C. 20006), and a quarterly publication (*Seasonal News*). But even though it represents an innovative mechanism for supporting small farmers and for delivering fresh produce to urban consumers, CSA is in the end an adaptation to a seriously flawed agricultural system. In my last chapter, I explore several policy options that have the potential to institutionalize both the spirit and substance of community-supported agriculture.

15. Finally, in reference to the microfarmers, I should add that my survey sample likely underrepresents their actual numbers in the general back-to-the-land population, since it was drawn from the subscriber list of a generalist back-to-the-country magazine, which would probably be of limited interest to full-time, professional farmers. The same would hold true for the purists and country romantics, though for a different reason: the subscription price for the magazine would be in the luxury category for most subsistence and low-income back-to-the-landers. By the same logic, the more affluent weekenders and pensioners are likely overrepresented in the *Countryside* subscription lists.

16. One should not confuse the weekenders who live full-time in their adopted rural communities with the weekenders who buy country property as a second home, part of an affluent group of urbanites seeking a temporary escape from the city, who in the process drive up land values to the point where locals cannot afford the housing, and generally disrupt community traditions. For a treatment of this second kind of weekender and their impact on small towns, see Ron Powers, *Far from Home: Life and Loss in Two American Towns* (New York: Anchor-Doubleday, 1992), and Raye Ringholz, *Little Town Blues: Voices from the Changing West* (Salt Lake City: Peregrine Smith, 1992).

17. For many people who want to move to the country, including back-to-the-landers, the only viable means for supporting themselves, in light of depressed rural and farm economies and in the absence of public-sector employment, is to start their own businesses. It should not be surprising, then, that a small but dynamic advice industry that focuses on starting a small business targets those thinking about a country move. For a general approach to the move to a simpler life, see, for example, M. M. Kirsch, *How to Get off the Fast Track and Live a Life Money Can't Buy* (Los Angeles: Lowell House, 1991); and for a specific treatment of becoming a country entrepreneur, see Jerry Germer, *Country Careers: Successful Ways to Live and Work in the Country* (New York: John Wiley, 1993). There are, however, not only books and magazines for the aspiring country entrepreneur, but also consultancy services (e.g., the Greener Pastures Institute), which sponsor newsletters, seminars, and 1–800 numbers (e.g., 1-800-OUT-OF-LA). For a brief overview for the country-move advice phenomenon, see Susan Ellicott, "Meet the 'Ralph Naders of Relocation,'" *San Diego Union*, November 17, 1993, B-7.

The following characterization of an exchange between an underling and his "boss" in a *Mother Earth News* advertisement illustrates the attractiveness of owning one's own business and, in addition, having country property (given the problematic nature of earning an income from farming and the sense of independence that comes from being a country entrepreneur):

Uh, Mr. Gridley?

What is it Perkins?

I'm just . . . I'm turning in my resignation, sir.

Resignation? Are you kidding? Look, if it's about that little bawling out at the meeting Thursday . . .

No, Mr. Gridley. It's not that. It's . . .

It's the overtime, right? Well wake up, boy! It's dog-eat-dog out there! No pain, no gain! Know what I mean?

Ironically sir, that may be part of it. You see, Kate and I are moving out of the city. We've put a down payment on a little piece of land and . . .

Leaving the city? I've got news for you, Perkins. I consider myself a pretty good judge of character, and believe me, you're no farmer!

But I'm not going to be a farmer, Mr. Gridley. You see, I'm a pretty good woodworker, and Kate's got a great head for numbers, so we're starting a little handmade furniture business.

Well it sounds pretty darn crazy to me, Perkins. Do you really think this is a smart move, future-wise?

I really don't know, sir. But it's a first step. ("The First Step," *Mother Earth News*, special ed., Spring 1985, 175)

18. Sara Pacher, "Wild Horse Plains Montana," *Mother Earth News*, November/December 1988, 78–84. One advantage of being a country entrepreneur is the ability, working at or close to home, to keep the homestead going. A California respondent to the *Countryside* survey in her early fifties wrote, "Since we run our business from home, my main extravagance is a portable phone so I can work in the garden and still not miss business calls."

19. This quotation and the following ones are from Helena Turner, "A Visit with David and Cathy Williams, Family Farmers on Saltspring Island," *Smallholder*, March 1978, 705–8.

20. A composite of two different classified ads from the *Smallholder*, May 1978, 628. The ad raises the question of back-to-the-landers and communal living. The communitarian label is a legitimate, *theoretical* back-to-the-country classification category, but only two of the 565 *Countryside* respondents said they were part of a communal lifestyle. And in my interviews and case studies I encountered no communitarian smallholders. Consequently, I do not attempt in this chapter either a description or an analysis of this intriguing kind of back-to-the-lander. In Chapter 6, "Organizing for Change: New Pioneers as Activists," however, I do explore the smallholders' attitudes toward communal living, the likelihood of their involvement in community organizing, and the frequency of cooperative behavior.

21. The responses to the happiness question and the *Countryside* respondents' reported family income figures place the back-to-the-landers in the broad mainstream of North American life. Typically, one-third of Americans report being "very happy" on quality-of-life surveys, and less than 10 percent claim to be either "somewhat unhappy" or "very unhappy"—percentages very close to the *Countryside* results. (For an excellent summary of this kind of quality-of-life research, including a discussion on the possibility that questionnaire respondents embellish the extent of the general happiness they feel, see David G. Myers, *The Pursuit of Happiness* [New York: Morrow, 1992], 22–30.) And with median family incomes of $30,000 to $40,000 (questionnaire respondents reported income by category rather than by a specific amount), the *Countryside* respondents are close to the U.S. 1993 median income of 31,241 (U.S. Bureau of the Census, "Income and Poverty," CD-ROM).

Chapter 3

1. An overview of the mindfulness phenomenon can be found in Ellen J. Langer, *Mindfulness* (Reading, Mass: Addison-Wesley, 1989), and Claude Whitmyer, ed., *Mindfulness and Meaningful Work: Explorations in Right Livelihood* (Berkeley: Parallax Press, 1994). "Flow," an experience similar to mindfulness, is described in Mihaly Csikszentmihalyi, *Flow: The Psychology of Optimal Experience* (New York: Harper & Row, 1990).

2. This description of the back-to-the-landers' experience with mindfulness raises the

question of just how unique the smallholders are in their ability to find tranquillity in a sense of communion with their natural surroundings. While there exist substantial popular and scholarly literature on the psychological aspects of mindfulness, there is little social survey work on the phenomenon. Nevertheless, it seems safe to assume that back-to-the-landers, and others with out-of-doors interests, have an advantage over city dwellers in the ready availability of the mindfulness encounters. This working hypothesis, however, does not deny that many urban residents are still able to find the serenity of mindfulness through a meditative apprehension of the ordinary in their immediate environments (see, for example, Thich Nhat Hanh, "Washing Dishes," in *Peace Is Every Step: The Path of Mindfulness in Everyday Life* (New York: Bantam, 1991), 26–27). I am suggesting, however, that mindfulness likely comes easier and more frequently to those, like the back-to-the-landers, who withdraw from fast-paced urban lives in order to make mindfulness itself a priority.

3. Carol Adamo, "A Tale of Two Homesteads," *Countryside*, December 1983, 16–19. The quotations that follow come from these pages.

4. Jd Belanger, "Jd Belanger Replies," *Countryside*, December 1983, 17–18.

5. Adamo, "A Tale of Two Homesteads," 18.

6. Duane Elgin, *Voluntary Simplicity: Toward a Way of Life That Is Outwardly Simple, Inwardly Rich*, rev. ed. (New York: William Morrow, 1993). David E. Shi's *Simple Life: Plain Living and High Thinking in American Culture* (New York: Oxford University Press, 1985) is a fine treatment of the historical attempts at voluntary simplicity. Shi's work demonstrates that there has often been a chasm between rhetoric and performance on matters of frugality, with advocates like William Penn and Thomas Jefferson unable to detach themselves from patrician habits. For a collection of historical and contemporary materials on living simply, see David E. Shi, ed., *In Search of the Simple Life: American Voices Past and Present* (Salt Lake City: Peregrine Smith, 1986).

7. Elgin, *Voluntary Simplicity*, 23.

8. The term "soft paths" was popularized by Amory B. Lovins, in *Soft Energy Paths* (New York: Harper & Row, 1977).

9. Gandhi's phrase comes from E. F. Schmacher, *Small Is Beautiful* (New York: Harper & Row, 1973).

10. The turn of phrase is from Lewis Mumford, *Technics and Civilization* (New York: Harcourt Brace Jovanovich, 1963), 105.

11. Haru Kanemitsu, "Frugality," *Smallholder*, March 1978, 697.

12. Julie Summers, "Escargot on a Slug Budget," *Smallholder*, July 1985, 1331–33.

13. Elgin, *Voluntary Simplicity*, 104.

14. The description that follows combines the Columbia River Barter Fair and the Okanogan Earth Song Festival.

15. Fraser Lang, "The Salmon Circle," *Columbiana* 4, no. 3 (1991): 25.

16. A factor that likely inhibits church activity is country isolation. As a Jewish correspondent explained, "We need to travel nearly forty miles one way to the closest synagogue, so our participation in group services is minimal."

17. The back-to-the-land perspective on religion is very much in harmony with that of Norman MacLean, who, in his novella *A River Runs Through It* (Chicago: University of Chicago Press, 1989), 1, observed that in his family "there was no clear line between religion and fly fishing."

18. E. L. Doctorow, "A Gangsterism of the Spirit," *Nation*, October 2, 1989, 349.

19. Although the new pioneers' mindfulness experiences mitigate the potential for a distortion of the principle of self-reliance into the "grotesque" of extreme individualism, the comments from the *Countryside* survey reveal self-sufficiency's underside: intolerance for those who are different or who need help. One respondent wrote, "We believe in taking

responsibility for our own health by eating natural foods (most of which we grow ourselves) and exercising daily. We do not have health insurance and are against socialized medicine where we will be forced to pay for all those who abuse their bodies or run to doctors for every little thing and take no responsibility for themselves." Another respondent amplified this sense of self-accomplishment in writing, "I may be better off financially than others, but I *earned* it. It wasn't given to me. My parents gave me the desire to succeed and set a good example. They were poor farmers. We had food, clothing, a warm home and were a family. *No one* gave me a dime to go to college, *no one*. You can be a success if you want to. Most people are satisfied with being a parasite."

The sentiments expressed by these two smallholders were not representative of the written comments from the *Countryside* questionnaire and at best reflect a small minority of survey respondents. These comments do, however, demonstrate that a thin line separates a self-reliance that celebrates independence and individual achievement from a self-reliance that becomes "a grotesque" through a kind of self-righteous pride.

Chapter 4

1. The ideas behind convivial technology are developed in Ivan Illich, *Tools for Conviviality* (New York: Harper & Row, 1973). For a treatment of convivial, or soft, technology that combines both philosophical perspectives on its democratic and community-enhancing potential and a compendium of specific applications (still relevant two decades after publication), see Godfrey Boyle and Peter Harper, eds., *Radical Technology* (New York: Pantheon, 1976).

2. The list is adapted from Robin Clarke's list of thirty-five characteristics of hard and soft technologies in *The Next Whole Earth Catalog* (New York: Point/Random House, 1980), 176.

3. James A. Montmarquet, in *The Idea of Agrarianism: From Hunter-Gatherer to Agrarian Radical in Western Culture* (Moscow: University of Idaho Press, 1989), 246–47, refers to Hector St. John de Crevecoeur, a contemporary of Thomas Jefferson, as a "man whose economic interest in such activities as beekeeping was hardly distinguishable from his naturalist's interest in bees—and in every part of the natural environment of his farm." Montmarquet also quotes Liberty Hyde Bailey, cochair of the Country Life Commission, on the idea of the farmer as naturalist: "Country living is essentially an outlook to nature, and the farmer is a naturalist. In proportion as he is a good naturalist he is a good farmer. The farmer, woodsman, hunter, explorer, knows as much about the things in the out-of-doors than you can find in any book . . . The best naturalists do not write" (Bailey, *Outlook to Nature* [New York: Macmillan, 1911], 54, cited in Montmarquet, *The Idea of Agrarianism*, 232).

4. This example comes from Nancy Jack Todd and John Todd, *Bioshelters, Ocean Arks, Fish Farms: Ecology as the Basis of Design* (San Francisco: Sierra Club Books, 1984). On the application of natural design principles, see also Bill Mollison, *Permaculture: A Designer's Manual* (Tyalgum, New South Wales: Tagari Publications, 1988). The Todds and Mollison have influenced much of the description of the homestead dream that follows.

5. The garden description draws on Jeff Ball, *Jeff Ball's Sixty-Minute Garden* (Emmaus, Pa.: Rodale, 1985).

6. For a description and analysis of a wide range of issues focused on the North American diet, including the treatment of animals from birth to slaughterhouse to table, see John Robbins, *Diet for a New America* (Walpole, N.H.: Stillpoint, 1987). On the specific issue of chickens, see Gene Bruce, "Public Health: Dirty Chicken," *Atlantic*, November 1990, 32–50.

The responses to Bruce's article, including his reply, are in the *Atlantic*'s letters-to-the-editor section, February 1991, 11–12.

7. John Vivian, "Raising Free-Range Chickens," *Mother Earth News*, July/August 1984, 75.

8. Helga Olkowski, Bill Olkowski, Tom Javits, and the Farallones Institute staff, *The Integral Urban House: Self-Reliant Living in the City* (San Francisco: Sierra Club Books, 1979), 96. The description of the composting toilet here draws on ibid., 96–97, 110–18. I would not want, however, to leave the impression that the kind of composting toilet I describe here is the only ecologically sound way to handle human excreta—any more than Anne Schwartz's weeder geese are the only way to take care of garden weeds. For one of a variety of innovative ways to reclaim water-contaminated sewage, see John Todd, "Solar Aquatics," in *Whole Earth Ecolog* (New York: Harmony Books, 1990), 85.

9. A good discussion on solar power is Michael Webster, "A Place in the Sun," *Harrowsmith* (Canadian ed.), June 1993, 62–67.

10. The unelaborated analogy comes from ibid., 67.

11. Olkowski et al., *The Integral Urban House*, 116.

12. I come back here to Donella Meadows and her coauthors' estimate, generated by their computer simulation models, of the need for an 80 percent reduction in the use of nonrenewable resources per unit of industrial production and a 90 percent reduction in pollution per unit of industrial production for the planet to reach a state of ecological sustainability by the mid–twenty-first century. Donella H. Meadows, Dennis L. Meadows, and Jorgen Randers, *Beyond the Limits: Confronting Global Collapse, Envisioning a Sustainable Future* (Post Mills, Vt.: Chelsea Green, 1992).

13. There were another six items of soft technology I included in the *Countryside* survey, and in Table 20 I summarize the questionnaire responses for these additional items.

Table 20.   Homestead technology: the remaining elements

Item	%	Effectiveness Score
Larger animals for home slaughter	34	3.4
Beef cattle	27	3.3
Pigs	24	3.2
Woodstove (cooking)	18	3.1
Sheep	17	2.8
Solar heat	13	3.0

Note: Total number of respondents = 565 (actual responses numbered from 561 to 563, since not all respondents answered each question)

In order to assess smallholders' commitment to the soft path, it is possible, in addition to reporting percentages for each item of technology they use, to calculate an index or indexes of soft-technological employment. One index, a technological self-reliance index, consists of the number of soft-technologies a smallholder possessed from the list of twenty-five in the questionnaire. On the technological self-reliance index, the *Countryside* survey respondents had an average score of 6.8 (a median of 6.0), with a range of scores from 0 to 18. A complimentary index, a technological self-reliance effectiveness index, consists of the number of items in use multiplied by the effectiveness score of each item. This index would have a theoretical range from 0 to 100. On the technological self-reliance effectiveness index, the *Countryside* respondents' scores actually fell in a range from 0 to 72, with a median score of 20.

14. John Cronin, "Choices Motivated by Aesthetic, Health, Environmental Concerns," *Countryside,* May/June 1993, 66.

15. Paul Molyneaux, "Techno-Tools Steal from Me . . . Isolate Me," *Countryside,* May/June, 1993, 67.

16. Wendell Berry, *What Are People For?* (San Francisco: North Point Press, 1990), 170–77. Originally published in the *New England Review and Bread Loaf Quarterly,* the essay was reprinted in *Harper's.* The North Point edition includes letters to *Harper's* in response to the essay and Berry's reaction to the letters. For a provocative debate on the technological issues with which Berry struggles, see the exchange between Kirkpatrick Sale (author of *Rebels Against the Future: The Luddites and Their War on the Industrial Revolution* [Reading, Mass.: Addison-Wesley, 1995]) and Kevin Kelly (editor of *Wired* and former editor of *Whole Earth Review*) in *Wired,* June 1995, 166–68, 211–16.

17. Berry, *What Are People For?* 170. Though he does "not see anything wrong with it" (his family's literary cottage industry), several of his readers who took time to write letters to the *Harper's* editors certainly did. One respondent wrote, "The value of a computer to a writer is that it is a tool not for generating ideas but for typing and editing words. It is cheaper than a secretary (or wife!) and arguably more fuel efficient. And it enables spouses who are not inclined to provide free labor more time to concentrate on *their* own work . . . Let the PCs come and the wives and servants go seek more meaningful work" (Ibid., 174, emphasis in original). In response to this attack, Berry vigorously defends himself and the idea of a household economy, but rather than summarize his counterarguments here, I shall wait until I can contextualize them within my report on the smallholders' division of family labor. I do so in note 24 below.

18. Ibid., 177.

19. Wendell Berry, *The Memory of Old Jack* (San Diego: Harcourt Brace Jovanovich, 1974), 177, 36.

20. Berry, *What Are People For?* 176, 196.

21. Ibid., 196.

22. There were actually five response categories for these questions in the *Countryside* survey. I have collapsed them to three categories in order to facilitate clarity in the data presentation. The original categories were: (1) usually the wife, (2) wife more than husband, (3) wife and husband about the same, (4) husband more than wife, and (5) usually the husband.

23. The difference between men's and women's evaluations of their respective contributions to the homestead work load is intriguing. On an aggregate basis, Table 13 shows a roughly symmetrical division of labor in respect to gardening and animal care. But when gardening and animal care are broken down by male and female responses, there is a remarkable divergence. Three out of five males (60 percent) report that usually the husbands do the gardening, while almost two-thirds of the females (66 percent) say it is the wives who usually do the gardening. With regard to animal care the same pattern continues: females claim most of the work load falls to them (51 percent), and males claim that on their homesteads husbands usually provide animal care (61 percent). This general pattern of divergent reporting also applies to the other farmstead and household tasks, but to a much lesser degree. One percent of the males, for example, admit that their wives usually cut the homestead wood, though 7 percent of the females say they usually do. This rough consensus carries over to household tasks, with 75 percent of the males reporting that wives usually do the house cleaning, though 86 percent of the females say wives do the household cleaning.

On the surface these sometimes contradictory estimations of who does the homestead work would appear to make a prima facie case for conflict and dissatisfaction in back-to-the-land relationships, particularly on the part of women who carry a disproportionate share of homestead responsibilities. But in spite of their differences, females are no more likely than males to be dissatisfied with their conjugal or family relationships. What, then, might be the significance of the divergent perspectives on homestead workloads? I believe the differences support the generalization that most smallholding couples do not work side by side on homestead chores, but labor separately as their individual schedules permit. Consequently, it is only to be expected that their separate experiences, and at times hectic schedules, would lead individual marriage partners to differing evaluations—perhaps overestimations for themselves and underestimations for their spouses—of their contributions to the farmstead workload.

24. One way to understand the smallholding families' division of labor is to see their households as possessing premodern characteristics (similar in a general way to nineteenth-century pioneer family structure or even that of contemporary peasants), rather than exclusively modern or postmodern characteristics. Independence, dependence, and interdependence are key variables in classifying these three distinct types of households. From the perspective of gender relations, the transition from modern to postmodern households entails, in part, the movement of women from positions of dependence on their spouses' income, while performing unpaid domestic labor, to situations where they achieve independence from their spouses by earning an income outside the household, ideally by developing a career. In the postmodern household, where women become "liberated" from domestic obligations though a career, conjugal bonds become based on mutual affection and negotiated agreements on rights and responsibilities in areas like domestic maintenance and child care. This brief summary, however, does not deny that many women work outside the modern household more often by necessity than by choice, and thus face the "double day" of a job and housework. Neither does the analysis here ignore the fact that relationships in the postmodern household are particularly fragile, since each partner in the relationship is often financially independent and affection does not always survive the contingencies of a postmodern existence.

The postmodern household, however, is not the only escape from what some see as the suffocating nature of the modern household. For many smallholders the alternative is not a move *ahead* to the postmodern family but a move *back* toward premodern family forms. In the premodern family (or "household mode of production"), spouses work together (though not necessarily side by side) as partners in a productive unit, which in the case of the back-to-the-landers is a subsistence or semisubsistence homestead. The "social glue" that holds the premodern household together, then, is not only affection but also an interdependent relationship in which each partner needs his or her spouse in order to accomplish common goals. Given the obvious commitment of the *Countryside* survey's female respondents to a back-to-the-land way of life, it seems safe to conclude that many women can and do find personal fulfillment outside of both the modern home *and* the postmodern domestic household.

One finds, nevertheless, a residual hostility toward the household mode of production, perhaps due in part to its critics failing to appreciate the important distinctions between modern and premodern households. This hostility manifests itself in classic form in the confrontation between Wendell Berry and his inquisitors (see note 17 above). Berry summarizes the letters to *Harper's* that take him to task for permitting his wife to type, on a Royal 1956 standard typewriter, and edit his essays, in the following way: "My offense is that I am a man who receives some help from my wife; my wife's offense is that she is a woman who does some work for her husband—which work, according to her critics and mine, make her a drudge, exploited by a conventional subservience" (Berry, *What Are People For?* 179–80). Though Berry offers no evidence on the nature of his household's division of labor beyond his wife's assistance in typing and editing, his detractors, he claims, rest their case on a syllogism "of the flimsiest sort": "My wife helps me in my work, some wives who have helped their husbands in their work have been exploited, therefore my wife is exploited" (182). Carrying this line of argument one step further, Berry observes: "If I had written in my essay that my wife worked as a typist and editor for a publisher, doing the same work that she does for me, no feminists, I daresay, would have written to *Harper's* to attack me for exploiting her—even though, for all they knew, I might have forced her to do such work in order to keep me in gambling money. It would have been assumed as a matter of course that if she had a job away from home she was a 'liberated woman,' possessed of a dignity that no home could confer upon her" (182).

Though Berry caricatures here the idea of the career woman as a liberated person, he does identify what he sees as a definite irony: women who escape domestic subservience in the home almost inevitably become organizational underlings of one sort or another, trading in domestic for corporate servitude. On the other hand, according to Berry's argument, the woman working as a partner in the premodern household economy has the potential for a genuine, rather than illusory, sense of freedom. Of course, in the end, the type of household one desires to attach oneself to is a matter of personal preference, with fulfillment a matter of one's values and expectations rather than objective circumstances. And Berry would likely be the first one to agree. But at the same time he still sees the separation of production from consumption in postmodern and modern households as ecologically insidious: "The modern household is the place where the consumptive couple do their consuming. Nothing productive is done there. Such work as is done there is done at the expense of the resident couple or family, and to the profit of suppliers of energy and household technology. For entertainment, the inmates consume television or purchase other consumable diversion elsewhere" (180).

25. I would not want to leave the impression that the rationality and efficiency of the soft path have been completely ignored by the research-and-development establishment. The Rocky Mountain Institute, under Amory and Hunter Lovins, for example, has been very active in winning government and private-sector grants and consultancies. Due in part to their efforts and the obvious benefits from conservation and efficiency, "renewable energy provided a third of all the nation's net increases in energy supply since 1979 and now delivers, for example, about a third of Maine's electricity" (*Rocky Mountain Institute Newsletter,* Spring 1991, 3). But while the hard path is more than willing to appropriate the soft path's efficiency innovations, the research-and-development establishment remains essentially oblivious to the philosophical foundations of the soft path, which emphasize restraint, the reduction of demand, the importance of physical involvement with technology, and, ultimately, the channeling of human energy away from material accumulation to the enhancement of social and environmental relationships.

26. The ideas behind ecological design are receiving a renewed emphasis in the mid-nineties, particularly in the pages of the *Whole Earth Review,* whose *Whole Earth Catalog* predecessors celebrated an ecological sensitivity in the sixties and seventies. In the 1980s and on through the early 1990s the *Whole Earth Review* became at least partially distracted by the microchip revolution, telecommunications, virtual reality, and nano-technology. But on Earth Day in 1995 *Whole Earth Review* associates founded the International Ecological Design Society, with a journal (*Journal of Ecological Design*), electronic conferencing, and a World Wide Web page. For the initial statement on the establishment of the society, see Stuart Cowan, "Cultivating Ecological Design Intelligence," *Whole Earth Review,* no. 85 [Spring 1995]: 44–47.

27. Hawken's criteria reflect the 80 percent reduction in nonrenewable energy use and 90 percent reduction in pollution called for by Meadows et al., *Beyond the Limits.* Hawken's assessment comes from his *Ecology of Commerce: A Declaration of Sustainability* (New York: Har-

per Business, 1993). For a summary of his position, see "The Hawken Guideposts for Designing Sustainable Commerce," *Yoga Journal*, September/October, 1994, 69.

28. Drawing on cross-cultural material, Wolfgang Sachs makes these same points in "The Virtue of Enoughness," *New Perspectives Quarterly*, Spring 1989, 16–19. Sachs criticizes soft-technology advocates like Amory Lovins and the Worldwatch Institute's Lester Brown for emphasizing efficiency over the reduction of demand in the sustainability equation. Counting on efficiency, rather than a reduction of demand, as the primary path to a sustainable future is potentially dangerous, since efficiency by itself, through a "rebound effect," can actually increase overall consumption. For example, "while energy use per dollar Gross National Product (GNP) decreased by 23 percent in the Western industrialized countries between 1973 and 1987, total annual energy consumption actually increased by 15 percent over the same time span" (Mathis Wackernagel and William Rees, *Our Ecological Footprint: Reducing the Human Impact on the Earth* [Philadelphia: New Society, 1996], 128). If consumers fail to subscribe to a conservation ethic beyond the immediate self-interest of saving dollars, they are likely to spend their savings on increasing levels of consumption, with serious ecological ramifications. A growing number of consumers worldwide only intensifies the problem.

29. See Karl Hess, *Community Technology* (New York: Harper & Row, 1979).

Chapter 5

1. Wendell Berry, *The Unsettling of America: Culture and Agriculture*, 3d ed. (San Francisco: Sierra Club, 1996).

2. Marsha Sinetar, *Do What You Love, the Money Will Follow: Discovering Your Right Livelihood* (Mahwah, N.J.: Paulist Press, 1987), 9–10. The title of Sinetar's book is an adaptation of Michael Phillips and Salli Rasberry's first law of money: "Do what you love. If you're doing the right thing, the money will follow" (*The Seven Laws of Money* [New York: Random House, 1974]). A more expansive treatment of right livelihood can be found in Claude Whitmyer, ed., *Mindfulness and Meaningful Work: Explorations in Right Livelihood* (Berkeley: Parallax Press, 1994).

3. Sinetar, *Do What You Love*, 37.

4. Ibid., 12, 111–12.

5. I consciously avoid here the use of the word "entrepreneur" (notwithstanding my previous categorization of some smallholders as "country entrepreneurs"), since it can imply a preoccupation with profit over service, an emphasis on speculative, rather than productive, ventures. Paul Hawken makes these same points in a letter to the *Utne Reader* [March/April, 1989, 4], "Ethical Business, Not Entrepreneurs," and suggests the term "proprietorship" in place of "entrepreneurship" to label businesses that operate on right-livelihood principles.

6. For an elaboration of these points, see Michael Phillips, "The Social Dimensions of Right Livelihood," in *Mindfulness and Meaningful Work*, ed. Whitmyer, 111–16.

7. Marianne's and Dean's volunteer work raises a natural question about the relationship between right livelihood and service: Is there a way individuals and communities can organize themselves in order to support those who find their right livelihood in presently nonremunerative service work such as literacy training, aid to the homeless, and the tutoring of high-needs children? Even though the debt and job preoccupations of the 1990s seem to preclude an optimistic response to the question, at least two intriguing proposals for the promotion of right livelihood are at present circulating in policy-discussion circles. The first proposal I want to discuss briefly comes from Joe Dominguez and Vicki Robin, *Your*

Money or Your Life: Transforming Your Relationship with Money and Achieving Financial Independence (New York: Viking, 1992). Dominguez and Robin outline a plan for individuals and families to become financially independent through the application of voluntary simplicity and a series of disciplined budgeting, savings, and investment strategies. Over a period of a relatively few years, they believe a person of even modest means can save enough to invest in treasury bonds, whose interest would then allow the bondholder to pursue his or her right livelihood through volunteer community service. One might still want to supplement the interest income with part-time or occasional employment, but the lifestyle and investment decisions would permit one the freedom to practice right livelihood.

The second proposal is developed by Jeremy Rifkin in *The End of Work: The Decline of the Global Labor Force* (New York: J. P. Tarcher/Putnam, 1994). Rifkin calls for a combination of income vouchers and tax credits that would permit individuals—either from choice or need—to work in the volunteer sector, a third sector he considers separate from the private and public sectors. This enhancement of an already dynamic third sector would obviously require a sharp increase in public spending, though Rifkin claims that these costs would be more than offset through an overall improvement in the quality of life (crime reduction, family stability, and investment in the country's human capital).

While these policies appear quixotic in an age of efficiency and unapologetic supply-side economics, they do demonstrate a significant counterstream interest in the principles of sustainability and the ideals of right livelihood.

8. The backyard salad garden was a temporary phase in both Marianne's and Dean's lives. It lasted one season for them, though there is still an active cohort of backyard farmers in Seattle. Dean has moved to California, where he keeps alive the dream of starting his own nursery. Marianne eventually moved back into the practice of medicine, though she now works in the specialized area of women's health in a Seattle-area clinic. She shares a house with three-quarters of an acre on the suburban fringe, where she continues to pursue an avocation, if not a vocation, in organic gardening.

9. My generalization here is not meant to discount the work of several fine support networks that have worked and continue to work with right-livelihood businesses, perhaps the most notable of these the Briarpatch Network in San Francisco (see Salli Rasberry, ed., *The Briarpatch Book* [Volcano, Ca.: Volcano/New Glide Publications, 1978]). In *Mindfulness and Meaningful Work*, 279–80, Claude Whitmyer lists seven organizations, three in the Bay Area, that support right-livelihood businesses. (See also the book Whitmyer coauthored with Salli Rasberry, *Running a One-Person Business*, 2d ed. [Berkeley: Ten Speed Press, 1994].) These voluntary educational efforts, however effective they may be, can hardly substitute for society-wide public policy that encourages and rewards the right-livelihood way of earning a living.

10. As this report on the back-to-the-land movement and its connection to a sustainable future comes down to its final two chapters, I do not want to leave the impression this book was written out of the conviction that sustainability depends on any kind of massive movement back to the countryside. I believe the battles for sustainability will have to be fought, and can be won, in our cities. Elsewhere, with Beverley A. Suderman, I have sketched the outlines of one version of what "green cities" might look like (see Jeffrey C. Jacob and Beverley A. Suderman, "Alternative Visions of Progress: The Multiple Meanings of Sustainable Development," in *Sustainable Development in the Twenty-First-Century Americas: Alternative Visions of Progress*, ed. Beverley A. Suderman, Jeffrey C. Jacob, and Merlin B. Brinkerhoff [Calgary, Alberta: University of Calgary, Division of International Development, 1995], 7–9). The transition to green cities will, however, require fundamental changes in the nature of the late-twentieth-century city, changes that will move metropolitan America in the general direction of pre–World War II cities, where there was less reliance on the private auto-

mobile, higher population densities rather than suburban sprawl, and mixed residential-business districts ("pedestrian pockets") rather than monocultural neighborhood enclaves. The details of these sustainable cities are elaborated in Richard Register, *Ecocity Berkeley: Building Cities for a Healthy Future* (Berkeley: North Atlantic Books, 1987); Peter Berg, Beryl Magilavy, and Seth Zuckerman, *A Green City Program for San Francisco Bay Area Cities and Towns* (San Francisco: Planet Drum Books, 1989); Peter Katz, *The New Urbanism: Toward an Architecture of Community* (New York: McGraw-Hill, 1993); and Peter Calthorpe, *The Next Metropolis: Ecology, Community, and the American Dream* (Princeton: Princeton Architecture Press, 1993).

Chapter 6

1. To explore the question of just how much time back-to-the-landers might have for activities like community and environmental organizing, I asked the *Countryside* respondents to choose one of the following four employment-time categories: full-time, part-time and/or seasonal, no outside employment, or retired. In answering this question, 62 percent of the male respondents reported working full-time, as did 36 percent of the female respondents; 21 percent of the males and 12 percent of the females said they were retired; 12 percent of the males and 27 percent of the females said they worked part-time or seasonally; and 5 percent of the males and 25 percent of the females reported no outside employment. Of course, the homestead itself will normally have first claim on any "free" time with which the smallholders find themselves.

2. After I completed my interview with Barry, he wrote me to explain the technicalities of his first confrontation with the Forest Service. "The Forest Service erred by not informing me of the proposed timber sale before they made the decision, and most certainly by not notifying me of the decision. NEPA, 40 CFR 1506.6(b), is explicit in mandating that the Forest Service 'provide public notice of NEPA-related hearings, public meetings, and availability of environmental documents so as to inform those persons and agencies who may be interested or affected.' Being a landowner adjacent to the proposed action, *and* having a permit to draw water, qualifies us under the above regulation" (correspondence, June 25, 1993).

3. Subsequent to my interview with Barry his life became more, rather than less, complicated. His successes with the appeal process brought him greater notoriety, making him a popular speaker and consultant for a wide variety of activist groups in the Pacific Northwest, in both the United States and Canada. His advocacy of sustainable forestry has also brought him before congressional committees as an expert witness. In June of 1993 Barry provided me with an update on his work. "My life as a forest activist continues at a blurring pace. A lot has been accomplished, some ecosystems have been spared and some have been lost . . . and of late I have been dancing with the devil, Louisiana Pacific Corporation, in attempts to find some common ground where trees can be logged in an ecologically sound manner. I'm off to Washington D.C. to spend the week dancing with more devils, politicians. The highlight of the week, hopefully, is my meeting with the Assistant Secretary of Agriculture who is the head of the Forest Service. My message: although everyone recognizes the need for change in the way our national forests are being managed, this change will never be realized as long as those who implemented the destructive policies of the past remain in top managerial positions in the Forest Service. Time to clean house and get rid of the old guard!" (correspondence, June 25, 1993).

4. Noel Perrin, *Third Person Rural: Further Essays of a Sometime Farmer* (Boston: David R. Godine, 1983), 186.

5. The 8 percent figure from the Sierra Club survey is cited by Paul Rauber, "With

Friends Like These . . . ," *Mother Jones*, November 1986, 47. Rauber elaborates, "Alluring to the leaders of the environmental organizations is that 8 out of every hundred Americans say they would like to belong to an environmental organization. Searching for that elusive 8 percent is the preoccupation of many environmental groups" (47).

6. Kirkpatrick Sale presents a more optimistic assessment of the current state of interest in mainstream environmental groups. Sales sees the evidence suggesting that one in every seven adults actually has membership in one of the major environmental groups, which together have twenty million members, with an overlapping membership of approximately 30 percent (*The Green Revolution* [New York: Hill & Wang, 1993], 79–80). In general sympathy for environmental organizations, Sale has the following to say: "Survey after survey indicated that Americans took environmentalism seriously: a 1990 CBS poll, for example, found that 74 percent of those questioned said that protecting the environment was so important that no standards could be set too high (up from 45 percent in 1981), and nearly half of them proclaimed a 'strong identification' with environmentalism; a 1990 Gallup poll found that 76 percent of Americans called themselves environmentalists" (80). Sale's assessment of the general population's sympathy for environmentalism makes the sentiments and behavior of the back-to-the-landers more typical than extraordinary, although at the same time Sale does characterize the population at large as being very concerned over ecological matters.

In this discussion of North American environmental sentiment, one might infer, both from Sale and from me, that environmental activism is necessarily associated with the work of the major environmental organizations, like the Sierra Club, the Environmental Defense Fund, and the Audubon Society. While many back-to-the-landers work with local chapters of these national organizations, most, like Barry Rosenberg, are likely to invest their time and money in local and regional ("grassroots") groups working for the protection of their immediate communities. This local focus by smallholder activists is not necessarily a refection of their provincialism. Recent chroniclers of the environmental movement see the dynamic, progressive work in environmentalism moving from the "majors" (who are currently preoccupied with the possibility of environmental-business accommodations) toward grassroots organizations, which have a much higher proportion of women and visible minorities as active members than do the majors. For an overview of this shift to localism, in addition to Sale, see Riley E. Dunlap and Angela G. Mertig, eds., *American Environmentalism: The U.S. Environmental Movement, 1970–1990* (Philadelphia: Taylor & Francis, 1992); Robert Gottlieb, *Forcing the Spring: The Transformation of the American Environmental Movement* (Washington, D.C.: Island Press, 1993); and Mark Dowie, *Losing Ground: American Environmentalism at the Close of the Twentieth Century* (Cambridge: MIT Press, 1995).

7. Sale, *The Green Revolution*, 80.

8. This is an edited version of the letter that appeared in the *Smallholder*, December 1981, 980–81. Another letter, also opposing the study, concluded, "The less informed our opposition is about us, the better" (*Smallholder*, February 1982, 1012).

9. Haru Kanemitsu, "Voluntary Simplicity," *Smallholder*, April 1985, 1299.

10. The phantom quality of back-to-the-country organizing is not exclusive to the smallholding movement. North American universities are littered with institutes and study groups that either never received funding or exhausted it and whose only remaining artifacts are stationery letterheads that reflect the organizers' frustrated ambitions.

11. Quoted by Sale, *The Green Revolution*, 56. Brower himself has been in the middle of the struggle for the soul of environmental organizations. He left the Sierra Club to found Friends of the Earth, which he left to organize the Earth Island Institute. On the question of the necessity of a dialectic to keep environmental organizations from compromising their ideals, Brower says, "The Sierra Club made the Nature Conservancy look reasonable. Friends of the Earth made the Sierra Club appear reasonable, and Earth First! makes FOE appear

reasonable. Now we need some people to make Earth First! appear reasonable. There's much to be done" (Rauber, "With Friends Like These . . . ," 49).

12. Sale, *The Green Revolution*.

13. Although back-to-the-lander Barry Rosenberg is a critical part of the Inland Empire Public Lands Council, it is not technically a back-to-the-land organization. It was initially organized by a physician and includes sportsmen (hunters and fishers) and urban conservationists, as well as rural members, like Barry, who are trying to protect the ecological integrity of their communities.

14. Nancy Jack Todd and John Todd, *Bioshelters, Ocean Arks, Fish Farms: Ecology as the Basis of Design* (San Francisco: Sierra Club Books, 1984), 5.

15. John Todd, "Solar Aquatics," in *Whole Earth Ecolog* (New York: Harmony Books, 1990), 85.

16. Nancy Jack Todd edits *Annals of the Earth;* see the citation in *Whole Earth Ecolog*, 84.

17. John Todd's phrase, as attributed by Judith Barnet, president of the board of directors of the New Alchemy Institute, in a letter to supporters of the institute, July 1992, 4. After my initial interview with him, Earle wrote to me to point out "[t]his quote was not originally John Todd's. Judy Barnet is wrong. The phrase came from either J. Baldwin or Stewart Brand" (correspondence, October 1993).

18. During the early period of Susan's activism, she publicly used the name Willis-Johnson, but now she uses Susan Willis.

19. A concrete illustration of Plum Creek's dedication to its shareholders' short-term interests was its insistence, at the height of RIDGE's campaign against its clear-cutting practices and through the time of this writing, on selling raw lumber to East Asia. Rather than sell all their logs to local mills for processing, thus creating local jobs, Plum Creek and the Northwest's other large timber companies export as much of their production to Japan, Korea, and China as the East Asian timber markets will bear. The Japanese, for example, are willing to pay 70 percent more for logs than the U.S. mills. Sandwiched between log exports on the one hand and the protection of old-growth forests on the other, small U.S. mills have had to close down for lack of lumber to cut, consequently laying off mill workers. In the process, the Pacific Northwest has been transformed into a resource colony, selling unprocessed natural resources to East Asia and buying in turn manufactured goods such as automobiles, electronic equipment, and microchips. The sale to East Asia of unprocessed logs from federal forests is prohibited, but Plum Creek is free to export logs from its own private land. For an overview of the conflicting issues involved in the sale of logs from private land, including the protection of old-growth forests, see Ronald Brownstein, "Facing West, Nervously," *National Journal*, October 28, 1989, 2624ff.

20. Articles in the *Seattle Times* where Susan Willis (Willis-Johnson) is quoted on the Roslyn Ridge–Plum Creek controversy appeared on June 18, 1990, A1; November 7, 1990, D1; November 22, 1990, F1; and November 27, 1990, A6. The *Wall Street Journal* article appeared on June 18, 1990, A1.

21. It is likely that the Moses Lake legislator saw his way clear to support RIDGE's position precisely because there were no timber interests in his district.

22. Given Susan's idealism and Plum Creek's desire to exploit Roslyn's resources, it should not come as a surprise to learn of her reentry into the Plum Creek–RIDGE battles, though it would have been difficult to anticipate the circumstances. To take advantage of Roslyn's notoriety as the location for *Northern Exposure*'s Cicely, Alaska, Plum Creek wants planning clearance to build a resort with hotels, golf courses, and up to five thousand housing units on a site close to the town. RIDGE opposes the development, taking the position that resort wages are low and that development drives up the price of local housing, pricing long-time residents out of the housing market. For an overview of the controversy, see

Nicholas K. Geranios, "Tiny 'Northern Exposure' Town Divided over Plans for Development," *Los Angeles Times,* May 23, 1993, Metro sec., pt. B, 3.

Although Susan takes an active role in the new "resort wars" with Plum Creek, her involvement is significantly lower than during RIDGE's first encounters with Plum Creek. She says, "There are many others who have come forward and given incredible amounts of time and energy to the fight. Now I see them tired, worn-out, and hurting just like I was." While she wonders where the new energy will come from for the continuing battles with Plum Creek, she is channeling her own enthusiasm in new directions. She took a leave of absence from her elementary school teaching position for the 1995–96 school year to work on a master's degree in English composition at Central Washington University in Ellensburg. As part of her graduate-degree responsibilities, Susan teaches English Composition 101 to first-year students. Her message to her students is a simple one: writing well and thinking clearly comes much easier when you have a passion for your subject matter. The educational project she started with elementary school students now continues with the consciousness raising of college freshmen.

23. Quoted in Sale, *The Green Revolution,* 95.

Chapter 7

1. It is instructive to note that 90 percent of farm operators lived on farms in 1940, whereas only one-third do in the early 1990s. Since farm residence does not say that much about being a farmer, the U.S. Census Bureau will no longer keep a data category for people who live on farms, bringing to an end forty-five years of reports on the resident farm population. "Farewell to the Farm Report," *American Demographics,* March 1994, 21–22.

2. Though she just wants to ride her bicycle or walk alongside the country roads in her area, the California back-to-the-lander's simple desire raises enormous questions about retrofitting rural America's infrastructure toward the goal of sustainability. Rural America's transportation arteries over the last century have devolved into two-lane farm and market roads that carry out natural resources and move commuters from home to job and back again. But as important as building bike and walking paths might be, the more compelling need is for efficient mass transportation to the countryside. In David Orr's judgment, "amidst all of the options for alternative transportation, the best and cheapest is to rebuild the railroad network that for nearly a century bound the country together . . . Railroads once serviced small towns throughout rural America. They will have to once again. This, too, is an old idea that was dismantled, not because it did not work, but because it was systematically subverted in the interest of capital" (*Earth in Mind: On Education, Environment, and the Human Prospect* [Washington, D.C.: Island Press, 1994], 197–98). With traffic in the countryside moving by train, walking and riding a bike on a country road should be much safer, and more pleasant.

3. Alternative agriculture is a significant social movement in its own right. For a description of one of its core elements, the Campaign for Sustainable Agriculture, which "is made up of nearly 600 organizations representing family farmers, consumers, environmentalists, rural communities, social justice advocates, fish and wildlife interests, animal protection supporters, farm workers, the religious community, people of color, and others," see Kathy Lawrence, "A Campaign for Sustainability," *In Context,* no. 42 (Fall 1995): 48–49, with "Action Resource Guide," 56–57.

4. Increased production through capital- and nonrenewable-energy-intensive farming is closely correlated with the degradation of rural ecosystems (topsoil loss, aquifer depletion, etc.). Regarding the link between agricultural subsidies and environmental damage, Paul Hawken makes the following observation: "Most of the fertilizers and pesticides employed

today are used on crops produced in overabundance and thus fall under the government subsidy programs that provide price supports for their overuse. Thus our taxes are being used not for restoration, but to subsidize environmental damage" (*Ecology of Commerce: A Declaration of Sustainability* [New York: Harper Business, 1993], 186).

5. Eric Bates, "Farmers Who Are Kicking the Habit," *Nation*, February 13, 1995, 195.

6. The discussion here on full-cost pricing follows closely on Hawken, *Ecology of Commerce*, 177–99. For an insightful analysis that complements the Hawken argument, see Thomas Power and Paul Rauber, "The Price of Everything: Free-Market Environmentalism," *Sierra*, November 1993, 86ff.

In proposing public policy, one has to face up to the feasibility question. With any policy analysis there is necessarily a dynamic tension between significance and feasibility—policy that is feasible by reason of its harmony with current legislation rarely qualifies as an instrument for significant change. At the same time, policy proposals that significantly challenge the status quo are almost by definition unfeasible, at least when they are initially proposed. Of course, the political climate can and does change, and what was once speculative becomes part of daily congressional debates.

On the surface, full-cost pricing and its associated green taxes and social tariffs would appear to be squarely in the unfeasible policy category in the 1990s free-market political climate. But since full-cost pricing builds on the logic of the marketplace, as well as the necessity of an activist government, it possesses the potential to appeal to a broad cross section of the political spectrum. By using tax incentives and disincentives rather than large-scale bureaucratic programs and by de-emphasizing regulatory controls, full-cost pricing has the capacity to attract political moderates and pragmatists, as well as progressives. A case in point is the U.S. Presidential Commission on Sustainable Development, which presented its report, "Sustainable America: A New Consensus for Prosperity, Opportunity, and a Healthy Environment for the Future," on February 15, 1996, after two years of public consultations. Corporate CEOs, directors of national environmental organizations (the "majors"), and elected and appointed government officials were prominent members of the commission. In reference to the kinds of tax and subsidy policies that would reflect full-cost pricing, the commission made the following recommendations: "Change tax policies—without increasing the overall tax burden—to encourage employment and economic opportunity, while discouraging environmentally damaging production and consumption decisions. Tax reforms should not place a disproportionate burden on lower income individuals and families. Eliminate government subsidies that are inconsistent with economic, environmental, and social goals" (from "Highlights of Policy Changes Needed to Achieve Sustainable Development," a section of the commission report, Internet version, http://www2.whitehouse.gov/ WH/EOP/pcsd/index.html). In addition, the Clinton-Gore administration's promotion of the "reinventing government" campaign, which includes full-cost pricing as a central policy option, suggests that impact fees and social tariffs are moving closer to the broad mainstream of current political thinking. See David Osborne and Ted Gaebler, *Reinventing Government: How the Entrepreneurial Spirit Is Transforming the Public Sector* (Reading, Mass.: Addison-Wesley, 1992).

On a more general level, full-cost pricing, green taxes, and social tariffs are part of a "social market" approach to government, in contrast to the unregulated "free market" approach. With precedents from the social democracies of Western Europe and Scandinavia, social markets recognize that individuals need to have the opportunity to exercise their entrepreneurial (proprietorship) talents, while at the same time government has the responsibility to structure the market place to reflect community and ecological interests. For a discussion of the desirability and the feasibility of social markets in North America, in addition to Hawken, *Ecology of Commerce*, see Charles Derber et al., *What's Left: Radical Politics in the Post-Communist Era* (Amherst: University of Massachusetts Press, 1995); and for a practical application in the contexts of the Netherlands, New Zealand, and Canada's green plans, which include environmental taxes as a key policy strategy, see Huey D. Johnson, *Green Plans: Greenprint for Sustainability* (Lincoln: University of Nebraska Press, 1995). And according to David Malin Roodman, "The world's first tax shift was passed by the Swedish parliament in 1991. It reduced income taxes by 4 percent. To pay for this reduction, the government instituted a variety of environmental charges, including taxes on sulfur dioxide emissions, which cause acid rain, and on carbon dioxide emissions, which contribute to the greenhouse effect" ("Green Tax Shift Begins in Europe," *World Watch*, March/April 1996, 6). These changes in environmental tax policies are tracked by the Wuppertal Institute for Climate, Environment, and Energy in Wuppertal Germany (P. O. Box 10 04 08, D-42004 Wuppertal, Germany). The Wuppertal Institute publishes a newsletter in English.

For additional sources on full-cost pricing and environmental taxes, see David Malin Roodman, "Environmental Taxes Spread," in *Vital Signs: The Trends That Are Shaping Our Future*, ed. Lester R. Brown, Christopher Flavin, and Hal Kane (New York: Norton, 1996), 114–15, and Hazel Henderson, *Building a Win-Win World: Life Beyond Global Economic Warfare* (San Francisco: Berett-Koehler, 1996). A perceptive article on the logistical difficulties of transferring to full-cost pricing is Doug Macdonald, "Beer Cans, Gas Guzzlers, and Green Taxes: How Using Tax Instead of Law May Affect Environmental Policy," *Alternatives*, July/August, 1996, 12–19. Finally, for a complimentary perspective on full-cost pricing that takes the form of a critique of the way we keep our national accounts, see Clifford Cobb, Ted Halstead, and Jonathan Rowe, "If the GDP Is Up, Why Is America Down?" *Atlantic Monthly*, October 1995, 59–78.

7. John Gever et al., *Beyond Oil* (Cambridge: Ballinger, 1986), 28–29.

8. For the human costs of export agriculture, see Angus Wright, *The Death of Ramón González: The Modern Agricultural Dilemma* (Austin: University of Texas Press, 1990).

9. Hawken, *Ecology of Commerce*, 197–99.

10. Wolfgang Sachs, "The Virtue of Enoughness," *New Perspectives Quarterly* 6 (Spring 1989): 16–19.

11. David Myers, *The Pursuit of Happiness* (New York: Avon, 1993) is an excellent summary of quality-of-life research. Myers's 207 pages of text are complimented by 103 pages of footnotes and bibliography; the research identifies a wide variety of relationships, rather than material accumulation, as the primary predictors of happiness. Complimenting Myers's work is the emerging field of "ecopsychology" (Theodore Roszak, Mary E. Gomes, and Allen D. Kanner, eds., *Ecopsychology: Restoring the Earth, Healing the Mind* [San Francisco: Sierra Club Books, 1995]). Ecopsychology maintains that the modern separation from nature is responsible for a broad range of psychodynamic illnesses, as well as many of the social, economic, and political crises. Healing and happiness, then, on both individual and community levels, can come from the kind of reconnection with nature that back-to-the-landers experience during their mindfulness interludes. For a brief and accessible treatment of ecopsychology, see Andy Fisher, "Toward a More Radical Ecopsychology: Therapy for a Dysfunctional Society," *Alternatives*, July/August 1996, 20–26.

INDEX